The Rest Is Commentary

Beacon Texts in the Judaic Tradition
N. N. Glatzer, Editor

The Rest Is Commentary

A Source Book of Judaic Antiquity

Edited and Introduced by

NAHUM N. GLATZER

Beacon Press   Boston

Also by Nahum N. Glatzer

The Philosophy of History of the Tannaites
(*Geschichtslehre der Tannaiten*)

History of the Talmudic Age
(*Geschichte der talmudischen Zeit*)

Dialogues of the Masters
(*Gespräche der Weisen*)

Moses Ben Maimon

A Short History of the Jews
(*Kitzur Toledot Yisrael*)

Maimonides Said

In Time and Eternity: A Jewish Reader

Language of Faith

Hammer on the Rock: A Midrash Reader

Franz Rosenzweig: His Life and Thought

Hillel the Elder: The Emergence of Classical Judaism

Leopold and Adelheid Zunz: An Account in Letters

Jerusalem and Rome: The Writings of Flavius Josephus

Published simultaneously in Canada by
S. J. Reginald Saunders and Co., Ltd., Toronto

Library of Congress catalog card number: 61–7250

Printed in the United States of America

To Fanny

with brotherly affection

A certain heathen came to Shammai and said to him:
Convert me provided that you teach me the entire Torah
      while I stand on one foot.
Shammai drove him away with the builder's cubit which
      was in his hand.
He went to Hillel who said to him:
What is hateful to you, do not do to your neighbor:
that is the entire Torah;
the rest is commentary;
go and learn it.

HILLEL THE ELDER

Preface

When the by now famous heathen asked for the briefest possible presentation of Judaism, Hillel the Elder quoted his version of the Golden Rule, adding: "The rest is commentary; go and learn it." This significant addition points to one of the main characteristics of Judaic literature: Modestly, it considers itself mere commentary, marginal note, exposition; however, it is deeply conscious of the fact that it is a commentary on what is, or should be, the most important, most basic, most sacred to man. Fortunately, this does not apply in equal measure to all writings; from time to time an all-too-human voice blends with the voices of the "commentators."

In this source book an attempt is made to introduce the modern reader to the little-known literature of Judaic antiquity, i.e., the period from the Second Temple (or, Second Jewish Commonwealth) through the talmudic age. This literature, which includes the so-called Apocrypha, the writings of the Dead Sea, or Qumran, sect, Philo of Alexandria, Flavius Josephus of Jerusalem and Rome and the works of Talmud and Midrash, appears here in representative selections. As distinct from the method followed by this editor in an earlier anthology (*In Time and Eternity*, published by Schocken in 1946), the present volume, especially in its first part, offers more comprehensive passages and, in addition to a thematic arrangement, adheres as much as possible to a chronological sequence. Only from talmudic-midrashic sources brief, pithy sayings have been chosen, as exemplary for at least one type of this literature.

The Introduction will present a sketch of the historic background against which the selections should be read. Further information, especially on the works from which the selections are culled, is given in the brief prefatory notes to the sections of the book; brief notes on dates and names appear bracketed in the text. Brackets, too, are used to indicate abridgments within the text. The translations from the original (see "Sources" and "Acknowledgments") have been revised in places.

With pleasure the editor acknowledges his gratitude to Professor Philip Rieff for his sincere interest in this volume and his good counsel.

N. N. GLATZER

Brandeis University
September 1960

Contents

VII. After the Fall of Jerusalem 152

VIII. From the Ordinances of the Talmudic Masters 182

IX. Beliefs and Opinions of the Talmudic Masters 189

Introduction

The era that commences about 500 B.C. and ends about A.D. 500 is the time in which Judaism originated and took shape. Ancient Biblical Israel, whose history came to an end with the destruction of the Jerusalem temple in 586 B.C. and the Babylonian captivity (586 to 538), underwent a thorough transformation before it became the religion, culture, world-view and destiny that we call Judaism.

An edict of Cyrus (538 B.C.), founder of the Persian Empire, made it possible for the Jewish exiles in Babylonia to return to Jerusalem and to rebuild the temple. Only a small group returned to Zion, and the land allotted to its members was small. It measured about one thousand square miles, and much of this territory was desert. But those who returned from exile were the first of a new people of Judaea, and the allotted land was the site of a new state, one which was to create a fateful chapter in the history of Western civilization.

Among the important men of the new Zion was the prophet Zechariah, who conceived what became the challenge both of Jerusalem and of the Jews dispersed in the various Near Eastern and Mediterranean centers: "Not by might, nor by power, but by my spirit, saith the Lord of hosts" (Zech. 4:6). In his vision Jerusalem, as yet an insignificant, much neglected city, became "the city of truth" (8:3) and of peace (8:12), the center of worship of a universal God (14:9). A short period later, the prophet Malachi saw monotheism spreading "from the rising of the sun even unto the going down of the same . . . and in every place offerings are presented unto my name" (1:11). Judaea was a more or less autonomous priestly state within the Persian Empire; but the priests, ever in peril of falling from their sacred mission into a temple bureaucracy, would do well, Malachi felt, to follow the example of Aaron, the first priest: "The law of truth was

in his mouth . . . he walked with Me in peace and uprightness. . . . For the priest's lips should keep knowledge . . .
for he is the messenger of the Lord" (2:6-7).

It was about a century after the Return that the Jewish
community was established on a solid foundation, politically,
culturally and economically. This was due largely to the work
of two Babylonian Jews: Nehemiah, who administered Judaea
as Persian governor, and Ezra the scribe. The latter, em-
powered by the Persian king, Artaxerxes, made the Torah of
Moses the basis of communal and private life. He is said to
have introduced the reading and interpretation of the Law
as the central element in the synagogue liturgy and in education. The Biblical books of Ezra and Nehemiah, based partly
on personal memoirs of the men concerned, include an account (chapter 8 of Nehemiah) of the great gathering of the
people of Jerusalem at which Ezra read the Law for the first
time, thus re-enacting on a more human, almost secular, stage,
the drama of the revelation on Sinai.

And when the seventh month was come, and the children of Israel were
in their cities, all the people gathered themselves together as one man into the
broad place that was before the water gate; and they spoke unto Ezra the
scribe to bring the book of the Law of Moses, which the Lord had commanded
to Israel.

And Ezra the priest brought the Law before the congregation, both
men and women, and all that could hear with understanding, upon the first
day of the seventh month.

And he read therein before the broad place that was before the water
gate from early morning until midday, in the presence of the men and the
women, and of those that could understand; and the ears of all the people were
attentive unto the book of the Law.

And Ezra the scribe stood upon a pulpit of wood, which they had made
for the purpose. . . .

And Ezra opened the book in the sight of all the people—for he was
above all the people—and when he opened it, all the people stood up. And
Ezra blessed the Lord, the great God. And all the people answered: "Amen,
Amen," with the lifting up of their hands; and they bowed their heads and
fell down before the Lord with their faces to the ground.

Also Jeshua, and Bani . . . caused the people to understand the Law;
and the people stood in their place. And they read in the book, in the Law of

God, distinctly; and they gave the sense, and caused them to understand the reading.

And Nehemiah . . . and Ezra, the priest, the scribe, and the Levites that taught the people, said unto all the people: "This day is holy unto the Lord your God; mourn not, nor weep." For all the people wept, when they heard the words of the Law.

Then he said unto them: "Go your way, eat the fat, and drink the sweet, and send portions unto him for whom nothing is prepared; for this day is holy unto our Lord; neither be ye grieved; for the joy of the Lord is your strength." . . .

And all the people went their way to eat, and to drink, and to send portions, and to make great mirth, because they had understood the words that were declared unto them.

Post-Exilic Judaism, therefore, was established upon the late-prophetic and Ezraic foundations. From the first source it drew its knowledge of God, its passion for justice, its vision of a new Zion; from the Ezraic, its will to translate prophetic ideals into the practice of daily life, its emphasis on learning, its dedication to the community. The cultivation of these virtues made for the spiritual unity of Israel under the various political constellations and fated difficulties. The synagogue, school and home were the centers of this culture, while the temple in Jerusalem remained its official symbol. True, the priest ministered to the elaborate ritual of the Jerusalem sanctuary and the high priest headed the Commonwealth; but the other functions of Judaism were open to all. Among the interpreters of the Law, bearers of tradition, teachers of wisdom and leaders of communities, we find priests and laymen, traditionalists and reformers, rich and poor, sons of Israel or descendants of heathens. What mattered here was knowledge, conduct, dedication. This application of the democratic principle to a religious civilization was the source of much vitality, color and creative tension, especially in the first half of the thousand years of history with which this book is concerned.

The reader will do well to keep in mind that the century of Malachi, Nehemiah and Ezra is also the age of Pericles and the century of the achievement of Greek drama by the poets Aeschylus, Euripides, Sophocles and Aristophanes; of histori-

ographers Herodotus and Thucydides and the creation of the
Acropolis; of the sculptor Phidias and those who, like Anaxagoras, advanced philosophical thought. Compared with this
profusion of beauty, the material culture of Judaea is negli-
gible indeed. There all energies were devoted to the education
of man as an individual, as a member of society, as a partner in
the sacred community of worshipers.

The fourth century, the second of the Persian rule over
Yehud, as Judaea was called, left us no dated documents from
which we could reconstruct the history of the period. Then
in 333 B.C., Alexander the Great conquered the Persian Empire and with it Syria and Palestine, and Judaea appeared as a
still small but internally mature, highly developed commonwealth. Around the urban center in Jerusalem were clustered
numerous agricultural communities. Within their own groups,
and in whatever contact they had with the world around
them, the farmers followed the teachings of simple piety and
of brotherly love. Biblical laws concerning release of debts, the
sabbatical year, gifts due to those in need of them, the regulations against interest on loans, all sought to establish justice
in practical life, to eliminate unfair profit and to safeguard
peace. In truly fascinating researches of recent date, Professor
Y. F. Baer of Jerusalem[1] has identified these farmers with the
Early Pious Men (*Hasidim ha-Rishonim*) known to us only
from later literature (the Mishnah); in many details of the
laws followed by these communities, Baer found parallels to
the laws of Solon, the Athenian reformer, and to the regulations of the classical Greek Polis as we read them in Plato's
Laws. Thus in the society of the Early Hasidim we recognize
a synthesis of the traditions of ancient Israel and some of the
tenets of the independent Greek republics.

Alexander's conquests brought East and West together,
and laid the foundation for a unified world civilization to
which both East and West were to contribute. The grandiose
idea did not materialize, but it remained a powerful cultural
stimulus for centuries to come. On a lower level, Hellenic
fashions, ways of life and modes of thought and belief pene-

trated the East, commingled with and at times replaced ancient cultures and religious disciplines.

After Alexander's death (323 B.C.), his generals ("Successors") divided his realm among themselves. Palestine came under Egyptian (Ptolomaic) domination. In the third century, thousands of Jews migrated to Alexandria, Egypt, the newly established center of the world commerce which gradually succeeded Athens as the capital of Greek learning and Hellenist civilization. In due course the Jews in Alexandria formed a community organization and enjoyed autonomous jurisdiction. They spoke Greek and accepted Greek modes of life. The educated class was, in various degrees, versed in Greek writings; its own literary products demonstrate a synthesis of Hebrew and Greek wisdom. The Greek translation of the Five Books of Moses (the Septuagint, later to include translations of the entire Hebrew Bible) became the authoritative sacred scripture of the Alexandrian and all Greek-speaking Jews. The high religious and ethical principles, expounded and propagated in the commonly understood language, attracted many proselytes. On the other hand, a measure of exclusiveness on the part of the Jews and resistance to indiscriminate mingling gave rise to anti-Semitism, which, in turn, accounted for a good number of apologetic writings in which the Jews tried to present their religion.

In this atmosphere grew some of the works later included in the Biblical Apocrypha, such as the Wisdom of Solomon (see "Wisdom and the Order of this World") which combines Greek notions about God, world and man with the Hebrew praise of simple piety, and the Fourth Book of Maccabees (see "Inspired Reason") which, in enumerating the forms of wisdom (prudence, justice, manliness, temperance) shows Stoic influence. Jewish Hellenist thought at its maturest stage is represented by Philo of Alexandria (see "Hellenist Exposition of Scripture") in whose thought Scriptures and Plato blended in profound harmony. As Professor Harry A. Wolfson of Harvard has demonstrated,[2] it was this Philonian system that provided the intellectual basis for the religious philosophy of Christian antiquity and the Middle Ages.

Judaea presumably continued in the cultivation of the Ezraic heritage, but lack of original sources prevents us from tracing this development. We are better informed about another strain of culture that found a renewed expression in post-Ezraic Judaea: the tradition of "wisdom" as the trusted guide to the good life. Schools of wisdom trained young men in the art of prudent living and counseled personal self-perfection and striving for the ever distant goal of wisdom, because "when a man has finished, then does he but begin." The Biblical Apocrypha preserve the Wisdom of (Joshua, Jesus) Ben Sira, a good example of this type of literature (see "In Praise of Wisdom" and "Manifestation of God in Nature").

In Judaea too there is evidence of a strong Hellenist influence on the Jewish population. Hellenic cities neighbored on Jewish areas; in addition, there were mixed settlements of Jews and Greeks. In the market place and in general contacts of life, the Jew met the Greek soldier, trader, artisan. The more advanced Greek technical civilization, the liberalizing physical culture as acquired in the gymnasia and at athletic games impressed the sons of the well-to-do, while the scholars and thinkers came to appreciate Greek rationalism, humanism and methods of thought.

The meeting of East and West resulted in many and intricate changes in the political, social, religious and personal life in Judaea. The extreme positions are marked on the one hand by the radical Hellenizers, who repudiated the traditional religious mores and advocated assimilation to the ways of the pagans, and on the other by the loyalists (the later Pharisees), who adhered to and cultivated their belief in the eternity of the Bible, its laws, its sacred history and promise for the future of Israel. Professors Elias Bickerman of Columbia University[3] and W. F. Albright of Johns Hopkins University[4] have shown that these advocates of Torah had adopted some important aspects of liberal Hellenism. Systematic rules of scriptural interpretation, certain forms of legal thinking and the emphasis on organized education are matters that have their roots in Biblical Israel and Ezraic Judaism, but their decisive development and final shape is due to the climate of Hellenism. In a way, this acceptance of Greek influence is a continuation of the process which we noted in the communities of the Early Hasidim. This voluntary, organic and creative Hellenization within Judaism must be clearly distinguished from the imitative, arrogant, opportunistic Hellenist assimilation of the upper classes in Jerusalem.

In the first decades of the second century B.C., the antagonism between Judaism and Hellenism gave way to open conflict. The aristocratic, well-to-do Jews in Jerusalem, supported by the higher echelons of the temple priesthood, cultivated Greek modes of social and cultural life: Greek language, gymnasia, games, dress, habits of eating and entertainment. Its advocates hoped that such assimilation would relieve Judaea's isolation in the Hellenist world around it. Jerusalem was to be counted among the Hellenist cities of the Eastern Mediterranean region; it was to become a second Antioch, the king's residence.

The Hellenist transformation of Judaism was opposed by the simple people of Jerusalem, the farming communities outside the city, the Hasidim ("the pious"), the lower clergy —men and women who best realized the threat to the God-given moral and religious order of Israel.

In 198 B.C., Antiochus III brought Palestine under the sway of the Syrian (Seleucid) power. When Antiochus IV Epiphanes inherited the Seleucids' throne (175 B.C.), a critical stage of the Hellenization problem was reached. This politically unsuccessful king (Rome interfered with his Egyptian expedition) pursued a policy of forced Hellenization which was to serve his narrow political ambitions. But Antiochus "Epimanes" (the mad man), as his title was parodied at home made Hellenization identical with heathenization. In 167 B.C. he abolished the Torah as the Jewish constitution, had an altar to Zeus erected in the Jerusalem temple and had a hog offered as sacrifice. This act provoked loyal, non-Hellenist Jews to an over-all revolt. The insurrection,

known as the Maccabean rebellion, turned both against the
king and against the Jewish Hellenist party in Jerusalem
(headed by the high priests, first Jason, then Menelaus),
which supported the king's aims and which, in turn, received
support from the king. Rebellion seemed to be the only means
of preventing Jerusalem from becoming a pagan center and
of regaining the freedom of religion. The rise of a small group
of volunteer fighters against the Seleucid armies did not hold
any promise of success. But the rebels were upheld by their
belief that the outcome of this war must matter to the Lord
of history. (See "The Origin of the Maccabean Rebellion,"
"The Rededication of the Temple" and "Simon's Beneficent
Rule").

The community of the Hasidim that joined the small
fighting force of Judah the Maccabee (the "hammerer")
found the ideology of its action in the Biblical Book of Daniel.
Its unknown author, witness to the events, interpreted his
time and the function of the hasidic supporters of the rebellion in the context of the ancient prophetic view of Israel and
within the scope of world history. In his apocalyptic vision
("revealing" events and their hidden meaning), past history
appeared to be a sequence of heathen empires that were permitted to rule the world: Babylonian, Medic, Persian and
Greek. The fourth of the kingdoms to quote from chapter 7,
"shall devour the whole earth, and shall tread it down, and
break it in pieces." The king "shall speak words against the
Most High, and shall wear out the saints of the Most High;
and he shall think to change the seasons and the law." But
"his dominion shall be taken away, to be consumed and to
be destroyed unto the end."

> I saw in the night visions,
> And, behold, there came with the clouds of heaven
> One like unto a son of man,
> And he came even to the Ancient of days [God],
> And he was brought near before Him.
> And there was given him dominion,
> And glory, and a kingdom,
> That all the peoples, nations, and languages

Should serve him;
His dominion is an everlasting dominion, which shall not pass away,
And his kingdom that which shall not be destroyed.

Thus "judgment was given for the saints of the Most High; and the time came, and the saints possessed the kingdom." "And the kingdom and the dominion, and the greatness of the kingdoms under the whole heaven, shall be given to the people of the saints of the Most High; their kingdom is an everlasting kingdom, and all dominions shall serve and obey them."

Thus, it was thought, the hour had come when the era of the "four kingdoms" would be superseded by the "Kingdom of God." The wickedness and the cruelty of the pagan world, symbolized in Daniel's vision by fierce beasts, was to be replaced by the realm symbolized by the image of man ("son of man"), and headed by Israel, the "people of the saints." Inspired by this view of the historic drama, the pious willingly fought, suffered—and waited.

The Maccabees (or, as they are also called, the Hasmoneans, i.e., from the family of Hasmon) won their fight. Independence of Judaea was achieved in 140 B.C. under Simon, a brother of Judah the Maccabee (see "Simon's Beneficent Rule"). Rulers, kings and high priests from the Hasmonean family headed the Jewish state and expanded its territory to its ancient Biblical frontiers. But these largely secular developments were not at all a realization of the hopes of the Book of Daniel. The power-minded, conquering Hasmonean kingdom was no "dominion of the saints of the Most High." The Hasidim withdrew as soon as religious liberty was achieved and left the field to those who knew that only political freedom would provide a basis for freedom of worship and for cultural growth. Daniel's visions, however, remained important for the future of religious and historical thought. They served as prototype and model for later apocalyptic writings (see "The Hope for a New Age" from the Book of Enoch, "The Vision of a New Era" and "The Vision of the Disconsolate Women" from the Fourth Book of Ezra and "The Consolation of Zion," from the Apocalypse of Baruch). Dan-

iel's attempt to interpret history as world history, as a mean-
ingful, interrelated progression of events, and the idea of the
"Four Kingdoms" were the concepts that excited the historical and political imagination of ages to come, Jewish and
Christian. Naturally, the fourth and last of the kingdoms to
precede the new, hoped-for age (which in the Book of Daniel
was referred to as Greece) was now interpreted to be the
Roman Empire. The enigmatic numbers of days (1,290, or
1,335) to expire before the inception of the Messianic age
(Dan. 12:11-12) occupied the speculative mind of Western
mankind for centuries. Also, the tales of martyrdom and of
steadfastness in the face of tyranny and oppression (see
"Martyrdom of the Seven Brothers and their Mother" from
the Second Book of Maccabees and "Inspired Reason" from
the Fourth Book of Maccabees) served as an example of dedication and personal heroism in both Judaism and Christianity.

The Maccabean uprising, as we have seen, was in the
main a reaction against the violent attempt to replace the
Judaic by Hellenic institutions. A peaceful, friendly penetra-
tion of Hellenism would have effected an entirely different
course of historic development. The Hellenist transformation
of Judaism might have succeeded and might have forced a
remnant of loyal Jews into a sectarian existence. It was, as
Emil Schürer said, "just the extreme and radical character of
this [Hellenist] attempt that saved Judaism,"[5] because the
Judaism that emerged from the Hellenist crisis was stronger
than before, a determined socioreligious entity, ever more
clearly conscious of its place in the world. Instead of permitting an expansion in all possible directions to face the threat
of superficiality of purpose and mediocrity of expression, Judaism now championed concentration on practically one field,
the religious, and that in its broadest sense. Within this
realm, Judaism could adapt freely from the Greeks. The scholarly vocabulary of the period contains some three thousand
borrowed words, mostly Greek. The Hebrew term *Keneset ha-
Gedolah* (Great Assembly) was replaced by the Hellenistic
term *Sanhedrin*. Platonic and Stoic ideas merged with the
ancient prophetic and Ezraic views and doctrines. While the

conduct of daily life was regulated by a sober discipline of the Law, the mind was trained to face argument and opposition, to cultivate discrimination and understanding. Socratic dialectic became one of the intellectual forces that molded thinking in the schools of Judaea. Unmediated divine revelation was regarded as a revered fact of the past, but it was no longer considered as the source of new human knowledge. Tradition of the elders counted as a treasure of accumulated experience but no longer as the sole guide to action. Only logical and systematic reasoning was recognized as a valid authority for the understanding of the inherited Scriptures (record of the word of God and His way in history) and in the search for norms of the good life. Rational argument and logical analysis became the instrument of discourse as recorded in the Talmud, that monumental record of life, thought and legal deliberation of some five hundred years following the Maccabean period. The list of logical rules to be applied to the exposition, mainly of legal texts in the Bible (until this day this list is being recited by pious Jews in the daily morning prayer), goes back to Hellenistic rhetoric. The principle of rationality and order is as much Hebraic as it is Greek.

The most representative scholar in Jerusalem of the post-Maccabean and early talmudic era is Hillel the Elder (ca. 60 B.C. to ca. A.D. 10), founder of the "House (or School) of Hillel." (See "Hillel the Elder"). His interests as scholar, legislator and teacher range over practically all fields of Jewish law, civil and ritual. In this respect Hillel, despite his new directions and emphases (which do not concern us here), is a link in the unbroken chain of the tradition of Israel. His ethical teachings, though in the main rooted in the same tradition, show remarkable parallels with Stoic thought, especially with the tenets of Seneca, in part his contemporary. Hillel spoke of the soul as a guest in the human body, and Seneca of God who dwells as a guest in the body. Hillel's saying, "If I am not for myself, who is for me?" runs parallel to Seneca's, "It is your duty to try your best . . . there is no dependency upon others." Hillel's admonition against an attitude of "when I shall have leisure I shall study" reminds one of Seneca's "Do not excuse yourself with: I shall have leisure later and then I shall seek wisdom." Hillel's "Do not judge your fellow man until you have stood in his place" differs only a little from Seneca's "We should put ourselves in that place in which the man with whom we are angry is to be found," and both point in the direction of Epictetus' advice: "Give no judgment from another tribunal before you have yourself been judged at the tribunal of absolute justice." [6]

These continued contacts between Jewish and Hellenic thought suggest a general atmosphere of rationalism and humanism that motivated the thinking of the intelligentsia in both Hellenism and Judaism. Both believed that education should aim at the "wise man," not the businessman or the politician. *Paideia*, the Greek idea of perfection through education, classically enunciated by Professor Werner Jaeger,[7] finds a corresponding motif in Judaism. Here, the dedicated study of the Torah, a study of the divine word which renews the experience of revelation of Sinai (see "Revelation and the Study of the Law"), is to lead to the perfection of the individual and to moral action.

At this point the correspondence ends. That in the end Judaism did not merge with Hellenism, as the pre-Maccabean Jewish Hellenists desired, is due to the differences between the two cultures, differences basic and contrasting.

The philosophic doctrines of late antiquity, lofty as they were, were mindful only of the upper classes. In Plato's ideal state the masses of men are held in bondage. Aristotle considers some human beings to be slaves by nature; the Stoa saw in the multitude, but *typhloi*, blind fools. To be sure, there is in the Stoa an awareness of the equality of men and a feeling of compassion with suffering humanity. But the words were purer than the deeds. The ideal remained *apatheia*, indifference towards any disturbance of the quiet inner life of the wise, and *ataraxia*, equanimity of mind. Judaism, on the other hand, was less concerned with the definition of the ideal than it was with the application of the ideal to real life. Here the affirmation of the ideal and social legislation had to be supplemented by active personal responsibility for the needs of one's neighbor. Compassion and charity were not to be only expressions of humaneness but *imitatio dei*. And not only moral action, but all other aspects of life as directed by the Law, liturgic and civil, dietary and criminal, ceremonial and agricultural, were considered an acknowledgment and fulfillment of the divine will. The determination to defend also this aspect of religion contributed greatly to the separation of Israel in the ancient world.

In the period of the Hasmonean kingdom (142 to 63 B.C.), the various cultural trends in Judaea crystallized to form three distinct groups, known as the Sadducees, the Pharisees and the Dead Sea, or Qumran, Brotherhood (Essenes).

The Sadducees had their origin in the temple hierarchy (the name, Hebrew, *Zedukim*, is probably derived from Zadok, chief priest under King Solomon). This group comprised the conservative element of the population, the priestly aristocracy, prosperous merchants and landowners. Worldly in politics and general view of life, they preserved rigidly the ancient religious traditions, as contained in the Biblical documents, and opposed innovations in religious practice and progress in doctrine. They "disregard fate entirely and place God beyond the commission or the very sight of evil. Good and evil, they contend, are man's choice, and everyone is free to embrace one or the other according to his will. The soul's permanence after death and the punishments and rewards of Hades they reject" (Josephus).[8]

The middle class was represented by the Pharisees (Hebrew, *Perushim*, indicating separation from "the unclean" and dedication to the sacred). Their liberal interpretation of Torah was meant to form a bridge between the ancient word and the requirements of the present, and, at the same time, to expand and deepen the relevance of Torah. They cultivated the personal element in religion and the spiritual meaning of the ritual. The center of their public life was less the official sanctuary in Jerusalem than the synagogues and houses of study. As compared with the Sadducees, the Pharisees were progressive, ever ready to prevent religious views from becoming rigid doctrines and dogmas. The New Testament mentions in one breath Pharisees and hyocrites. Hypocrisy and intolerance undoubtedly existed among the Pharisees, but this hardly suggests what the movement was. Rather it is the humble and humane Hillel the Elder and his disciples who are a living demonstration of Pharisaism.

As the supporters of nonradical Hellenism or their descendants, merged with the Sadducees, so, we may assume, some of the descendants of the early Hasidim became a part of the Pharisaic movement, and within it continued to represent some of the hasidic ideals. The radical Jewish Hellenists disappeared in the mainstream of Eastern Mediterranean Hellenism. The uncompromising adherents of the hasidic ideology, and those of the Pharisees of a related persuasion, alienated by the conduct of public affairs at the Hasmonean court and by the secularization of the Jerusalem priesthood, went to the wilderness in the Dead Sea region. There they established the order of the Essenes, or joined already existing groups of pious hermits. The exact composition of this sectarian movement is not yet established. Its history is still a matter of conjecture, but the importance of the sect for the understanding of contemporaneous Judaism and for early Christianity is generally recognized. The oath of a newly admitted member of the brotherhood is an indication of its general tendency; the initiated one swore that

> he will exercise piety toward God;
> observe justice towards men;
> do no harm to any one . . . ;
> he will abhor the wicked and be helpful to the good;
> show fidelity to all men . . . ;
> he will be a lover of truth and reprove those who tell lies,
> he will keep his hands clear from theft
> and his soul from unlawful gains.[9]

This is what Josephus says in his detailed description of the Essenes. For Philo's presentation of this sect, see "The Essenes," taken from his essay Every Good Man Is Free. (See also "The Dead Sea, or Qumran, Brotherhood" from the Manual of Discipline, and "Hymns of the Dead Sea Brotherhood" from its collection of Thanksgiving Hymns.)

In the caves which for many centuries preserved parts of the library of the Dead Sea community have been found some portions of the apocryphal book the Testaments of the Twelve Patriarchs (see "A New Priesthood") and fragments of the apocalyptic Book of Enoch (see "The Judgment and the New Age"), works which illustrate the deep disappointment with their time and the passionate awaiting of a better day in the future for those who shall deserve a future. The loyal Jews in Jerusalem shared this hope with the sectarians in the wilderness.

A sect of Jewish hermits, the Therapeutae, existed also in Egypt, a description of which is offered by Philo (see "The Therapeutae").

Rome, with its gradual conquest of all countries in the Eastern Mediterranean region, first interfered in Judaea in 63 B.C., when Pompey entered Jerusalem. Herod the Great (37 to 4 B.C.), descendant of the Idumaeans (a people converted to Judaism by the Hasmonean ruler, John Hyrcanus), ruled in Judaea by the grace of Rome (see "Thou Art Our King" from the Psalms of Solomon). Judaea's dependence on Rome (see "The Emperor's Statue") strained the endurance of those who wished to preserve inner independence. It was probably during this period that an unknown, sensitive author reread the Book of Job and recast the story of the tragic tension between the inscrutable Creator and rebellious man into a song of love between a silently suffering creature and a gracious God, a late outpouring of the hasidic spirit (see "Testament of Job the Saint").

The Judaeo-Roman war of A.D. 66, which had resulted from the unbearable tension between Jerusalem and Rome, ended in A.D. 73 with the destruction of Jerusalem and the temple. The last fortress to hold out against the overwhelming Roman forces was Masada (see "The Heroes of Masada," described by Flavius Josephus). Judaea became a Roman province.

The catastrophe of the fall of Jerusalem evoked different reactions. The apocalyptic visionaries, spiritual descendants

of Daniel, tried to interpret the event in a cosmic context and
to keep alive the hope in a new Jerusalem (see "The Vision
of a New Era" and "The Vision of the Disconsolate Woman"
from the Fourth Book of Ezra, and "The Consolation of
Zion" from the Apocalypse of Baruch). The early Christian
community saw in the fall of Zion a confirmation of its beliefs in God's rejection of the people of Israel and His election
of a New Israel, the Church. The Pharisees, founders of rabbinic (or normative, or classical) Judaism, rallied around
Johanan ben Zakkai (called the youngest disciple of Hillel
the Elder), who taught that the central institutions of Jerusalem were to be replaced by an intensified cultivation of
learning and practice of *hesed,* loving-kindness. He emphasized the prophetic dictum: "I desire mercy (*hesed*), not
sacrifices."

The Dead Sea Brotherhood ceased to exist. The party
of the Sadducees disappeared from sight. The Jewish community of Alexandria suffered destruction. On the other hand,
the Jewish communities in Babylonia, established long ago,
were augmented by refugees of the war in Judaea and developed into major centers of Judaism and Jewish studies in the
centuries to come. Among the numerous Jewish communities
scattered throughout the Roman Empire, the one in Rome
should be mentioned. There lived Flavius Josephus, the
former Judaean general (defending Galilee) and later ad-
viser to the Roman army besieging Jerusalem. In Rome, under
the patronage of the ruling house, Josephus wrote his *Jewish
War, Antiquities* and his outline of Judaic thought and institutions (see "In Defense of Judaism" from *Against Apion*).

The subjugated Jews in Judaea rose once more against
Rome (under Bar Kokhba, 132 to 135), and were again defeated. A period of martyrdom followed. The victims, lovingly
remembered (see "The Ten Martyrs"), became a prototype
of those who suffered persecution in the Middle Ages.

All intellectual and spiritual energies of the post-destruc-
tion period were concentrated on the interpretation and the
formulation of the laws (*Halakhah,* the rule to go by), and on
reflection upon past history, the lives of great men, on issues

of faith and wisdom, ethics and folklore (*Haggadah*, homiletics). Stress was laid on precision of expression, on brevity of report; stylistic beauty for beauty's sake, literary elegance, was no longer practiced. The originally oral character of transmission, the pointed discussion among scholars in the houses of study, the dialogue between master and disciple, the pithy comment on a Biblical passage—all these traits are evident in the voluminous records that emerged from this activity: the Mishnah, codification of the laws, completed about A.D. 200, the Palestinian and Babylonian Talmuds, interpretations of the Mishnah, completed at the end of the fourth and fifth centuries respectively, the Midrashim (plural of Midrash, exposition, scriptural exegesis), and collections of Haggadah material, compiled in the talmudic period and in the following centuries. (See "The Order of Benedictions" and "The Seder Ceremony" as samples from the Mishnah, "The Ways of Good Life" as a sample of Haggadah from one of the talmudic tractates, the following eight selections as samples of haggadic material culled from various talmudic-midrashic sources, and "Reflections on Life" from *Tanna debe Eliyahu*, a late haggadic compendium. Talmudic discussion of legal and ritual material is not included here.)

Information on what really mattered to the talmudic teachers is given in the one nonlegal treatise of the Mishnah, *Abot* (Fathers), which includes the chief sayings and religio-ethical maxims attributed to about sixty masters. The following condensation of this treatise may provide some background to our selections from the talmudic and midrashic writings.

Chief among the virtues is the study of the Law. Torah is one of the three things upon which the universe is based (the other two being the divine worship and loving-kindness). A person ought to attach himself to a master and to a companion for joint study; irregular hours of study are to be avoided. Those who grow up among the sages will cultivate silence; they will say little and do much. The study of Torah is to be combined with some worldly occupation (for such an arrangement will not leave time for idleness), but business

tends to overly occupy a person's mind. Therefore, it is better
to reduce such activity in order to concentrate one's efforts on
Torah. The true way of learning is: Eat a morsel of bread
with salt, drink water by measure, sleep upon the ground, live
a life of trouble while you toil in the Law; then you will be
happy in this world and in the world to come. He who fulfills
the Torah in the midst of poverty shall in the end fulfill
it in plenty; he who neglects it in plenty shall in the end
neglect it in poverty. Knowledge cannot be inherited; man
must "prepare himself" for this serious pursuit. The day is
short and work is plentiful. It is not one's function to finish
the work, yet he is not free to desist from it. He who takes
upon himself the yoke of Torah frees himself from the yoke
of government and the yoke of worldly troubles. When
people sit together—a group of ten, or five, or three or two—
and study Torah, or even if a man alone meditates on the
Law, the divine presence abides there. An assembly which is
for the sake of heaven will in the end be established. Equally,
a controversy which is for the sake of heaven will in the end
be established.

But learning has to result in action. He that studies in
order to teach is granted the means to learn and to teach; he
who learns in order to practice (what he learns) is granted the
means to learn and to teach, to observe and to practice. Wisdom will endure if it is exceeded by proper action; he whose
wisdom exceeds his deeds, his wisdom will not endure. No
selfish motive may prompt a person in the pursuit of learning.
The Torah may not be made a crown for the aggrandizement
of the student nor a spade wherewith to dig. He who makes
profit from the words of the Torah removes his life from the
world.

As the disciple honors his master, so will the teacher have
regard for his pupil. His honor will be dear to him as the
honor of his associate, the honor of his associate as the reverence of his master, and the reverence of his master as the fear
of God in heaven.

The learned man will go out and practice charity and
good deeds toward his fellow man. He will be guided by a

humble consideration of man's origin, his ultimate disintegration and the final day of judgment. He will emulate the Patriarch Abraham and cultivate good will, a humble spirit and soul. He will avoid jealousy, lust and ambition. He will never despise a human being or discriminate against anything, for there is no man who has not his hour, and there is no thing that has not its place. There are three crowns: the crown of Torah, the crown of priesthood and the crown of royalty; yet there is a higher crown still: the crown of a good name. Three things uphold this world: truth, judgment and peace. The realm of human action borders on the realm of the divine. He in whom the spirit of men takes delight, in him the spirit of God takes delight. It is a sign of God's love for man that He created him in His image; but it is a sign of even greater love that man was made to be aware of this fact. An unexplainable tension exists between divine providence and human choice. Everything is foreseen by God, yet the right of choice is given to man. God judges the world by grace, but human works are decisive. Man lives in a divine universe; whatever He has created in His world He created but for His glory.

In such a spirit did the "sages" and their disciples construct their lives and their view of the world.

In the centuries after the destruction of Jerusalem (the talmudic period), Judaism had further withdrawn from the stage of world history. The greatness of Rome ceased to be a problem. Concentrating on its spiritual heritage, Israel was satisfied with serving the Lord in its tiny synagogues and schools and with creating islands of sanctity in the world. But contacts with the world did not cease. The theory of Israel as a completely segregated community in exile can no longer be maintained as correct. But contacts rarely implied communion; the world had fallen apart into mutually exclusive entities in which tolerance was a rare virtue.

The diversity of writings, representative examples of which are offered in this volume, will gain a measure of coherence if we understand them as attempts on the part of the Jewish community to face the encounter with a variety of cultural and human situations and as responses to their challenges. While fixing its gaze on what is ultimately essential, Israel endeavored to translate it into the language of any given hour in history, thus cultivating the "rest" of the teaching "which is commentary."

I. Wisdom—Divine and Human

In Praise of Wisdom

FROM THE WISDOM OF BEN SIRA

A note on Ben Sira. The ancient Near East—and, for that matter, the ancient world—developed early a type of writing which deals with human life and its personal, social, political and religious problems. The source of this "wisdom" is neither divine revelation nor philosophical reason but the actual experience of life, both as handed down from the forefather and as personally encountered. The wise man (Hebrew, *Hakham*), as distinguished from the priest, prophet or philosopher, taught first and foremost that the good life was a life of righteousness before God and man. Then, love and regard for one's fellow man, self-respect, contentment, pursuit of knowledge and understanding that the beginning and the end of wisdom is "the fear of the Lord" were emphasized.

Wisdom (or *Hokhmah*) literature is represented in the Hebrew Bible by the Proverbs (*Mishle*), Ecclesiastes (*Kohelet*), a number of Psalms and Job—the latter being a profound challenge of the self-sufficiency of human knowledge and wisdom, and of the theory that there is a connection between righteous living and happiness.

The Apocrypha preserve in this literary form the Wisdom of Ben Sira and the Wisdom of Solomon.

The Wisdom of Joshua (Jesus) Ben Sira (or Sirach), or Ecclesiasticus of the English Versions, was written in Jerusalem, between 200 and 180 B.C. About half a century later, the author's grandson translated the book from its original Hebrew into Greek for the benefit of the Jewish community in Egypt. This version became a part of the Greek Bible; similarly, a Syriac translation, incorporated into the Syriac Bible (*Peshitta*), is based on the Hebrew original. The original Hebrew text, quotations of which appear in the talmudic literature, went out of circulation in the later Middle Ages. Only in 1896 and shortly afterward were parts of the Hebrew text (eleventh to twelfth centuries) that go back to the original discovered in the *Genizah* (storeroom) of an old Cairo synagogue.

Ben Sira's work offers an invaluable picture of life in Jerusalem before the Maccabean uprising. The nation, according to him, was divided into two groups: (1) the wealthy, worldly and morally unrestrained; (2) the poor, humble and pious. However, the differences had not yet taken shape in the form of organized factions or doctrinal leadership, and the point had not yet been reached where coexistence became impossible.

The origin of wisdom

All wisdom cometh from the Lord,
    And is with Him forever.
The sand of the seas, and the drops of rain,
    And the days of eternity—who can number them?
The height of the heaven, and the breadth of the earth,
    And the deep—who can trace them out?
Before them all was Wisdom created,
    And prudent insight from everlasting.
The root of Wisdom, to whom hath it been revealed?
    And her subtle thoughts, who hath known them?
One there is, greatly to be feared,
    The Lord sitting upon His throne;
He himself created her, and saw, and numbered her,
    And poured her out upon all His works;
Upon all flesh in measure,
    But without measure doth He grant her to them that love
    Him.

The fear of the Lord is the true wisdom

The fear of the Lord is glory and exultation,
    And gladness, and a crown of rejoicing.
The fear of the Lord delighteth the heart,
    And giveth gladness, and joy, and length of days.
Whoso feareth the Lord, it shall go well with him at the last,

And in the day of his death he shall be blessed.
To fear the Lord is the beginning of Wisdom,
  And with the faithful was she created in the womb.
With faithful men is she, and she hath been established from
      eternity;
  And with their seed shall she continue.
To fear the Lord is the fullness of Wisdom,
  And she satiateth men with her fruits.
She filleth all her house with pleasant things,
  And her garners with her produce.
The crown of Wisdom is the fear of the Lord,
  And increaseth peace and life and health.
She is a strong staff and a glorious stay,
  And everlasting honor to them that hold her fast.
To fear the Lord is the root of Wisdom,
  And her branches are length of days.

If thou desire Wisdom, keep the commandments,
  And the Lord will give her freely unto thee.
For the fear of the Lord is wisdom and instruction,
  And faith and meekness are well-pleasing unto Him.
My son, disobey not the fear of the Lord,
  And approach it not with a double heart.
Be not a hypocrite in the sight of men,
  And take good heed to thy lips.
Exalt not thyself lest thou fall,
  And bring disgrace upon thyself,
And the Lord reveal thy hidden thoughts,
  And cast thee down in the midst of the assembly,
Because thou camest not unto the fear of the Lord,
  And thy heart was full of deceit.

On free will

Say not: "From God is my transgression,"
  For that which He hateth made He not.
Say not: "It is He that made me to stumble,"
  For there is no need of evil men.
Evil and abomination doth the Lord hate,

And He doth not let it come nigh to them that fear Him.
God created man from the beginning,
　　And placed him in the hand of his inclination.[1]
If thou so desirest, thou canst keep the commandment,
　　And it is wisdom to do His good pleasure.
Poured out before thee are fire and water,
　　Stretch forth thine hand unto that which thou desirest.
Life and death are before man,
　　That which he desireth shall be given to him.
Sufficient is the wisdom of the Lord,[2]
　　He is mighty in power, and seeth all things.
And the eyes of God behold his works,
　　He knoweth every deed of man.
He commanded no man to sin,
　　Nor gave strength to men of lies.

A man's duties

Despise no man who is in bitterness of spirit,
　　Remember that there is one who exalteth and humbleth.
Devise not evil against a brother,
　　Nor do the like against a friend or a neighbor withal.
Take no delight in lies of any sort,
　　For the outcome thereof will not be pleasant.
Prate not in the assembly of elders,
　　And repeat not words in thy prayer.
Hate not laborious work,
　　Nor husbandry, for it was ordained of God.
Number not thyself among sinful men,
　　Remember that wrath will not tarry.
Humble thy pride greatly,
　　For the expectation of man is decay.

Change not a friend for money,
　　Nor a natural brother for gold of Ophir.
Reject not a wise wife;
　　And a well-favored wife is above pearls.
Maltreat not a servant that serveth truly,
　　Nor a hireling who giveth his life for thee.

A wise slave love as thyself,
  And withhold not from him his freedom.
Hast thou cattle, look to them thyself,
  And if they are profitable, keep them.
Hast thou sons, correct them,
  And give them wives in their youth.
Hast thou daughters, keep their bodies,
  And show them not a pleasant countenance.
Marry thy daughter, and sorrow will depart,
  But bestow her upon a man of understanding.
Hast thou a wife, forsake her not,
  But trust not thyself to one that hateth thee.
Honor thy father with thy whole heart,
  And forget not thy mother who bare thee.
Remember that of them thou wast begotten,
  And how canst thou recompense them for what they have
    done for thee?

Also to the poor stretch out thy hand,
  That the blessing may be perfected.
A gift hath grace in the sight of every man living,
  And also from the dead withhold not kindness.
Withdraw not thyself from them that weep,
  And mourn with them that mourn.
Forget not to visit the sick,
  For thou wilt be loved for that.
In all thy doings remember thy last end,
  Then wilt thou never do corruptly.

Of women

Be not jealous over the wife of thy bosom,
  Lest she learn malice against thee.
Give not thyself unto a woman,
  So as to let her trample down thy manhood.
Meet not a strange woman,
  Lest thou fall into her nets.
With a female singer have no converse,
  Lest thou be taken in her snares.

On a maiden fix not thy gaze,
    Lest thou be entrapped in penalties with her.
Give not thyself unto the harlot,
    Lest thou lose thine inheritance.
Look not round about thee in the streets of a city,
    And wander not about in the broad places thereof.
Hide thine eye from a lovely woman,
    And gaze not upon beauty which is not thine;
By the comeliness of a woman many have been ruined,
    And this way passion flameth like fire.
With a married woman sit not at table,
    And mingle not wine in her company;
Lest thou incline thine heart towards her,
    And in thy blood fallest into destruction.

I would rather dwell with a lion and a dragon,
    Than keep house with a wicked woman.
The wickedness of a woman maketh black her look,
    And darkeneth her countenance like that of a bear.
In the midst of his friends her husband sitteth,
    And involuntarily he sigheth bitterly.
There is but little malice like the malice of a woman,
    May the lot of the wicked fall upon her!
As a sandy ascent to the feet of the aged,
    So is a woman of tongue to a quiet man.
Fall not because of the beauty of woman,
    And be not ensnared for the sake of what she possesseth;
For hard slavery and a disgrace it is,
    If a wife support her husband.
A humbled heart and a sad countenance,
    And a heart-wound, is an evil wife.
Hands that hang down, and palsied knees,
    Thus shall it be with a wife that maketh not happy her
        husband.
From a woman did sin originate,
    And because of her we all must die.
Give not water an outlet,

Nor to a wicked woman power.
If she go not as thou would have her,
    Cut her off from thy flesh.

A good wife—blessed is her husband,
    The number of his days is doubled.
A worthy wife cherisheth her husband,
    And he fulfilleth the years of his life in peace.
A good wife is a good gift:
    She shall be given to him that feareth God, for his portion.
Whether rich or poor, his heart is cheerful,
    And his face is merry at all times.

The training of children

He that loveth his son will continue to lay strokes upon him,[3]
    That he may rejoice over him at the last.
He that disciplineth his son shall have satisfaction of him,
    And among his acquaintance glory in him.
He that teacheth his son maketh his enemy jealous,
    And in the presence of friends exulteth in him.
When his father dieth he dieth not altogether,[4]
    For he hath left one behind him like himself.
In his life he saw and rejoiced,
    And in death he hath not been grieved.
Against enemies he hath left behind an avenger,
    And to friends one that requiteth favor.
He that pampereth his son shall bind up his wounds,
    And his heart trembleth at every cry.

An unbroken horse becometh stubborn,
    And a son left at large becometh headstrong.
Cocker thy son and he will terrify thee;
    Play with him and he will grieve thee.
Laugh not with him, lest he vex thee,
    And make thee gnash thy teeth at the last.
Let him not have freedom in his youth,
    And overlook not his mischievous acts.
Bow down his neck in his youth,

And smite his loins sore while he is little—
Lest he become stubborn and rebel against thee,
　　And thou experience anguish of soul on his account.
Discipline thy son, and make his yoke heavy,
　　Lest in his folly he stumble.

The physician

Cultivate the physician in accordance with the need of him,
　　For him also hath God ordained.[5]
It is from God that the physician getteth wisdom,
　　And from the king he receiveth gifts.
The skill of the physician lifteth up his head,
　　And he may stand before nobles.
God hath created medicines out of the earth,
　　And let not a discerning man reject them.
Was not the water made sweet by the wood,[6]
　　That He might make known to all men His power?
And He gave men discernment,
　　That they might glory in His mighty works,
By means of them the physician assuageth pain,
　　And likewise the apothecary prepareth a confection:
That His work may not cease,
　　Nor health from the face of His earth.
My son, in sickness be not negligent;
　　Pray unto God, for He can heal.
Turn from iniquity, and purify thy hands;
　　And from all transgressions cleanse thy heart.[7]
Give a meal-offering with a memorial,
　　And offer a fat sacrifice to the utmost of thy means.
And to the physician also give a place;
　　Nor should he be far away, for of him there is need.
For there is a time when successful help is in his power;
　　For he also maketh supplication to God,
To make his diagnosis successful,
　　And the treatment, that it may promote recovery.
But he that sinneth before his Maker
　　Let him fall into the hands of the physician.

The Ideal Scribe

FROM THE WISDOM OF BEN SIRA

He that applieth himself to the fear of God,
    And setteth his mind upon the Law of the Most High,
He searcheth out the wisdom of all the ancients,
    And is occupied with the prophets of old.
He heedeth the discourses of men of renown,
    And entereth into the deep things of parables;
Searcheth out the hidden meaning of proverbs,
    And is conversant with the dark sayings of parables;
He serveth among great men,
    And appeareth before princes;
He traveleth through the lands of the peoples,[8]
    Testeth good and evil among men;
He is careful to seek unto his Maker,
    And before the Most High entreateth mercy;
He openeth his mouth in prayer,
    And maketh supplication for his sins.

If it seem good to God Most High,
    He shall be filled with the spirit of understanding.
He himself poureth forth wise sayings in double measure,
    And giveth thanks unto the Lord in prayer.
He himself directeth counsel and knowledge,
    And setteth his mind on their secrets.
He himself declareth wise instruction,
    And glorieth in the law of the Lord.
His understanding many do praise,
    And never shall his name be blotted out:
His memory shall not cease,
    And his name shall live from generation to generation.
His wisdom doth the congregation tell forth,

And his praise the assembly publisheth.
If he live long, he shall be accounted happy more than a
    thousand;
And when he cometh to an end, his name sufficeth.

Manifestation of God in Nature

FROM THE WISDOM OF BEN SIRA

The beauty of the [heavenly] height is the pure firmament,
    And the firm heaven poureth out light.
The sun when it goeth forth maketh heat to shine—
    How awe-inspiring is the work of the Lord.
At noontide it bringeth the world to boiling heat,
    And before its scorching ray who can maintain himself?
Like a glowing furnace which keepeth the casting hot,
    So the sun's dart setteth the mountains ablaze:
A tongue of flame consumeth the inhabited world,
    And with its fire the eye is scorched.
For great is the Lord that made it,
    And His word maketh His mighty [servant] brilliant.
Moreover, the moon He made for its due season,
    To rule over periods and for an everlasting sign:
By the moon are determined the feasts and times prescribed,
    A light-giver waning with her course:
Month by month she reneweth herself—
    How wonderful is she in her changing!
The army-signal of the cloud-vessels on high,
    She paveth the firmament with her shining.

The beauty of heaven, and the glory, are the stars,
    And a gleaming ornament in the heights of God.
At the word of the Holy One they take their prescribed place,
    And they sleep not at their watches.
Behold the rainbow and bless its Maker,
    For it is majestic exceedingly in majesty:

It encompasseth the heavenly vault with its glory,
  And the hand of God hath spread it out in pride.
His might marketh out the lightning,
  And maketh brilliant the flashes of His judgment.
On that account He hath created a treasure house,
  And He maketh the clouds fly like birds.
By His mighty power He maketh strong the clouds,
  And the hailstones are broken.
His thunder's voice maketh His earth to be in anguish
  And by His strength He shaketh mountains.
The terror of Him stirreth up the south wind,
  The whirlwind of the north, hurricane, and tempest;
Like flocks of birds, He sheddeth abroad His snow,
  And like settling locusts is the fall thereof.
The beauty of the whiteness dazzleth the eyes,
  And the heart marveleth at the raining thereof.
The hoarfrost also He poureth out like salt,
  And maketh the crystals sparkle like sapphire.
The icy blast of the north wind He causeth to blow,
  And hardeneth the pond like a bottle.
Over every basin of water He spreadeth a crust,
  And the pond putteth on as it were a breastplate.
It burneth up the produce of the mountains as a drought,
  And the sprouting pasture as a flame.
A healing for all such is the distillation of the clouds,
  Even the dew, alighting to bring refreshment after heat.
By His counsel He hath stilled the deep,
  And hath planted the islands in the ocean.
They that go down to the sea tell of its extent,
  And when our ears hear it we are astonished.
Therein are marvels, the most wondrous of His works,
  All kinds of living things, and whales created.
By reason of Him their end prospereth,
  And at His word what He wills is done.

More like this we will not add,
  And the conclusion of the matter is: He is all.
We will sing praises, because we cannot fathom;

For greater is He than all His works.
Terrible is the Lord exceedingly,
    And wonderful are His mighty acts.
Ye that magnify the Lord, lift up your voice,
    As much as ye can, for there is still more!
Ye that exalt Him, renew your strength,
    And weary not, for ye cannot fathom Him!
Who hath seen Him, that he may tell thereof?
    And who shall magnify Him as he is?
The number of things mysterious is greater even than these,
    And I have seen but few of His works.
Everything hath the Lord made,
    And to the pious hath He given wisdom.

The High Priest, Simon, Son of Johanan

FROM THE WISDOM OF BEN SIRA

Great among his brethren and the glory of his people
    Was Simon, son of Johanan the priest.[9]
In whose time the House[10] was renovated,
    And in whose days the Temple was fortified;
In whose days the wall was built,
    Having turrets for protection like a king's palace;
In whose time a reservoir was dug,
    A water cistern like the sea in its abundance.
He took thought for his people to preserve them from robbers,
    And fortified his city against the enemy.
How glorious was he when he looked forth from the Tent,[11]
    And when he came out from the sanctuary!
Like a morning star from between the clouds,
    And like the full moon on the feast days;
Like the sun shining upon the Temple of the Most High,
    And like the rainbow becoming visible in the cloud;
Like a flower on the branches in the days of the first-fruits,[12]
    And as a lily by the water brooks,

As the sprout of Lebanon on summer days,
    And as the fire of incense in the censer;
Like a golden vessel beautifully wrought,
    Adorned with all manner of precious stones;
Like a luxuriant olive tree full of berries,
    And like an oleaster abounding in branches.
When he put on his glorious robes,
    And clothed himself in perfect splendor,
When he went up to the altar of majesty,
    And made glorious the court of the sanctuary;
When he took the portions from the hand of his brethren,
    While standing by the blocks of wood,
Around him the garland of his sons,
    Like young cedar trees in Lebanon;
And like willows by the brook did they surround him,
    All the sons of Aaron in their glory,
And the Lord's fire-offering in their hands,
    In the presence of the whole congregation of Israel.

Until he had finished the service of the altar
    And arranging the rows of wood of the Most High,
And stretched forth his hand to the cup,
    And poured out of the blood of the grape;
Yet, poured it out at the foot of the altar,
    A sweet-smelling savor to the Most High, the All-King.
Then the sons of Aaron sounded
    With the trumpets of beaten work;
Yea, they sounded and caused a mighty blast to be heard
    For a remembrance before the Most High.
Then all flesh hasted together
    And fell upon their faces to the earth,
To worship before the Most High,
    Before the Holy One of Israel.
And the sound of the song was heard,
    And over the multitude they made sweet melody;
And all the people of the land cried
    In prayer before the Merciful One,
Until he had finished the service of the altar,

And His ordinances had brought him nigh unto Him.
Then he descended, and lifted up his hands
    Upon the whole congregation of Israel,
And the blessing of the Lord was upon his lips,
And he glorified himself with the name of the Lord.
And again they fell down, now to receive
    The pardon of God from him.

Now bless the God of all,
    Who doeth wondrously on earth,
Who exalteth man from the womb,
    And dealeth with him according to His will.
May He grant you wisdom of heart,
    And may there be peace among you.
May His mercy be established with Simon,
    And may He raise up for him the covenant of Phinehas;[13]
May one never be cut off from him;
    And as to his seed, may it be as the days of heaven.

Wisdom and the Order of This World

FROM THE WISDOM OF SOLOMON

A note on the Wisdom of Solomon. Wisdom is not merely a guide to a prudent and most efficient way of life, or an advocation of righteousness. Reminiscent of the position of the *Logos* in Stoic philosophy, Wisdom is held to be "the holy spirit from on high," "penetrating all things by reason of her pureness." It is "the breath of the power of God," the source of all truth. Such exaltation of the cosmic rôle of Wisdom, implied in earlier works of this category, is the hallmark of the Wisdom of Solomon.

There are various scholarly opinions on the authorship and date of the book. The soundest seems to be the view of Charles Cutler Torrey, who considers it to be a composite work, the first half (chapters 1 to 10) having been originally a Hebrew poetical composition, that the author of the second half, which is Greek rhetoric of the Alexandrian type, translated into Greek. The book as a whole presents a beautiful blend of Hebraic piety and elements of Greek philosophy. Its doctrine of the immortality of the soul is Platonic. To give the work greater authority it was, like Proverbs and Ecclesiastes, attributed to King Solomon, the wisest of men. The most probable date of its composition seems to be around 100 B.C.

Wisdom is a spirit that loveth man

Love righteousness, ye that be judges of the earth,
Thank ye of the Lord with a good mind,
And in singleness of heart seek ye him;
Because he is found of them that tempt him not,
And is manifested to them that do not distrust him.
For crooked thoughts separate from God;
And the [supreme] Power, when it is brought to the proof,
         putteth to confusion the foolish;
Because wisdom will not enter into a soul that deviseth evil,
Nor dwell in a body held in pledge by sin.
For the holy spirit of discipline will flee deceit,
And will start away from thoughts that are without
         understanding,
And will be scared away when unrighteousness approacheth.

For wisdom is a spirit that loveth man,
And she will not hold a blasphemer guiltless for his lips;
Because God is witness of his reins,
And is a true overseer of his heart,
And a hearer of his tongue:
Because the spirit of the Lord filleth the world,
And that which holdeth all things together[14] hath knowledge
         of every voice.
Therefore no man that uttereth unrighteous things shall be
         unseen;
Neither shall justice, when it punisheth, pass him by.
For the counsels of the ungodly shall be searched out;
And the report of his words shall come unto the Lord
For the punishment of his lawless deeds:
Because there is a zealous ear that listeneth to all things,
And the noise of murmurings is not hid.
Beware then of unprofitable murmuring,
And refrain your tongue from blasphemy;

Because no secret utterance shall go forth with impunity;
And a mouth that lieth destroyeth the soul.

Court not death in the error of your life;
Neither draw upon yourselves destruction by the works of your
    hands:[15]
Because God made not death;
Neither delighteth he when the living perish:
For he created all things that they might have being:
And the products of the world are healthsome,
And there is no poison of destruction in them:
Nor hath Hades royal dominion upon earth;
For righteousness is immortal.

God—lover of souls

To be greatly strong is Thine at all times;
And the might of Thine arm who shall withstand?
Because the whole world before Thee is as a grain in a balance,
And as a drop of dew that at morning cometh down upon the
    earth.
But Thou hast mercy on all men, because Thou hast power to
    do all things,
And Thou overlookest the sins of men to the end they may
    repent.[16]
For Thou lovest all things that are,
And abhorrest none of the things which Thou didst make;
For never wouldst Thou have formed anything if Thou didst
    hate it.
And how would anything have endured, except Thou hadst
    willed it?
Or that which was not called by Thee, how would it have
    been preserved?
But Thou sparest all things, because they are Thine,
O Sovereign Lord, Thou lover of souls;
For Thine incorruptible spirit is in all things.
Wherefore Thou dost chastise by little and little them that
    fall from the right way,

And, putting them in remembrance by the very things wherein
    they sin, dost Thou admonish them,
That escaping from their wickedness they may believe on
    Thee, O Lord.

Wisdom is a breath of the power of God

There is in wisdom a spirit: understanding, holy,
Alone in kind, manifold,
Subtile, freely moving,
Clear in utterance, unpolluted,
Distinct, that cannot be harmed,
Loving what is good, keen, unhindered,
Beneficent, loving toward man,
Steadfast, sure, free from care,
All-powerful, all-surveying,
And penetrating through all spirits
That are quick of understanding, pure, subtile.
For wisdom is more mobile than any motion;
Yea, she pervadeth and penetrateth all things by reason of her
    pureness.
For she is a breath of the power of God,
And a clear effluence of the glory of the Almighty;
Therefore can nothing defiled find entrance into her.
For she is a radiance from everlasting light
And an unspotted mirror of the working of God,
And an image of his goodness.
And she, though but one, hath power to do all things;
And remaining in herself, reneweth all things:
And from generation to generation passing into holy souls
She maketh them friends of God[17] and prophets.[18]
For nothing doth God love save him that dwelleth with
    wisdom.
For she is fairer than the sun,
And above all the constellations of the stars:
Being compared with light, she is found to be before it;
For the light of day succeedeth night,

But against wisdom evil doth not prevail;
But she reacheth from one end of the world to the other with
    full strength,
And ordereth all things well.

Solomon desired wisdom as a bride

Her I loved and sought out from my youth,[19]
And I sought to take her for my bride.
And I became enamored of her beauty.
She proclaimeth her noble birth in that it is given her to live
    with God,
And the Sovereign Lord of all loved her.
For she is initiated into the knowledge of God,
And she chooseth out for him his works.
But if riches are a desired possession in life,
What is richer than wisdom, which worketh all things?
And if understanding worketh,
Who more than wisdom is an artificer of the things that are?
And if a man loveth righteousness,
The fruits of wisdom's labor are virtues,
For she teacheth self-control and understanding, righteous-
    ness, and courage;[20]
And there is nothing in life for men more profitable than
    these.
And if a man longeth even for much experience,
She knoweth the things of old, and divineth the things to
    come:
She understandeth subtilties of speeches and interpretations
    of dark sayings:
She foreseeth signs and wonders, and the issues of seasons and
    times.
I determined therefore to take her unto me to live with me,
Knowing that she is one who would give me good thoughts
    for counsel,
And encourage me in cares and grief.
Because of her I shall have glory among multitudes,
And honor in the sight of elders, though I be young.
I shall be found of a quick discernment when I give judgment,

And in the presence of princes I shall be admired.
When I am silent, they shall wait for me;
And when I open my lips, they shall give heed unto me;
And if I continue speaking, they shall lay their hand upon
    their mouth.
Because of her I shall have immortality,
And leave behind an eternal memory to them that come after
    me.
I shall govern peoples,
And nations shall be subjected to me.
Dread princes shall fear me when they hear of me:
Among my people I shall show myself a good ruler, and in war
    courageous.
When I come into my house, I shall find rest with her;
For converse with her hath no bitterness,
And to live with her hath no pain, but gladness and joy.
When I considered these things in myself,
And took thought in my heart how that in kinship unto
    wisdom is immortality,
And in her friendship is good delight,
And in the labors of her hands is wealth that faileth not,
And in assiduous communing with her is understanding,
And great renown in having fellowship with her words,
I went about seeking how to take her unto myself.

Immortality

God created man for eternal life,
And made him an image of His own proper being;
But by the envy of Satan death entered into the world,[21]
And they that belong to his realm experience it.
But the souls of the righteous are in the hand of God,
And no torment shall touch them.
In the eyes of fools they seemed to die;
And their departure was accounted to be their hurt,
And their going from us to be their ruin:
But they are in peace.[22]
For though in the sight of men they be punished,
Their hope is full of immortality;

And having borne a little chastening, they shall receive great
      good;
Because God tested them, and found them worthy of Himself.
As gold on the furnace He proved them,
And as a whole burnt offering He accepted them.
And in the time of their visitation they shall shine forth,
And like sparks among stubble they shall run to and fro.
They shall judge nations, and have dominion over peoples;
And the Lord shall reign over them for evermore.
They that trust on Him shall understand truth,
And the faithful shall abide with Him in love;
Because grace and mercy are to His chosen,
And He will graciously visit His holy ones.

II. For the Sake of Freedom of Religion

A *Note on the First and the Second Book of Maccabees.* When in 168 B.C. King Antiochus IV Epiphanes of Syria, in pursuit of a forced Hellenization in his realm, decreed the abolition of the Mosaic law and commanded the introduction of the pagan cult in the Temple of Jerusalem, people were ready to rebel against both the Syrian overlord and the Jewish Hellenist party within, to fight for the freedom of religion and, later, for the political independence of Judaea. This rebellion, its progress and its outcome, are the theme of the First Book of Maccabees. It tells the story of the accession of Antiochus IV Epiphanes, the dramatic rise of the priest Mattathias of Modin and his five sons, the battles waged, primarily by the most heroic among the sons, Judah the Maccabee ("the Hammer"), the rededication of the Temple (commemorated in the *Hanukkah* ["dedication"] festival), the military pursuits of Judah's brother Jonathan and the actions of the last surviving brother, Simon (died 134 B.C.). It was Simon who brought the war to an end, secured independence, renewed a treaty of friendship with Sparta and Rome and established his family as the ruling house in Judaea.

The unknown author, a witness of the rebellion, wrote his book around 125 B.C.; the Hebrew original disappeared in the first Christian century; the extant Greek text is a translation from the Hebrew. The author, a skilled historian who took the historical writings of the Bible as his model, stands on the side of the Maccabean fighters. His aim is not propaganda but an objective, straightforward account of the events. His book is the most important source for this crucial period in history.

In contradistinction to the factual, down-to-earth history of the First Book of Maccabees, the Second is a passionate tale of the indomitable faith and spirit of resistance to tyranny that motivated the rebels. The book, whose content corresponds, roughly, to the first seven chapters of First Maccabees, is a condensation of a no longer extant history of the period in five books by a certain Jason of Cyrene. The unknown epitomist lived in Egypt, possibly in

Alexandria, and wrote in Greek towards the end of the second pre-Christain century. The book aimed at making Jews in the Diaspora aware of the heroism of their brethren in Jerusalem and at deepening their affection for the Temple. This purpose was served by the story of the steadfast old scribe, Eleazar, who chose death to transgression of the dietary laws, and the account of the martyrdom of the mother and her seven sons (our selection). In periods of religious persecution, Jews and Christians alike drew strength and comfort from the memory of these witnesses for the "faith," a term that gained prominence in Jewish thought of the era.

The Origin of the Maccabean Rebellion

FROM THE FIRST BOOK OF MACCABEES

The victory of Alexander the Great

And it came to pass after Alexander [356–323 B.C.], the son of Philip the Macedonian, who came from the land of Chittim [Greece], had smitten Darius [III, Codomannus], king of the Persians and Medes, that he reigned in his stead. He waged many wars, and won strongholds, and slew kings, and pressed forward to the ends of the earth, and took spoils from many peoples. But when the land was silenced before him, he became exalted, and his heart was lifted up. Then he gathered together a very mighty army, and ruled over lands and peoples and principalities; they became tributary unto him.

After these things he took to his bed, and perceived that he was about to die. Then he called his chief ministers, men who had been brought up with him from his youth, and divided his kingdom among them while he was yet alive. Alexander had reigned twelve years [336–323 B.C.] when he died. And his ministers ruled, each in his particular domain. After he was dead they all assumed the diadem, as did their sons after them for many years; they wrought much evil on the earth.

Antiochus Epiphanes and the Hellenists

A sinful shoot came forth from them, Antiochus Epiphanes, the son of Antiochus [III] the king [reigned 223–187 B.C.], who had been a hostage in Rome.[1] He became king in the one hundred and thirty-seventh year of the Greek kingdom.[2] In those days there came forth out of Israel lawless men[3] who persuaded many, saying: "Let us go and make a covenant with the nations around us; for since we separated ourselves from them many evils have come upon us."

The saying appeared good in their eyes; and certain of the people went eagerly to the king who gave them authority to introduce the customs of the heathen. They built a gymnasium in Jerusalem according to the manner of the heathen. They also submitted themselves to uncircumcision[4] and repudiated the holy covenant; yea, they joined themselves to the heathen and sold themselves to do evil.

Antiochus subdues Egypt

When, in the opinion of Antiochus, the kingdom was sufficiently established, he determined to exercise dominion also over the land of Egypt, in order that he might rule over two kingdoms. So he pushed forward into Egypt [171–170 B.C.] with an immense force, with chariots, elephants and horsemen, together with a great fleet. He waged war against Ptolemy [VI, Philometor], king of Egypt. Ptolemy turned back from before him and fled while many were wounded. They captured the fortified cities in Egypt; and he took the spoils from the land of Egypt.[5]

The desecration of the Temple

After he had smitten Egypt, Antiochus returned in the one hundred and forty-third year [170 B.C.], and went up against Israel and Jerusalem with a great army. In his arrogance he entered the Temple, and took the golden altar, the candlestick for the light and all its accessories, the table of the shewbread, the cups, the bowls and the golden censers, the veil, the crowns; and the golden adornment on the facade of the Temple he scaled off entirely. He took the silver, the gold, and the choice vessels; he also took the hidden treasures which he found. Having taken everything, he returned to his own land. He made a great slaughter and spoke most arrogantly.

And there was great mourning in Israel in every place;
Both the rulers and elders groaned;
Virgins and young men languished,
The beauty of the women faded away;
Every bridegroom took up lament,
She that sat in the bridal chamber mourned.
The land was moved for her inhabitants,
And all the house of Jacob was clothed with shame.

Jerusalem occupied by Apollonius

After two years, the king sent a chief collector of tribute[6] to the cities of Judah; and he came to Jerusalem with a great host. He spoke to them peaceful words in subtilty, so that they had confidence in him. Then he fell upon the city suddenly, and smote it with a grievous stroke, destroying much people in Israel. He took the spoils of the city, burned it with fire, and pulled down its houses and the walls surrounding it. They led captive the women and the children, and took possession of the cattle. They fortified the city of David with a great and strong wall with strong towers, so that it was made into a citadel[7] for them. They placed there a sinful nation, lawless men; and they strengthened themselves in it. They stored up arms and provisions, and after collecting together the spoils of Jerusalem, they laid them up there. It became a sore menace, for it was a place to lie in wait in against the sanctuary, an evil adversary to Israel continually.

They shed innocent blood on every side of the sanctuary,
And they defiled the sanctuary.
Because of them the inhabitants of Jerusalem fled,
She became a dwelling for strangers,
Being herself estranged to her offspring,

And her children forsook her.
Her sanctuary became desolate as a wilderness,
Her feasts were turned into mourning,
Her sabbaths into shame,
Her honor into contempt.
According as her glory had been so was now her dishonor
        increased,
And her high estate was turned to mourning.

Edict of Antiochus; religious persecution

Then the king wrote to his whole kingdom, that all should be one people, and that every one should give up his laws. All the nations acquiesced in accordance with the command of the king. Even many in Israel took delight in his worship and began sacrificing to idols and profaned the Sabbath.

Furthermore, the king sent letters by messengers to Jerusalem and to the cities of Judah to the effect that they should practice customs foreign to the land, and that they should cease the whole burnt offerings and sacrifices, and drink offerings in the sanctuary, that they should profane the Sabbaths and feasts, and pollute the sanctuary and those who had been sanctified; that they should build high places, and sacred groves and shrines for idols, and that they should sacrifice swine and other unclean animals; that they should leave their sons uncircumcised, and defile themselves by every kind of uncleanness and profanation, so that they might forget the Law and change all the ordinances.[8] Whoever should not act according to the word of the king, should die.

In this manner he wrote to all his kingdom, and appointed overseers over all the people and commanded the cities of Judah to sacrifice, every one of them. Many of the people joined them, all those who had forsaken the Law; these did evil in the land, and caused Israel to hide in all manner of hiding places.

On the twenty-fifth day of Kislev [December] in the one hundred and forty-sixth year [168 B.C.] they set up upon the

altar an "abomination of desolation," [9] and in the cities of
Judah on every side they established altars; they offered sacrifice at the doors of the houses and in the streets. The books of
the Law which they found they rent in pieces and burned.
With whomsoever was found a book of the covenant, and if
he was found consenting unto the Law, such an one was, according to the king's sentence, condemned to death. Thus did
they in their might to the Israelites who were found month by
month in their cities.

On the twenty-fifth day of the month they sacrificed
upon the altar which was upon the altar of burnt-offering. According to the decree, they put to death the women who had
circumcised their children, hanging their babes round their
necks, and they put to death their families, together with
those who had circumcised them. Nevertheless many in Israel
stood firm and determined in their hearts that they would not
eat unclean things, and chose rather to die so that they might
not be defiled with meats, thereby profaning the holy covenant; and they did die. Exceeding great wrath came upon
Israel.

The uprising under Mattathias

In those days Mattathias, the son of John, the son of
Simeon, a priest of the sons of Joarib,[10] moved from Jerusalem
and dwelt at Modin.[11] He had five sons: John, who was surnamed Gaddi, Simon, who was called Thassi, Judah who was
called Maccabee, Eleazar, who was called Auaran, and Jonathan, who was called Apphus.

When Mattathias saw the blasphemous things that were
done in Judah and in Jerusalem, he said, "Woe is me, why
was I born to behold the ruin of my people and the ruin of the
holy city, and to sit still there while it was being given into
the hand of enemies, and the sanctuary into the hand of
strangers?"

Her house has become as a man dishonored;
Her glorious vessels are carried away captive;
Her infants have been slain in her streets,

Her young men with the sword of the enemy.
What nation hath the kingdom not taken possession of,
Of what nation hath it not seized the spoils?
Her adornment hath all been taken away,
Instead of a free woman she is become a slave.
And, behold, our holy things, and our beauty, and our glory
    have been laid waste,
The heathen have profaned them! To what purpose should we
    continue to live?

Mattathias and his sons rent their garments, covered themselves with sackcloth, and mourned greatly.

Then the king's officers who were enforcing the apostasy came to the city of Modin to make them sacrifice. Many from Israel went unto them; but Mattathias and his sons gathered themselves together. The king's officers said to Mattathias: "A leader art thou, illustrious and great in this city, and upheld by sons and brothers. Do thou, therefore, come first, and carry out the king's command, as all the nations have done, and all the people of Judah, and they that have remained in Jerusalem; then shalt thou and thy house be numbered among the friends of the king, and thou and thy sons shall be honored with silver and gold and many gifts."

Mattathias answered and said in a loud voice: "If all the nations within the king's dominions obey him by forsaking, every one of them, the worship of their fathers, and have chosen for themselves to follow his commands, yet will I and my sons and my brethren walk in the covenant of our fathers. Heaven forbid that we should forsake the Law and the ordinances; but the law of the king we will not obey by departing from our worship either to the right or to the left."

As he ceased speaking these words, a Jew came forward in the sight of all to sacrifice upon the altar in Modin, in accordance with the king's command. When Mattathias saw it, his zeal was kindled, and his heart quivered with wrath. His indignation burst forth for judgment so that he ran and slew him on the altar; at the same time he also killed the king's officer who had come to enforce the sacrificing, pulled down the altar. Thus he showed his zeal for the Law, as Phinehas had done in the case of Zimri the son of Salom.[12] Then Mattathias cried out with a loud voice in the city, saying, "Let everyone that is zealous for the Law and would maintain the covenant follow me!"

He and his sons fled unto the mountains, and left all that they possessed in the city.

At that time many who were seeking righteousness and judgment went down to the wilderness to abide there, they and their sons, their wives, and their cattle, for misfortunes fell hardly upon them. It was reported to the king's officers and to the troops that were in Jerusalem, the city of David, that men who had rejected the king's command had gone down to hiding places in the wilderness. Many ran after them, overtook them, encamped against them, and set the battle in array against them on the Sabbath day. They said to them: "Let it suffice now; come forth and do according to the command of the king, and ye shall live." But they answered, "We will not come forth, nor will we do according to the command of the king and thereby profane the Sabbath day." Thereupon they attacked them. But they answered them not nor did they cast a stone at them, nor block up their hiding places, saying, "Let us all die in our innocence; Heaven and earth bear us witness that ye destroy us wrongfully." They attacked them on the Sabbath, and they died, they, their wives, their children, and their cattle, about a thousand souls.

When Mattathias and his friends heard this, they mourned greatly for them. One said to another, "If we all do as our brethren have done, and do not fight against the heathen for our lives and our ordinances, they will soon destroy us from off the earth." They took counsel on that day, saying, "Whosoever attacketh us on the Sabbath day, let us fight against him, that we may not all die as our brethren died in their hiding places."

Then were there gathered unto them a company of the Hasidim,[13] mighty men of Israel, each one willingly offering themselves in defense of the Law. All they that fled from the evils joined them and reinforced them. They mustered a host and smote sinners in their anger, and lawless men in their wrath; and the rest fled to the heathens to save themselves. Mattathias and his friends went about, and pulled down the altars, and circumcised by force the children that were uncircumcised, as many as they found within the borders of Israel. They pursued after the sons of pride, and the work prospered in their hand. Thus they rescued the Law out of the hand of the heathen and the kings, neither suffered they the sinner to triumph.

His last words

When the days drew near that Mattathias should die, he said unto his sons:

Now have pride and arrogance gotten strong; this is a season of destruction and wrath of indignation. My children, be zealous for the Law, and give your lives for the covenant of your fathers. Call to mind the deeds of the fathers which they did in their generations, that ye may receive great glory and everlasting name.

Was not Abraham found faithful in temptation,[14] and it was reckoned unto him for righteousness? Joseph in the time of his distress,[15] kept the commandment and became lord of Egypt. Phinehas, our father,[16] for that he was zealous exceedingly, obtained the covenant of an everlasting priesthood. Joshua[17] for fulfilling the word became a judge in Israel. Caleb[18] for bearing witness in the congregation obtained land as an heritage. David[19] for being merciful inherited the throne of a kingdom for ever and ever. Elijah[20] for that he was exceeding zealous for the Law was taken up into heaven. Hananiah, Azariah and Mishael,[21] believing in God, were saved from the flame. Daniel,[22] for his innocence, was delivered from the mouth of the lions.

And thus consider ye from generation to generation: all who hope in Him shall want nothing. Be not afraid of the words of a sinful man, for his glory shall be dung and worms. Today he shall be lifted up, and to-morrow he shall in no wise be found, because he is returned unto his dust, and his thought will have perished. And ye, my children, be strong and show yourselves men on behalf of the Law, for therein shall ye obtain glory. Behold Simon your brother, I know that he is a man of counsel; give ear unto him always; he shall be a father unto you. Judah the Maccabee, he hath been strong and mighty from his youth; he shall be your leader and shall fight the battle of the people. And ye, take you unto you all those who observe the Law, and avenge the wrong of your people. Render a recompense to the heathen, and take heed to the commandments of the Law.

Then he blessed them and was gathered to his fathers. He died in the one hundred and forty-sixth year [168–167 B.C.], and his sons buried him in the sepulchres of his fathers at Modin; and all Israel made great lamentation for him.

The Rededication of the Temple

FROM THE FIRST BOOK OF MACCABEES

Judah and his brethren said: "Behold, our enemies are discomfited,[23] let us go up to cleanse the sanctuary and dedicate it."

All the army was gathered together, and they went up to mount Zion. They saw our sanctuary laid desolate and the altar profaned, the gates burned up, and shrubs growing in the courts as in a forest or upon one of the mountains, and the chambers of the priests pulled down; they rent their garments and made great lamentation, and put ashes on their heads, and fell on their faces to the ground, blew solemn blasts upon the trumpets, and cried unto heaven.

Judah appointed a certain number of men to fight against those in the citadel, until he should have cleansed the sanctuary. He chose blameless priests, such as had delight in the Law, and they cleansed the sanctuary, carrying out the stones that had defiled it into an unclean place. They took counsel concerning the altar of burnt offerings, which had been profaned, what they should do with it. A good idea occurred to them, namely, to pull it down, lest it should be a reproach unto them, because the heathen had defiled it; so they pulled down the altar, and laid down the stones in the Temple mount, in a convenient place, until a prophet should come and decide as to what should be done concerning them. They took whole stones according to the Law,[24] and built a new altar after the fashion of the former one; they built the sanctuary and the inner parts of the Temple, and hallowed the courts. They made the holy vessels new, and brought the candlestick, the altar of incense and the table into the Temple. They burned incense on the altar, and lighted the lamps that were on the candlestick in order to give light in the Temple. They set loaves of bread upon the table, hung up the veils, and finished all the works which they had undertaken.

They rose up early in the morning on the twenty-fifth day of the ninth month which is the month Kislev [December], in the one hundred and forty-ninth year [165 B.C.], and offered sacrifice according to the Law upon the new altar of burnt offerings which they had made. At the corresponding time and on the day on which the heathen had profaned it, on that day was it rededicated, with songs and harps and lutes and cymbals. All the people fell upon their faces and worshiped, and gave praise to Heaven, to Him who had prospered them. They celebrated the dedication of the altar for eight days,[25] brought burnt offerings with gladness, and offered a sacrifice of deliverance and praise.

They also decked the front of the Temple with crowns of gold and small shields, and rededicated the gates and the chambers of the priests, and furnished them with doors. Thus there was exceeding great gladness among the people, and the reproach of the heathen was turned away. Judah and his brethren and the whole congregation of Israel ordained that the days of the dedication of the altar should be kept in their seasons year by year for eight days, from the twenty-fifth of the month Kislev, with gladness and joy. At that season they built high walls and strong towers around mount Zion, lest the heathen should come and tread them down, as they had

done before. He set there a force to keep it, and they fortified
Beth Zur to keep it, that the people might have a stronghold
facing Idumaea.[26]

Simon's Beneficent Rule

FROM THE FIRST BOOK OF MACCABEES

The land of Judah had rest all the days of Simon;[27] he
sought the good of his nation; his authority and glory pleased
them all his days. In addition to all his other glory was this
that he took Joppa[28] for a harbor, and made it a place of entry
for the ships of the sea.

An ode in his honor

He enlarged the borders of his nation,
And ruled over the land.
He gathered together many that had been in captivity,
And he ruled over Gazara, and Beth Zur, and the citadel.
He took away uncleannesses therefrom,
And there was none that could resist him.
They tilled their land in peace,
The land gave her increase,
And the trees of the plains their fruit.
Old men sat in the streets,
All spoke together of the common weal,
And the young men put on glorious and warlike apparel.
For the cities he provided food,
And furnished them with defensive works,
Until his glorious name was proclaimed to the end of the
            earth.
He made peace in the land,
And Israel rejoiced with great joy.
Everyone sat under his vine and his fig tree,
There was none to make them afraid;
No one was left in the land to fight them

And the kings were discomfited in those days.
He strengthened all that were brought low of his people.
He sought out the Law,
And put away the lawless and wicked.
He glorified the sanctuary,
And multiplied the vessels of the Temple.

Renewal of the alliance with Rome

When it was heard in Rome that Jonathan[29] was dead, and even unto Sparta,[30] they were exceeding sorry. But as soon as they heard that his brother Simon was made high priest in his stead, and ruled the country and the cities therein, they wrote to him on tablets of brass, to renew with him the friendship and the confederacy which they had established with Judah and Jonathan his brethren; they were read before the congregation in Jerusalem.

Now this is the copy of the letter which the Spartans sent:

The rulers and the city of the Spartans, unto Simon the high priest, and unto the elders, the priests and the rest of the people of the Jews, our brethren, greeting. The ambassadors that were sent to our people made report to us of your glory and honor, and we were glad for their coming. We did register the things that were spoken by them in the public records, as follows: "Numenius, son of Antiochus, and Antipater, son of Jason, the Jews' ambassadors, came to us to renew the friendship with us." It pleased the people to receive the men honorably and to place the copy of their words among the public records, to the end that the people of the Spartans might have a memorial thereof. Moreover they wrote a copy of these things unto Simon the high priest.

After this Simon sent Numenius to Rome having a great shield of gold of a thousand pound weight,[31] to confirm the confederacy with them.

Elevation to high priesthood

When the people heard these things, they said: "What

thanks shall we give to Simon and his sons? For he, and his brethren and his father's house have made themselves strong, and have chased away in fight the enemies of Israel from them, and established liberty for it."

They wrote on tablets of brass, and set them upon a pillar on mount Zion. This is the copy of the writing:

On the eighteenth day of Elul [August-September], in the one hundred and seventy-second year [141 B.C.]—that is the third year of Simon the high priest, prince of the people of God—in a great congregation of priests and people and princes of the nation and elders of the country, the following was promulgated by us. Forasmuch as oftentimes there have been wars in the country, Simon the son of Mattathias, the son of the children of Joarib, and his brethren put themselves in jeopardy, and withstood the enemies of their nation, that their sanctuary and the Law might be upheld; thus they glorified their nation with great glory. Jonathan assembled their nation together, and became their high priest and was gathered to his people.

Then their enemies determined to invade their country and stretch forth their hands against their sanctuary. Then rose up Simon and fought for his nation, and spent much of his own substance, armed the valiant men of his nation and gave them wages. He fortified the cities of Judaea and Beth Zur on the borders of Judaea, where the arms of the enemies were formerly held, and set there a garrison of Jews. He fortified Joppa which is by the sea, and Gazara which is upon the borders of Ashdod, wherein the enemies formerly dwelt; he placed Jews there, and whatsoever things were needed for the sustenance of these he put in them.

When the people saw the faith of Simon and the glory which he sought to bring to his nation, they made him their leader and high priest,[32] because he had done all these things, and because of the justice and faith which he kept to his nation, and because he sought in every manner to exalt his people. In his days things prospered in his hands, so that the heathen were taken away out of their country, as well as those that were in the city of David, in Jerusalem, who had made themselves a citadel, out of which they used to issue and pollute all things around the sanctuary, doing great hurt unto its purity. He made Jews to dwell therein and fortified it for the safety of the country and of the city, and he made high the walls of Jerusalem.

King Demetrius [of Syria] confirmed him in the high priesthood in consequence of these things, and made him one of his Friends, and treated him with great honor. For he had heard that the Jews had been proclaimed by the Romans friends and confederates and brethren, and that they had met the ambassadors of Simon honorably. And the Jews and the priests were well pleased that Simon should be their leader and high priest for ever, until a faithful prophet should arise; and that he should be a captain over them, so that he would set them over their works, and over the country, the arms or the strongholds; that he should take charge of the sanctuary, and that he should be obeyed by all, and that all contracts in the country should be written in his name; that he should be clothed in purple and wear gold; that it should not be lawful for anyone among the people or among the priests to set at nought any of these things, or to gainsay the things spoken by him, or to gather an assembly in the country without him, or that any other should be clothed in purple or wear a buckle of gold; but that whoever should do otherwise, or set at nought any of these things, should be liable to punishment.

All the people consented to ordain for Simon that it should be done according to these words. Simon accepted and consented to fill the office of high priest, to be captain and governor of the Jews and of the priests and to preside over all matters.

They commanded to put this writing on tablets of brass and to set them up within the precinct of the sanctuary in a conspicuous place; copies of this they caused to be placed in the treasury, to the end that Simon and his sons[33] might have them.

Martyrdom of the Seven Brothers and Their Mother

FROM THE SECOND BOOK OF MACCABEES

It also came to pass that seven brothers and their mother were arrested and shamefully lashed with whips and scourges, by the king's orders, that they might be forced to taste the forbidden swine's flesh. But one of them spoke up for the others and said: "Why question us? What wouldst thou learn from us? We are prepared to die rather than transgress the laws of our fathers."

The king in his exasperation ordered pans and cauldrons to be heated, and, when they were heated immediately, ordered the tongue of the speaker to be torn out, had him scalped and mutilated before the eyes of his brothers and mother, and then had him put on the fire, all maimed and crippled as he was, but still alive, and set to fry in the pan. As the vapor from the pan spread abroad, the sons and their mother exhorted one another to die nobly, uttering these words: "The Lord God beholdeth this, and truly will have compassion on us, even as Moses declared in his Song, which testifieth against them to their face, saying, 'And he will have compassion on His servants'" (Deut. 32:36).

When the first had died after this manner, they brought the second to the shameful torture, tearing off the skin of his head with the hair and asking him: "Wilt thou eat, before we punish thy body limb by limb?" But he answered in the language of his fathers and said to them, "No." So he too underwent the rest of the torture, as the first had done. But when he was at the last gasp, he said: "Thou cursed miscreant! Thou dost dispatch us from this life, but the King of the Universe shall raise us up, who have died for His laws, and revive us to life everlasting."

After him the third was made a mocking-stock. When he was told to put out his tongue, he did so at once, stretching forth his hands courageously, with the noble words: "These I had from heaven; for His name's sake I count them naught; from Him I hope to get them back again." So much so that the king himself and his company were astounded at the spirit of the youth, for he thought nothing of his sufferings.

When he too was dead, they tortured the fourth in the same shameful fashion. When he was near his end, he said: "It is better for those who perish at men's hands to cherish hope divine that they shall be raised up by God again; but thou—thou shalt have no resurrection to life."

Next they brought the fifth and handled him shamefully. But he looked at the king and said: "Holding authority among men, thou doest what thou wilt, poor mortal; but dream not that God hath forsaken our race. Go on, and thou shalt find how His sovereign power will torment thee and thy seed!"

After him they brought the sixth. When he was at the point of death he said: "Deceive not thyself in vain! We are suffering this on our own account, for sins against our own God. That is why these awful horrors have befallen us. But think not thou shalt go unpunished for daring to fight against God."

The mother, however, was a perfect wonder; she deserves to be held in glorious memory. Thanks to her hope in God, she bravely bore the sight of seven sons dying in a single day. Full of noble spirit and nerving her weak woman's heart with the courage of a man, she exhorted each of them in the language of their fathers, saying: "How you were ever conceived in my womb, I cannot tell! It was not I who gave you the breath of life or fashioned the elements of each! It was the Creator of the Universe who fashioneth men and deviseth the generation of all things, and He it is who in mercy will restore to you the breath of life even as you now count yourselves naught for his laws' sake."

Now Antiochus [Epiphanes] felt that he was being humiliated, but overlooking the taunt of her words, he made an appeal to the youngest brother, who still survived, and even promised on oath to make him rich and happy and a Friend and a trusted official of State, if he would give up his fathers' laws. As the young man paid no attention to him, he summoned his mother and exhorted her to counsel the lad to save himself. So, after he had exhorted her at length, she agreed to persuade her son.

She leaned over to him and, jeering at the cruel tyrant, spoke thus in her fathers' tongue: "My son, have pity on me. Nine months I carried thee in my womb, three years I suckled thee; I reared thee and brought thee up to this age of thy life. My child, I beseech thee, lift thine eyes to heaven and earth, look at all that is therein, and know that God did not make them out of the things that already existed. So is the race of men created. Fear not this butcher, but show thyself worthy of thy brothers; accept thy death, that by God's mercy I may receive thee again together with thy brothers."

Ere she had finished, the young man cried: "What are you waiting for? I will not obey the king's command, I will obey the command of the law given by Moses to our fathers. But thou, who hast devised all manner of evil against the Hebrews, thou shalt not escape the hands of God. We are suffering for our own sins, and though our living Lord is angry for a little, in order to rebuke and chasten us, He will again be reconciled to His own servants. But thou, thou impious wretch, vilest of all men, be not vainly uplifted with thy proud, uncertain hopes, raising thy hand against His servants; thou hast not yet escaped the judgment of the Almighty God who seeth all. These our brothers, after enduring a brief pain, have now drunk of everflowing life, in terms of God's covenant, but thou shalt receive by God's judgment the just penalty of thine arrogance. I, like my brothers, give up body and soul for our fathers' laws, calling on God to show favor to our nation soon, and to make thee acknowledge, in torment and affliction, that He alone is God, and to let the Almighty's wrath, justly fallen on the whole of our nation, end in me and in my brothers."

Then the king fell into a fury and had him handled

worse than the others, so exasperated was he at being mocked. Thus he also died pure, trusting absolutely in the Lord. Finally, after her sons, the mother also perished.

Let this suffice for the enforced sacrifices and the excesses of barbarity.

III. The Hope for a New Age

A note on the Book of Enoch. Enoch is the early Biblical personage who "walked with God, and he was not; for God took him" (Gen. 5:24). His name, therefore, lent itself well as a title for apocalyptic writings. Our Book of Enoch is preserved mainly in an Ethiopic version, made from the Greek translation of a Hebrew (or Aramaic) original. The book—written probably in or soon after the year 95 B.C.— is a composite structure. Its several sections represent revelations accorded to Enoch on his journeys through heavenly and earthly regions.

The book deals with the origin of sin, angels and demons, the judgment of the wicked, bliss of the righteous, resurrection and future life, the Messiah (having supernatural characteristics), and the new Jerusalem. One of the sections (chapters 85 to 90) is a vision of the history of the world up to the founding of the Messianic kingdom. Enoch's notions of the kingdom, the anointed one (Messiah), the son of man, the elect one, exerted an influence on the teachings of early Christianity.

The Day of Judgment

FROM THE BOOK OF ENOCH

In those days[1] when He hath brought a grievous fire upon you,
Whither will ye flee, and where will ye find deliverance?
And when He launches forth His word against you
Will you not be affrighted and fear?
And all the luminaries shall be affrighted with great fear,
And all the earth shall be affrighted and tremble and be
    alarmed.

And all the angels shall execute their commands[2]
And shall seek to hide themselves from the presence of the
        Great Glory,
And the children of earth shall tremble and quake;
And ye sinners shall be cursed for ever,
And ye shall have no peace.
Fear ye not, ye souls of the righteous,
And be hopeful ye that have died in righteousness.
And grieve not if your soul into Sheol[3] has descended in grief,
And that in your life your body fared not according to your
        goodness,
But wait for the day of the judgment of sinners
And for the day of cursing and chastisement.
And yet when ye die the sinners speak over you:[4]
"As we die, so die the righteous,
And what benefit do they reap for their deeds?
Behold, even as we, so do they die in grief and darkness,
And what have they more than we?
From henceforth we are equal.
And what will they receive and what will they see for ever?
Behold, they too have died,
And henceforth for ever shall they see no light."

I tell you, ye sinners, ye are content to eat and drink, and
rob and sin, and strip men naked, and acquire wealth and see
the good days. Have ye seen the righteous how their end falls
out, that no manner of violence is found in them till their
death? [The sinners answer:] "Nevertheless they perished and
became as though they had not been, and their spirits descended into Sheol in tribulation."

Now, therefore, I swear to you, the righteous, by the glory
of the Great and Honored and Mighty One in dominion, and
by His greatness I swear to you.
I know a mystery
And have read the heavenly tablets,
And have seen the holy books,
And have found written therein and inscribed regarding them:

That all goodness and joy and glory are prepared for them,
And written down for the spirits of those who have died in
      righteousness,
And that manifold good shall be given to you in recompense
      for your labors,
And that your lot is abundantly beyond the lot of the living.
And the spirits of you who have died in righteousness shall
      live and rejoice,
And their spirits shall not perish, nor their memorial from
      before the face of the Great One
Unto all the generations of the world: wherefore no longer
      fear their contumely.

The Victory of the Righteous

FROM THE BOOK OF ENOCH

In those days a change shall take place for the holy and elect,
And the light of days shall abide upon them,
And glory and honor shall turn to the holy,
On the day of affliction on which evil shall have been treas-
      ured up against the sinners.
And the righteous shall be victorious in the name of the Lord
      of Spirits:
And He will cause the others to witness this
That they may repent
And forgo the works of their hands.
They shall have no honor through the name of the Lord of
      Spirits,
Yet through His name shall they be saved,
And the Lord of Spirits will have compassion on them,
For His compassion is great.
And He is righteous also in His judgment,
And in the presence of His glory unrighteousness also shall
      not maintain itself:
At his judgment the unrepentant shall perish before Him.

And from henceforth I will have no mercy on them, saith the
Lord of Spirits.

In those days shall the earth also give back that which has
been entrusted to it,[5]
And Sheol also shall give back that which it has received,
And hell shall give back that which it owes.
For in those days the Elect One[6] shall arise,
And he shall choose the righteous and holy from among them:
For the day has drawn nigh that they should be saved.
And the Elect One shall in those days sit on My throne,
And his mouth shall pour forth all the secrets of wisdom and
counsel:
For the Lord of Spirits hath given them to him and hath
glorified him.
And in those days shall the mountains leap like rams,
And the hills also shall skip like lambs satisfied with milk,
And the faces of all the angels in heaven shall be lighted up
with joy.
And the earth shall rejoice,
And the righteous shall dwell upon it,
And the elect shall walk thereon.

The Elect One

FROM THE BOOK OF ENOCH

For wisdom is poured out like water,
And glory faileth not before him for evermore.
For he is mighty in all the secrets of righteousness,
And unrighteousness shall disappear as a shadow,
And have no continuance;
Because the Elect One standeth before the Lord of Spirits,
And his glory is for ever and ever,
And his might unto all generations.
And in him dwells the spirit of wisdom,
And the spirit which gives insight,

And the spirit of understanding and of might,
And the spirit of those who have fallen asleep in righteousness.
And he shall judge the secret things,
And none shall be able to utter a lying word before him;
For he is the Elect One before the Lord of Spirits according to
    His good pleasure.

A New Priesthood

FROM THE TESTAMENT OF LEVI

A note on the Testaments of the Twelve Patriarchs. The Biblical narratives of the blessings given by Jacob and Moses before their deaths, the former addressing his sons (chapter 49 of Genesis), the latter the tribes of Israel (chapter 33 of Deuteronomy), became in a later period a ready framework for ethical and religious teaching. The Testaments of the Twelve Patriarchs, dating from the first pre-Christian century or the first years of the present era, lets each of the twelve sons of Jacob, before his end came, review his life and impart instruction to his descendants. In these accounts Biblical stories blend with later midrashic legends. In their ethics the Testaments view man's love for God and for his fellow-man as complementary tenets ("Love the Lord through all your life, and one another with a true heart," Testament of Dan 5:3). This love is unconditional: "If a man sin against thee, cast forth the poison of hate and speak peaceably to him, and in thy soul hold no guile" (Testament of Gad 6:3). It is universal: in the last Temple "the twelve tribes shall be gathered together and all the Gentiles" (Testament of Benjamin 9:2). In the following passage the author envisages a new, Messianic priesthood, which will replace the priesthood that had failed its office.

The work, written in Hebrew, is preserved in Greek translation and in versions, such as the Armenian, based on the Greek. Early church writers made additions to the text.

. . . Then[7] shall the Lord raise up a new priest.
And to him all the words of the Lord shall be revealed;
And he shall execute a righteous judgment upon the earth
    for a multitude of days.
And his star shall arise in heaven as of a king,
Lighting up the light of knowledge as the sun the day,

And he shall be magnified in the world.
He shall shine forth as the sun on the earth,
And shall remove all darkness from under heaven,
And there shall be peace in all the earth.
The heavens shall exult in his days.
And the earth shall be glad,
And the clouds shall rejoice;
And the knowledge of the Lord shall be poured forth upon
    the earth, as the water of the seas;
And the angels of the glory of the presence of the Lord shall
    be glad in him.
The heavens shall be opened,
From the temple of glory shall come upon him sanctification,
With the Father's voice as from Abraham to Isaac.
And the glory of the Most High shall be uttered over him,
And the spirit of understanding and sanctification shall rest
    upon him.
For he shall give the majesty of the Lord to His sons in truth
    for evermore;
And there shall none succeed him for all generations for ever.
And in his priesthood the heathens shall be multiplied in
    knowledge upon the earth,
And enlightened through the grace of the Lord:
In his priesthood shall sin come to an end,
And the lawless shall cease to do evil,
And the just shall rest in him.
And he shall open the gates of the garden of Eden,[8]
And shall remove the threatening sword against man.
And he shall give to the saints to eat from the tree of life,
And the spirit of holiness shall be on them.
Beliar[9] shall be bound by him,
And he shall give power to His children to tread upon the evil
    spirits.
And the Lord shall rejoice in His children,
And be well pleased in His beloved ones for ever.
Then shall Abraham and Isaac and Jacob exult,
And I will be glad,
And all the saints shall clothe themselves with joy.

Thou Art Our King

FROM THE PSALMS OF SOLOMON

A note on the Psalms of Solomon. After initial successes, the rule of
the Hasmonean kings proved to be a failure; the great hopes attached to
Jewish kingship had not materialized. Kings Alexander Jannaeus (103–76) and
Aristobulus II (67–63) had favored the worldly, aristocratic Sadducean party
and had forsaken the Pharisees, defenders of the heritage of Israel. The quar-
rel about the throne of Jerusalem between the brothers Hyrcanus II and
Aristobulus II brought about the invasion of the holy city by Pompey (63
B.C.). The unknown psalmist, writing in Judaea about the middle of the first
pre-Christian century, voices the sentiments of the pious in the land. His
fervent hope is for the coming of the true—Messianic—king "to purge
Jerusalem, making it holy as of old."

The original Hebrew form of the Psalms is lost; they have been preserved in Greek translation. An ancient Syrian version was made from
Greek. The most important of the eighteen psalms is the seventeenth, here
reproduced.

O Lord, Thou art our King for ever and ever,
For in Thee, O God, doth our soul glory.
How long are the days of man's life upon the earth?
As are his days, so is the hope set upon him.
But we hope in God, our deliverer;
For the might of our God is for ever with mercy,
And the kingdom of our God is for ever over the nations in
      judgment.

Thou, O Lord, didst choose David to be king over Israel,
And swaredst to him touching his seed that never should his
      kingdom fail before Thee.
But, for our sins, sinners[10] rose up against us;
They assailed us and thrust us out;
What Thou hadst not promised to them,[11] they took away
      with violence.
They in no wise glorified Thy honorable name;

They set a [worldly] monarchy in place of that which was
      their excellency;
They laid waste the throne of David in tumultuous arrogance.

But Thou, O God, didst cast them down, and remove their
      seed from the earth,
In that there rose up against them a man that was alien to our
      race.[12]
According to their sins didst Thou recompense them, O God;
So that it befell them according to their deeds.
God showed them no pity;
He sought out their seed and let not one of them go free.
Faithful is the Lord in all His judgments
Which He doeth upon the earth.

The lawless one[13] laid waste our land so that none inhabited it,
They destroyed young and old and their children together.
In the heat of his anger he sent them away even unto the
      west,[14]
And he exposed the rulers of the land unsparingly to derision.
Being an alien the enemy acted proudly,
And his heart was alien from our God.
And all . . . Jerusalem,
As also the nations . . .
And the children of the covenant in the midst of the mingled
      peoples . . .
There was not among them one that wrought in the midst of
      Jerusalem mercy and truth.
They that loved the assemblies of the pious[15] fled from them,
As sparrows that fly from their nest.
They wandered in deserts that their lives might be saved from
      harm,
And precious in the eyes of them that lived abroad was any
      that escaped alive from them.
Over the whole earth were they scattered by lawless men.
Therefore the heavens withheld the rain from dropping upon
      the earth,
Springs were stopped that sprang perennially out of the deeps,
      that ran down from lofty mountains.

For there was none among them that wrought righteousness
and justice;
From the chief of them to the least of them all were sinful;
The king was a transgressor, and the judge disobedient, and
the people sinful.

Behold, O Lord, and raise up unto them their king, the son of
David,[16]
At the time in the which Thou seest, O God, that he may
reign over Israel Thy servant.
And gird him with strength, that he may shatter unrighteous
rulers,
And that he may purge Jerusalem from nations that trample
her down to destruction.
Wisely, righteously he shall thrust out sinners from the in-
heritance,
He shall destroy the pride of the sinner as a potter's vessel.
With a rod of iron he shall break in pieces all their substance,
He shall destroy the godless nations with the word of his
mouth;
At his rebuke nations shall flee before him,
And he shall reprove sinners for the thoughts of their heart.

And he shall gather together a holy people, whom he shall
lead in righteousness,
And he shall judge the tribes of the people that has been sanctified by the Lord his God.
And he shall not suffer unrighteousness to lodge any more in
their midst,
Nor shall there dwell with them any man that knoweth wickedness,
For he shall know them, that they are all sons of their God.
And he shall divide them according to their tribes upon the
land,
And neither sojourner nor alien shall sojourn with them any
more.
He shall judge peoples and nations in the wisdom of his right-
eousness. Selah.

And he shall have the heathen nations to serve him under his
     yoke;

And he shall glorify the Lord in a place to be seen of all the
     earth;

And he shall purge Jerusalem, making it holy as of old:

So that nations shall come from the ends of the earth to see
     his glory,

Bringing as gifts her sons who had fainted,

And to see the glory of the Lord, wherewith God hath glori-
     fied her.

And he shall be a righteous king, taught of God, over them,

And there shall be no unrighteousness in his days in their
     midst,

For all shall be holy and their king the anointed of the Lord.

For he shall not put his trust in horse and rider and bow,

Nor shall he multiply for himself gold and silver for war,

Nor shall he gather confidence from a multitude for the day
     of battle.

The Lord Himself is his king, the hope of him that is mighty
     through his hope in God.

All nations shall be in fear before him,

For he will smite the earth with the word of his mouth for
     ever.

He will bless the people of the Lord with wisdom and glad-
     ness,

And he himself will be pure from sin, so that he may rule a
     great people.

He will rebuke rulers, and remove sinners by the might of his
     word;

And relying upon his God, throughout his days he will not
     stumble;

For God will make him mighty by means of His holy spirit,

And wise by means of the spirit of understanding, with
     strength and righteousness.

And the blessing of the Lord will be with him: he will be
     strong and stumble not;

His hope will be in the Lord: who then can prevail against
    him?
He will be mighty in his works, and strong in the fear of God,
He will be shepherding the flock of the Lord faithfully and
    righteously,
And will suffer none among them to stumble in their pasture.
He will lead them all aright,
And there will be no pride among them that any among them
    should be oppressed.
This will be the majesty of the king of Israel whom God
    knoweth;
He will raise him up over the house of Israel to correct him.
His words shall be more refined than costly gold, the choicest;
In the assemblies he will judge the peoples, the tribes of the
    sanctified.
His words shall be like the words of the holy ones in the midst
    of sanctified peoples.
Blessed be they that shall be in those days,
In that they shall see the good fortune of Israel which God
    shall bring to pass in the gathering together of the
    tribes.
May the Lord hasten His mercy upon Israel!
May He deliver us from the uncleanness of unholy enemies!
The Lord Himself is our king for ever and ever.

IV. Sectarian Brotherhoods

The Rules of the Dead Sea, or Qumran, Brotherhood

FROM THE MANUAL OF DISCIPLINE

A note on the Dead Sea Manual of Discipline. This document, which introduces us to some of the beliefs and practices of the Dead Sea Brotherhood, is so far the most significant historically of the scrolls which began to be discovered in 1947. Qumran, one of the chief seats of the sect, was situated at the northern end of the western shore of the Dead Sea. The sect, which is either identical with the brotherhood of the Essenes (known to us from the accounts of Philo, Josephus and Pliny the Elder) or closely related to it, flourished from the second half of the second pre-Christian century to the time of the Judaeo-Roman war in A.D. 68.

Among the reasons that led to the exodus of this "remnant" of the faithful from the centers of Judaea and to the formation of the desert brotherhood were: the protest against the worldly character of the Hasmonean kingdom and the priesthood; differences in calendar calculation; the determination to establish a true community of brethren, to lead a life dedicated to purity of body and soul, observance of the law, community of goods, continuous study, obedience to authority, and the preparation for the Day of Judgment which would bring the victory of the "sons of light" over the "sons of darkness." Rigid laws regulated the admittance of new members and the details of life in the community.

The manuscript of the Manual (known also as Rule of the Community) consists of eleven columns. The prose text of the order of the brotherhood is followed (on columns X-XI) by a closing hymn, a statement of the sect's religious beliefs and a fair example of its poetic style.

Social relations

Now this is the practice of the men of the Community

who dedicate themselves to turn from all evil and to hold
firmly to all that He commanded according to His good pleasure: to separate themselves from the congregation of perverse
men, to become a Community in Torah and in property, answering [their legal questions] according to the sons of Zadok,[1]
the priests who keep the covenant, and according to the majority[2] of the men of the Community who hold firmly to the
covenant.

According to their judgment the divinely guided decision
is reached with regard to every matter, whether Torah, or
property, or laws, to practice truth, unity and humility, righteousness, and justice, and loving devotion, and walking humbly
in all their ways, in which none shall walk in the stubbornness
of his heart to go astray after his own heart and his own eyes
and his own impulsive desire; but EAM[3] is to circumcise in
the Community the uncircumcision of desire and the stiff
neck, to lay a foundation of truth for Israel (for the Community of eternal covenant), to atone for all those who dedicate themselves for holiness among Aaron and for a house of
truth in Israel and for those who join them for Community,
and for suit, and for judgment, so as to convict all transgressors of ordinances.

The oath of admission

Now these are to direct their ways according to all these
ordinances:

When they are admitted into the Community: everyone who enters into the council of the Community, shall enter
into the covenant of God in the sight of all the dedicated
ones. Then he shall take a binding oath to return to the Torah
of Moses according to all that he commanded, with wholeness
of heart and wholeness of soul towards all that is revealed of it
to [or, for] the Sons of Zadok, the priests who keep the covenant and who seek His good pleasure, and to [or, for] the
majority of the men of their covenant who communally dedicate themselves to His truth and to walking in His good
pleasure.

He shall further bind himself by a covenant to separate

himself from all perverse men who walk in the way of wickedness. For these are not reckoned in His covenant, for they
have not sought or inquired after Him in His ordinances to
know the unconscious sins into which they have strayed in-
curring guilt; while the conscious sins they have done wilfully,
with the result that they raise up anger unto judgment and
unto the exacting of vengeance through the curses of the covenant, bringing upon themselves the great judgments unto an
eternal destruction without remnant.

Separation from the wicked

These may not enter into water to [be permitted to]
touch the Purity of the holy men,[4] for they will not be
cleansed unless they have turned from their wickedness, for
uncleanness clings to all transgressors of His word. He [who
enters the covenant must] further [swear that he will] not
unite with a [perverse] man in his labor and in his property,
lest he cause him to incur guilt of transgression; for he must
keep far from him in every matter, for thus it is written:
"Thou shalt keep far from every false matter" (Exod. 23:7).

And further, no man of the men of the community may
answer [legal questions] according to their opinion in regard
to any teaching or laws. Moreover, he may not eat anything
of theirs, nor drink, nor take from their hand anything whatsoever except for a price, as it is written:

"Cease ye from man whose breath is in his nostrils,
For of what value is he to be reckoned?" Isa. 2:22).

For all who are not reckoned in His covenant are to be
separated, both they and all they have; and the holy men may
not rely upon any of the deeds of vanity. For vain are all who
do not recognize His covenant; and all who despise His word
He will destroy from the world, since all their deeds are uncleanness before Him and uncleanness is in all their property.

The examination of those entering the community

Now, when he [the neophyte] enters into the covenant
to do according to all these ordinances, to be united to a holy

congregation, they shall examine his spirit in the Community between a man and his fellow with respect to his understanding and his deeds in Torah, in accordance with the views of the sons of Aaron who are dedicated unitedly to establish His covenant and to administer all His ordinances which He commanded [them] to do, and in accordance with the views of the majority of Israel[5] who are dedicated to turn unitedly to His covenant.

Then one shall enroll them in order, each before his fellow, according to his understanding and his deeds, that they all may obey each his fellow, the lesser the greater; and they shall examine their spirit and their deeds, year by year to promote each according to his understanding and the perfection of his way, or to retard him according to his perversions, that each may reprove his fellow in truth and humility and loving devotion to each other.

Complaints and accusations

One shall not speak to his brother in anger, or in complaint, or with a [stiff] neck, or a wicked spirit; nor shall he hate him [in the uncircumcision] of his heart—though he shall reprove him on the very day so as not to incur guilt because of him. Indeed, a man shall not bring accusation against his fellow in the presence of the Many[6] who has not been subject to [previous] reproof before witnesses.

The common life

In these [regulations] let them walk in all their dwellings, everyone who is present, each with his fellow. The lesser shall obey the greater, in regard to goods and means. They shall eat communally, and bless communally, and take counsel communally; and in every place where there are ten men of the council of the Community, there shall not cease from among them a man who is priest. And let each one according to his assigned position sit before him; and in that order let them be asked for their counsel with regard to every matter.

And it shall be when they arrange the table to eat, or

[arrange] the wine to drink, the priest shall first stretch out his hand to invoke a benediction with the first of the bread and the wine. And in whatever place the ten are, there shall not cease to be a man who expounds the Torah day and night continually, [expounding] in turns each to his fellow. And let the Many keep awake in Community a third of all the nights of the year in order to read aloud from the Book and to expound laws and to bless in Community.

The Supreme Council

In the Council of the Community [there shall be] twelve laymen and three priests who are perfect in all that is revealed of the whole Torah, through practicing truth and righteousness and justice and loving devotion and walking humbly each with his fellow in order to maintain faithfulness in the land with a steadfast intent and with a broken spirit, and to expiate iniquity through practicing justice and [through] the anguish of the refining furnace, and to walk with all in the measure of truth and in the proper reckoning of the time.

The community during the eschatological period

When these things came to pass in Israel, the Council of the Community will have been established in truth:

As an eternal planting, a holy house for Israel,
A most holy institution of Aaron,
True witnesses with regard to judgment,[7]
And the chosen of divine acceptance to atone for the earth,
And to render to the wicked their desert.
That is the tried wall, the costly corner bulwark,
Whose foundations shall not be shaken asunder,
Nor be dislodged from their place!

A most holy abode belongs to Aaron in the knowledge of them all that they may be a covenant of religion and offer up an agreeable odor; and a house of perfection and truth is in Israel to establish a covenant with eternal ordinances. These will be acceptable to make atonement for the earth and to decree the condemnation of wickedness that there may be no more perversity.

The separate life and the going to the wilderness

When these [men] have become established in the institution of the Community for two years' time in perfection of way, they shall separate themselves as holy [or, as a sanctuary] within the council of the men of the Community; and every matter which was hidden from Israel and is found by a man who searches [studies], let him not hide it from these out of fear of an apostate spirit.

Now when these things come to pass in Israel to the Community, according to these rules, they will separate themselves from the midst of the habitation of perverse men to go to the wilderness to clear there the way of God,[8] as it is written:

In the wilderness clear the way of [the Lord];[9]

Level in the desert a highway for our God (Isa. 40:3):[10] that [means] studying the Torah which He commanded through Moses, so as to do according to all that was revealed time after time and according to that which the prophets revealed through His Holy Spirit.

Temporary exclusion

As for anyone of the men of the Community, [in] the covenant of the Community, who wilfully removes a word from all that He commanded, he shall not touch the Purity of the holy men; nor shall he have any knowledge of any of their counsel, until his deeds are purified from every kind of perversity that he may walk in perfection of way. Then he shall be admitted to the Council according to the judgment of the Many; and afterward he shall be enrolled in his assigned position; and according to this law shall it be for every one who joins the Community.

From the Source of His Knowledge: A Psalm

FROM THE MANUAL OF DISCIPLINE

With thanksgiving I will open my mouth,
the righteous acts of God shall my tongue recount always
and the faithlessness of men until their transgression is
 complete.
Empty words I will banish from my lips,
unclean things and perversions from the knowledge of my
 mind.
With wise counsel I will conceal knowledge,[11]
and with knowing prudence I will hedge about wisdom
with a firm limit, to preserve fidelity
and strong justice according to the righteousness of God.
I will exalt the decree with the measuring-line of times,
and will teach the practice of righteousness,
loyal love for the humble,
and strengthening of hands for the fearful of heart;
for the erring in spirit understanding;
to instruct the fainting with doctrine,
to answer humbly before the haughty of spirit,
and with a broken spirit to men of injustice,
who point the finger and speak wickedly
and are envious of wealth.

But as for me, my judgment belongs to God,
and in His hand is the blamelessness of my conduct
together with the uprightness of my heart;
and in His righteousness my transgression will be wiped out.
For from the source of His knowledge He has opened up my
 light;
my eye has gazed into His wonders
and the light of my heart penetrates the mystery that is to be.
That which is eternal is the staff of my right hand;
on a strong rock is the way I tread;

before nothing will it be shaken.
For the faithfulness of God is the rock I tread,
and His strength is the staff of my right hand.
From the source of His righteousness is my judgment.
A light is in my heart from His marvelous mysteries;
my eye has gazed on that which is eternal,
sound wisdom which is hidden from the man of knowledge,
and prudent discretion from the sons of man,
a source of righteousness and reservoir of strength
together with a spring of glory hidden from the company of
        flesh.
To those whom God has chosen He has given them for an
        eternal possession;
He has given them an inheritance in the lot of the holy ones
and with the sons of heaven has associated their company
for a council of unity and a company of a holy building,
for an eternal planting
through every period that is to be.

But I belong to wicked mankind,
to the company of erring flesh;
my iniquities, my transgression, my sin,
with the iniquity of my heart
belong to the company of worms and those who walk in
        darkness.

For the way of a man is not his own,
a man does not direct his own steps;
for judgment is God's
and from His hand is blamelessness of conduct.
By His knowledge everything comes to pass
and everything that is He establishes by His purpose;
and without Him nothing is done.

As for me, if I slip,
the steadfast love of God is my salvation forever;
and if I stumble in the iniquity of flesh,
my vindication in the righteousness of God will stand to
        eternity.

If He lets loose my distress,
from the pit He will deliver my soul;
He will direct my steps to the way.

In His mercy He has brought me near,
And in His righteousness He will cleanse me from the im-
      purity of man,
from the sin of the sons of man.
Thanks be to God for His righteousness,
to the Most High for His majesty!

Hymns of the Dead Sea Brotherhood

FROM THE THANKSGIVING HYMNS

Among the manuscripts found in the caves where the Dead Sea Brotherhood deposited its literary treasures are some thirty-five chapters and numerous
fragments of Hymns. In them the unknown poet gives utterance to his faith.
He thanks his Lord for protecting him from his adversaries, for "illumining
his face," and for having chosen him for the task of interpreting the knowledge
of "wondrous mysteries." Man sins, but God's steadfast love "redeems the
soul of the poor." E. L. Sukenik, one of the first interpreters of the Dead
Sea scrolls, and his son Yigael Yadin suggested that the writer of the Hymns
is none other than the leader of the Brotherhood, the "Teacher of Righteousness."

Streams in dry ground

I thank Thee, O Lord, because Thou hast put me
at a source of flowing streams in dry ground,
a spring of water in a land of drought,
channels watering a garden of delight,
a place of cedar and acacia,
together with pine for Thy glory,
trees of life in a fount of mystery,
hidden amid all trees that drink water.
They shall put forth a branch for an eternal planting,
taking root before they sprout,

They shall send out their roots to the stream;
its stump shall be exposed to the living water;
and it shall become an eternal source.
When there is a branch on it,
all the beasts of the forest will feed on it;
its stump will be trampled by all that pass by,
its branches by every winged bird;
and all the springs of water shall rise against it.
For in their planting they go astray,
and do not send out a root to the stream.
But he who causes a holy branch
to sprout for a planting of truth
is hiding his mystery, without its being thought of;
without its being known, he is sealing it up.
And Thou, O God, hast put a hedge about its fruit
in the mystery of mighty men of valor and holy spirits;
and a flame of fire turning every way.

They seek Thee with a double heart

I thank Thee, O Lord,
for Thou hast enlightened my face for Thy covenant. . . .
I shall seek Thee . . .
As the perfect dawn Thou shinest upon me.
But they . . . have made smooth their words
false phrases . . .
Distraught without understanding,
they have turned their deeds to folly,
   . . . for they have become loathsome to themselves.
When Thou dost work mightily in me, they do not regard me,
but drive me from my land like a bird from its nest,
and all my neighbors and friends are driven far from me;
they have regarded me as a broken vessel.

They are interpreters of lies and seers of deceit;
they devised baseness against me,
exchanging Thy law, which Thou didst cut into my heart,
for smooth things for Thy people.
They withheld the draught of knowledge from the thirsty,

and for their thirst made them drink vinegar;
so that God beheld their error,
going mad at their feasts,
being caught in their nets.

But Thou, O God, dost despise every purpose of Belial;[12]
it is Thy counsel that will stand,
and the purpose of Thy heart that is established forever.
But they are hapless, they plan devices of Belial;
they seek Thee with a double heart,
and are not established in Thy truth.
A root bearing poisonous and bitter fruit is in their plans,
and with the stubbornness of their hearts they go about.
They have sought Thee among idols,
and have set the stumbling block of their iniquity before their
          faces.
They have come to seek Thee
following the directions of false prophets, enticed by error.
Then, with strange lips
and an alien tongue they speak to Thy people,
making foolish by deceit all their works.
For they did not heed Thy instruction;
they did not listen to Thy word;
for they said of the vision of knowledge, "It is not right,"
and of the way of Thy heart, "It is not that."

But Thou, O God, wilt answer them,
judging them in Thy power
according to their idols and their many transgressions,
that they may be caught in their own plans,
in which they are estranged from Thy covenant.
Thou wilt cut off in judgment all men of deceit,
and seers of error will be found no more;
for there is no foolishness in all Thy works
or deceit in the devices of Thy heart.
Those who please Thee will stand before Thee forever;
those who walk in the way of Thy heart will be established
          to eternity.

As for me, while leaning upon Thee
I will rise and stand up against those who despise me,
and my hand will be against all who scorn me;
for they do not regard me,
though Thou didst work mightily in me
and didst appear to me in Thy strength to enlighten them;
Thou didst not plaster with shame
the faces of all those who consulted me,
who assembled for Thy covenant and heard me,
those who walk in the way of Thy heart
and present themselves to Thee in the company of the holy
      ones.
Thou wilt bring forth their judgment forever,
and truth with equity.
Thou wilt not mislead them by the hand of the hapless,
according to their plotting against them;
but wilt put the fear of them on Thy people,
a shattering for all the peoples of the lands,
to cut off in judgment all transgressors of Thy words.

Through me Thou hast enlightened the faces of many,
and hast made them strong until they were numberless;
for Thou hast given me knowledge of Thy wondrous mysteries,
and in Thy wondrous company Thou hast wrought powerfully
      with me;
Thou hast wrought wondrously in the presence of many,
for the sake of Thy glory
and to make known to all the living Thy mighty works.

Who that is flesh could do aught like this,
what thing formed of clay could do such wonders?
For man lives in iniquity from the womb,
and in faithless guilt to old age.
I know that righteousness does not belong to a man,
nor to a son of man blamelessness of conduct;
to the Most High God belong all works of righteousness.
A man's way is not established
except by the spirit which God created for him,
to make blameless a way for the sons of man,

that they may know all His works
in the might of His power and the greatness of His mercy
to all the sons of His good pleasure.

As for me, shaking and trembling have seized me,
and all my bones are broken;
my heart melts like wax before the fire,
and my knees go like water falling on a slope.
For I remember my guilty deeds,
together with the faithlessness of my fathers,
when the wicked rose against Thy covenant,
the hapless against Thy word.
Then I said, " For my transgression
I am left outside of Thy covenant."
But when I remembered the strength of Thy hand,
together with the abundance of Thy mercy,
I rose and stood up, and my spirit became strong,
standing firm before affliction;
for I leaned on Thy steadfast love
and Thy abundant mercy.

The Order of The Essenes

FROM PHILO: EVERY GOOD MAN IS FREE

In Philo of Alexandria (*ca.* 30 B.C.–A.D. 40) Hebraic (Biblical and early rabbinic) traditions and Greek critical philosophy, revelation and reason, meet and merge. In his ingeniously constructed integration of the two sources of truth, Philo, as H. A. Wolfson has demonstrated, laid the foundation for the entire realm of medieval European philosophy. The theology of Origen, Augustine and Thomas Aquinas is built upon Philo's reading of Plato in the light of Biblical faith.

In one of his minor works, *Every Good Man Is Free* (*Quod omnis probus liber sit*), written in his youth, Philo expounded the Stoic doctrine that the wise man alone is free, for true freedom and independence consist in "following God." Among the examples for his thesis, Philo cites the order of the Essenes and offers a description of their way of life.

For other accounts of the Essenes, see Flavius Josephus, *The Jewish War*, Book II, chapter 8, and the Manual of Discipline of the Dead Sea Brotherhood, which is identical with, or closely related to, the Essenes.

Introduction

Palestinian Syria, too, has not failed to produce high moral excellence. In this country live a considerable part of the very populous nation of the Jews, including as it is said, certain persons, more than four thousand in number, called the Essenes. Their name which is, I think, a variation, though the form of the Greek is inexact, of *hosiotes* (holiness), is given them, because they have shown themselves especially devout in the service of God, not by offering sacrifices of animals, but by resolving to sanctify the minds.

Ways of life

The first thing about these people is that they live in villages and avoid the cities because of the iniquities which have become inveterate among city dwellers, for they know that their company would have a deadly effect upon their own souls, like a disease brought by a pestilential atmosphere. Some of them labor on the land and others pursue such crafts as cooperate with peace and so benefit themselves and their neighbors. They do not hoard gold and silver or acquire great slices of land because they desire the revenues therefrom, but provide what is needed for the necessary requirements of life.

For while they stand almost alone in the whole of mankind in that they have become moneyless and landless by deliberate action rather than by lack of good fortune, they are esteemed exceedingly rich, because they judge frugality with contentment to be, as indeed it is, an abundance of wealth. As for darts, javelins, daggers, or the helmet, breastplate or shield, you could not find a single manufacturer of them, nor, in general, any person making weapons or engines or plying any industry concerned with war, nor, indeed, any of the peaceful kind, which easily lapse into vice, for they have not the vaguest idea of commerce either wholesale or retail or marine, but pack the inducements to covetousness off in disgrace.

No slavery

Not a single slave is to be found among them, but all are free, exchanging services with each other, and they denounce the owners of slaves, not merely for their injustice in outraging the law of equality, but also for their impiety in annulling the statute of Nature, who mother-like has born and reared all men alike, and created them genuine brothers, not in mere name, but in very reality, though this kinship has been put to confusion by the triumph of malignant covetousness, which has wrought estrangement instead of affinity and enmity instead of friendship.

Teachings

As for philosophy they abandon the logical part to quibbling verbalists as unnecessary for the acquisition of virtue, and the physical to visionary praters as beyond the grasp of human nature, only retaining that part which treats philosophically of the existence of God and the creation of the universe. But the ethical part they study very industriously, taking for their trainers the laws of their fathers, which could not possibly have been conceived by the human soul without divine inspiration.

The Sabbath

In these they are instructed at all other times, but particularly on the seventh days. For that day has been set apart to be kept holy and on it they abstain from all other work and proceed to sacred spots which they call synagogues. There, arranged in rows according to their ages, the younger below the elder, they sit decorously as befits the occasion with attentive ears. Then one takes the books and reads aloud and another of especial proficiency comes forward and expounds what is not understood. For most of their philosophical study takes the form of allegory, and in this they emulate the tradition of the past. They are trained in piety, holiness, justice, domestic and civic conduct, knowledge of what is truly good, or evil, or indifferent, and how to choose what they should and avoid the opposite, taking for their defining standards these three, love of God, love of virtue, love of men.

Love of God and man

Their love of God they show by a multitude of proofs, by religious purity[13] constant and unbroken throughout their lives, by abstinence from oaths, by veracity, by their belief that the Godhead is the cause of all good things and nothing bad; their love of virtue, by their freedom from the love of money or reputation or pleasure, by self-mastery and endurance, again by frugality, simple living, contentment, humility, respect for law, steadiness and all similar qualities; their love of men by benevolence and sense of equality, and their spirit of fellowship, which defies description, though a few words on it will not be out of place. First of all then no one's house is his own in the sense that it is not shared by all, for besides the fact that they dwell together in communities, the door is open to visitors from elsewhere who share their convictions.

Community of goods

Again they all have a single treasury and common disbursements; their clothes are held in common and also their food through their institutions of public meals. In no other community can we find the custom of sharing roof, life and board more firmly established in actual practice. And that is no more than one would expect. For all the wages which they earn in the day's work they do not keep as their private property, but throw them into the common stock and allow the benefit thus accruing to be shared by those who wish to use it. The sick are not neglected because they cannot provide anything, but have the cost of their treatment lying ready in the common stock, so that they can meet expenses out of the greater wealth in full security. To the elder men too is given the respect and care which real children give to their parents, and they receive from countless hands and minds a full and generous maintenance for their latter years.

Athletes of virtue

Such are the athletes of virtue produced by a philosophy free from the pedantry of Greek wordiness, a philosophy which sets its pupils to practise themselves in laudable actions, by which the liberty which can never be enslaved is firmly established. Here we have a proof. Many are the potentates who at various occasions have raised themselves to power over the country. They differed both in nature and the line of conduct which they followed. Some of them carried their zest for outdoing wild beasts in ferocity to the point of savagery. They left no form of cruelty untried. They slaughtered their subjects wholesale, or like cooks carved them piecemeal and limb by limb whilst still alive, and did not stay their hands till justice who surveys human affairs visited them with the same calamities. Others transformed this wild frenzy into another kind of viciousness. Their conduct showed intense bitterness, but they talked with calmness, though the mask of their milder language failed to conceal their rancorous disposition. They fawned like venomous hounds yet wrought evils irremediable and left behind them throughout the cities the unforgettable sufferings of their victims as monuments of their impiety and inhumanity. Yet none of these, neither the extremely ferocious nor the deep-dyed treacherous dissemblers, were able to lay a charge against this congregation of Essenes or holy ones here described. Unable to resist the high excellence of these people, they all treated them as self-governing and freemen by nature and extolled their communal meals and that ineffable sense of fellowship, which is the clearest evidence of a perfect and supremely happy life.

The Sect of the Therapeutae

FROM PHILO: ON THE CONTEMPLATIVE LIFE

Philo of Alexandria presented the Essenes as pursuing the "active life" within their brotherhoods. In his treatise On the Contemplative Life (*De vita contemplativa*) he describes a sect of Jewish hermits, men and women, settled on Lake Mareotis in the neighborhood of Alexandria, in Egypt, who follow a "life of contemplation," completely renouncing the world. Philo maintains that other such ascetic settlements existed "in many places in the inhabited world," but there is no evidence for this fact. The church historian Eusebius of Caesarea (third to fourth centuries) believed the Therapeutae to have been a society of early Christian monks. This assumption is historically erroneous; the sect adhered to the laws and institutions of Judaism. But the interest of the Church in this religious retreat helped to preserve Philo's treatise.

Introduction

[14]. . . By sight I do not mean the sight of the body but of the soul, the sight which alone gives a knowledge of truth and falsehood. But it is well that the Therapeutae, a people always taught from the first to use their sight, should desire the vision of the Existent and soar above the sun of our senses and never leave their place in this company which carries them on to perfect happiness. And those who set themselves to this service, not just following custom nor on the advice and admonition of others but carried away by a heaven-sent passion of love, remain rapt and possessed like bacchanals or Corybants until they see the object of their yearning.

Then such is their longing for the deathless and blessed life that thinking their mortal life already ended they abandon their property to their sons or daughters or to other kinsfolk, thus voluntarily advancing the time of their inheritance, while those who have no kinsfolk give them to comrades and friends. For it was right that those who have received ready to their hand the wealth that has eyes to see should surrender, the blind wealth to those who are still blind in mind. [. . .]

Community

So when they have divested themselves of their possessions and have no longer aught to ensnare them they flee
without a backward glance and leave their brothers, their
children, their wives, their parents, the wide circle of their
kinsfolk, the groups of friends around them, the fatherlands
in which they were born and reared, since strong is the attrac-
tion of familiarity and very great its power to ensnare. And
they do not migrate into another city like the unfortunate or
worthless slaves who demand to be sold by their owners and
so procure a change of masters but not freedom. For every
city, even the best governed, is full of turmoils and disturb-
ances innumerable which no one could endure who has ever
been even once under the guidance of wisdom. Instead of this
they pass their days outside the walls pursuing solitude in
gardens or lonely bits of country, not from any acquired habit
of misanthropical bitterness but because they know how unprofitable and mischievous are associations with persons of
dissimilar character.

This kind exists in many places in the inhabited world,
for perfect goodness must needs be shared both by Greeks and
the world outside Greece, but it abounds in Egypt in each of
the nomes as they are called and especially round Alexandria.
But the best of these votaries journey from every side to settle
in a certain very suitable place which they regard as their
fatherland. This place is situated above the Mareotic Lake on
a somewhat low-lying hill very happily placed both because
of its security and the pleasantly tempered air. The safety is
secured by the farm buildings and villages round about and
the pleasantness of the air by the continuous breezes which
arise both from the lake which debouches into the sea and
from the open sea hard by. For the sea breezes are light, the
lake breezes close and the two combining together produce a
most healthy condition of climate.

The houses of the society thus collected are exceedingly
simple, providing protection against two of the most pressing
dangers, the fiery heat of the sun and the icy cold of the air.

They are neither near together as in towns, since living at close quarters is troublesome and displeasing to people who are seeking to satisfy their desire for solitude, nor yet at a great distance because of the sense of fellowship which they cherish, and to render help to each other if robbers attack them.

Sanctuary

In each house there is a consecrated room which is called a sanctuary or closet and closeted in this they are initiated into the mysteries of the sanctified life. They take nothing into it, either drink or food or any other of the things necessary for the needs of the body, but laws and oracles delivered through the mouth of prophets, and psalms and anything else which fosters and perfects knowledge and piety. They keep the memory of God alive and never forget it, so that even in their dreams the picture is nothing else but the loveliness of divine excellences and powers. Indeed many when asleep and dreaming give utterance to the glorious verities of their holy philosophy.

Prayer and readings

Twice every day they pray, at dawn and at eventide; at sunrise they pray for a fine, bright day, fine and bright in the true sense of the heavenly daylight which they pray may fill their minds. At sunset they ask that the soul may be wholly relieved from the press of the senses and the objects of sense and sitting where she is consistory and council chamber to herself pursue the quest of truth. The interval between early morning and evening is spent entirely in spiritual exercise. They read the Holy Scriptures and seek wisdom from their ancestral philosophy by taking it as an allegory, since they think that the words of the literal text are symbols of something whose hidden nature is revealed by studying the underlying meaning.

They have also writings of men of old, the founders of their way of thinking, who left many memorials of the form used in allegorical interpretation and these they take as a kind of archetype and imitate the method in which this principle is carried out. And so they do not confine themselves to contemplation but also compose hymns and psalms to God in all sorts of metres and melodies which they write down with the rhythms necessarily made more solemn.

The Sabbath

For six days they seek wisdom by themselves in solitude in the closets mentioned above, never passing the outside door of the house or even getting a distant view of it. But every seventh day they meet together as for a general assembly and sit in order according to their age in the proper attitude, with their hands inside the robe, the right hand between the breast and the chin and the left withdrawn along the flank. Then the senior among them who also has the fullest knowledge of the doctrines which they profess comes forward and with visage and voice alike quiet and composed gives a well-reasoned and wise discourse. He does not make an exhibition of clever rhetoric like the orators or sophists of today but follows careful examination by careful expression of the exact meaning of the thoughts, and this does not lodge just outside the ears of the audience but passes through the hearing into the soul and there stays securely. All the others sit still and listen showing their approval merely by their looks or nods.

This common sanctuary in which they meet every seventh day is a double enclosure, one portion set apart for the use of the men, the other for the women. For women too regularly make part of the audience with the same ardor and the same sense of their calling. The wall between the two chambers rises up from the ground to three or four cubits built in the form of a breastwork, while the space above up to the roof is left open. This arrangement serves two purposes; the modesty becoming to the female sex is preserved, while the women sitting within earshot can easily follow what is said since there is nothing to obstruct the voice of the speaker.

Daily life

They lay self-control to be as it were the foundation of

their soul and on it build the other virtues. None of them would put food or drink to his lips before sunset since they hold that philosophy finds its right place in the light, the needs of the body in the darkness, and therefore they assign the day to the one and some small part of the night to the other. Some in whom the desire for studying wisdom is more deeply implanted even only after three days remember to take food. Others so luxuriate and delight in the banquet of truths which wisdom richly and lavishly supplies that they hold out for twice that time and only after six days do they bring themselves to taste such sustenance as is absolutely necessary.

They have become habituated to abstinence like the grasshoppers who are said to live on air[15] because, I suppose, their singing makes their lack of food a light matter. But to the seventh day as they consider it to be sacred and festal in the highest degree they have awarded special privileges as its due, and on it after providing for the soul refresh the body also, which they do as a matter of course with the cattle too by releasing them from their continuous labor. Still they eat nothing costly, only common bread with salt for a relish flavored further by the daintier with hyssop, and their drink is spring water. For as nature has set hunger and thirst as mistresses over mortal kind they propitiate them without using anything to curry favor but only such things as are actually needed and without which life cannot be maintained. Therefore they eat enough to keep from hunger and drink enough to keep from thirst but abhor surfeiting as a malignant enemy both to soul and body.

As for the two forms of shelter, clothes and housing, we have already said that the house is unembellished and a makeshift constructed for utility only. Their clothing likewise is the most inexpensive, enough to protect them against extreme cold and heat, a thick coat of shaggy skin in winter and in summer a vest or linen shirt. For they practise an all-round simplicity knowing that its opposite, vanity, is the source of falsehood as simplicity is of truth, and that both play the part of a fountainhead of other things, since from falsehood flow the manifold forms of evil and from truth abundant streams of goodness both human and divine. [. . .]

Festal meetings

I will [now] describe the festal meetings of those who have dedicated their own life and themselves to knowledge and the contemplation of the verities of nature, following the truly sacred instructions of the prophet Moses [. . .].

They assemble, white-robed and with faces in which cheerfulness is combined with the utmost seriousness, but before they recline, at a signal from a member of the Rota,[16] which is the name commonly given to those who perform these services, they take their stand in a regular line in an orderly way, their eyes and hands lifted up to heaven, eyes because they have been trained to fix their gaze on things worthy of contemplation, hands in token that they are clean from gain taking and not defiled through any cause of the profit-making kind. So standing they pray to God that their feasting may be acceptable and proceed as He would have it.

After the prayers the seniors recline according to the order of their admission, since by senior they do not understand the aged and grey headed who are regarded as still mere children if they have only in late years come to love this rule of life, but those who from their earliest years have grown to manhood and spent their prime in pursuing the contemplative branch of philosophy, which indeed is the noblest and most godlike part. The feast is shared by women also, most of them aged virgins, who have kept their chastity not under compulsion, like some of the Greek priestesses, but of their own free will in their ardent yearning for wisdom. Eager to have her for their life mate, they have spurned the pleasures of the body and desire no mortal offspring but those immortal children which only the soul that is dear to God can bring to the birth unaided[17] because the Father has sown in her spiritual rays enabling her to behold the verities of wisdom.

The order of reclining is so apportioned that the men sit by themselves on the right and the women by themselves on the left. Perhaps it may be thought that couches though not costly still of a softer kind would have been provided for people of good birth and high character and trained practice in philosophy. Actually they are plank beds of the common kinds of wood, covered with quite cheap strewings of native papyrus, raised slightly at the arms to give something to lean on.

For while they mitigate somewhat the harsh austerity of Sparta, they always and everywhere practice a frugal contentment worthy of the free, and oppose with might and main the love-lures of pleasure. They do not have slaves to wait upon them as they consider that the ownership of servants is entirely against nature. For nature has borne all men to be free, but the wrongful and covetous acts of some who pursued that source of evil, inequality, have imposed their yoke and invested the stronger with power over the weaker.

In this sacred banquet there is, as I have said, no slave, but the services are rendered by free men who perform their tasks as attendants not under compulsion nor yet waiting for orders, but with deliberate good will anticipating eagerly and zealously the demands that may be made. For it is not just any free men who are appointed for these offices but young members of the association chosen with all care for their special merit who as becomes their good character and nobility are pressing on to reach the summit of virtue. They give their services gladly and proudly like sons to their real fathers and mothers, judging them to be the parents of them all in common, in a closer affinity than that of blood, since to the right minded there is no closer tie than noble living. And they come in to do their office ungirt and with tunics hanging down, that in their appearance there may be no shadow of anything to suggest the slave.

In this banquet—I know that some will laugh at this, but only those whose actions call for tears and lamentation—no wine is brought during those days but only water of the brightest and clearest, cold for most of the guests but warm for such of the older men as live delicately. The table too is kept pure from the flesh of animals; the food laid on it is loaves of bread with salt as a seasoning, sometimes also flavored with hyssop as a relish for the daintier appetites. Abstinence from wine is enjoined by right reason as for the priest when sacrificing, so to these for their lifetime. For wine acts like a drug producing folly, and costly dishes stir up that most insatiable of animals,[18] desire.

Learned discourse

Such are the preliminaries. But when the guests have laid themselves down arranged in rows, as I have described, and the attendants have taken their stand with everything in order ready for their ministry, the President of the company, when a general silence is established—here it may be asked when is there no silence—well at this point there is silence even more than before so that no one ventures to make a sound or breathe with more force than usual—amid this silence, I say, he discusses some question arising in the Holy Scriptures or solves one that has been propounded by someone else.

In doing this he has no thought of making a display, for he has no ambition to get a reputation for clever oratory but desires to gain a closer insight into some particular matters and having gained it not to withhold it selfishly from those who if not so clear-sighted as he have at least a similar desire to learn. His instruction proceeds in a leisurely manner; he lingers over it and spins it out with repetitions, thus permanently imprinting the thoughts in the souls of the hearers, since if the speaker goes on descanting with breathless rapidity the mind of the hearers is unable to follow his language, loses ground and fails to arrive at apprehension of what is said. His audience listen with ears pricked up and eyes fixed on him always in exactly the same posture, signifying comprehension and understanding by nods and glances, praise of the speaker by the cheerful change of expression which steals over the face, difficulty by a gentler movement of the head and by pointing with a fingertip of the right hand. The young men standing by show no less attentiveness than the occupants of the couches.

The exposition of the sacred scriptures treats the inner meaning conveyed in allegory. For to these people the whole book of the law seems to resemble a living creature with the literal ordinances for its body and for its soul the invisible meaning laid up in its wording. It is in this meaning especially that the rational soul begins to contemplate the things akin to itself and looking through the words as through a mirror beholds the marvelous beauties of the concepts, unfolds and removes the symbolic coverings and brings forth the thoughts and sets them bare to the light of day for those who need but a little reminding to enable them to discern the inward and hidden through the outward and visible.

When then the President thinks he has discoursed enough and both sides feel sure that they have attained their object, the speaker in the effectiveness with which his discourse has carried out his aims, the audience in the substance of what they have heard, universal applause arises showing a general pleasure in the prospect of what is still to follow. Then the President rises and sings a hymn composed as an address to God, either a new one of his own composition or an old one by poets of an earlier day who have left behind them hymns in many measures and melodies, hexameters and iambics, lyrics suitable for processions or in libations and at the altars, or for the chorus whilst standing or dancing, with careful metrical arrangements to fit the various evolutions. After him all the others take their turns as they are arranged and in the proper order while all the rest listen in complete silence except when they have to chant the closing lines or refrains, for then they all lift up their voices, men and women alike.

When everyone has finished his hymns the young men bring in the tables mentioned a little above on which is set the truly purified meal of leavened bread seasoned with salt mixed with hyssop [. . .].

Sacred vigil

After the supper they hold the sacred vigil which is conducted in the following way. They rise up all together and standing in the middle of the refectory form themselves first

into two choirs, one of men and one of women, the leader
and precentor chosen for each being the most honored
amongst them and also the most musical. Then they sing
hymns to God composed of many measures and set to many
melodies, sometimes chanting together, sometimes taking up
the harmony antiphonally, hands and feet keeping time in accompaniment, and rapt with enthusiasm reproduce sometimes
the lyrics of the procession, sometimes of the halt and of the
wheeling and counterwheeling of a choric dance.

Then when each choir has separately done its own part
in the feast, having drunk as in the Bacchic rites of the strong
wine of God's love they mix and both together become a
single choir, a copy of the choir set up of old beside the Red
Sea[19] in honor of the wonders there wrought. [. . .] It is on
this model above all that the choir of the Therapeutae of
either sex, note in response to note and voice to voice, the
treble of the women blending with the bass of the men, create
an harmonious concent, music in the truest sense. Lovely are
the thoughts, lovely the words and worthy of reverence the
choristers, and the end and aim of thoughts, words and choristers alike is piety. Thus they continue till dawn, drunk with
this drunkenness in which there is no shame, then not with
heavy heads or drowsy eyes but more alert and wakeful than
when they came to the banquet, they stand with their faces
and whole body turned to the east and when they see the sun
rising they stretch their hands up to heaven and pray for
bright days and knowledge of the truth and the power of
keen sighted thinking. And after the prayers they depart each
to his private sanctuary once more to ply the trade and till the
field of their wonted philosophy.

So much then for the Therapeutae, who have taken to
their hearts the contemplation of nature and what it has to
teach, and have lived, in the soul alone, citizens of heaven
and the world, presented to the Father and Maker of all by
their faithful sponsor Virtue, who has procured for them
God's friendship and added a gift going hand in hand with it,
true excellence of life, a boon better than all good fortune and
rising to the very summit of felicity.

V. Re-Reading a Biblical Work

Job the Saint

THE TESTAMENT OF JOB

Following the pattern of Biblical and apocryphal "testaments" (see the introductory note to the Testaments of the Twelve Patriarchs), this midrashic work recasts and reinterprets the story of Job in the form of parting words which the sufferer addresses to the children born to him after his restoration. It bears the title: "Testament of Job, the blameless, the sainted, the conqueror in many contests."

The Hebrew original of the work, composed in the last pre-Christian century, is lost. Two Greek versions made from the Hebrew, each represented by one manuscript, became known in the nineteenth century. In 1897 Kaufmann Kohler published an English translation and introduction to this fascinating document.

The Biblical Book of Job presents a Job whose experience of evil causes him to question God's interest in His creation. Justice, central in prophetic religion, seems to have been renounced by God Himself, who absurdly "destroyeth the innocent and the wicked" (Job 9:22). "The earth is given into the hand of the wicked" (9:24), God is remote, and man, "knowing" this true state of reality, is isolated from both God and world. Job's anguished cry "Answer Thou me" (13:22) is heeded and the voice of the remote, silent God is heard "out of the whirlwind" (chapters 38 to 40). The Creator allows man to behold the vast panorama of the universe. One thing alone is missing in this majestic picture of heaven and earth: man. Now Job realizes ("knows") his insignificance. But it is God who has revealed this knowledge to man.

In recasting the drama of Job, the unknown author of the Testament did not need to work toward what is the culmination of the story in the Biblical Book of Job: God's appearance and answer to the rebellious sufferer. In the Testament, Job never doubts divine justice. His agony affects the faith of the world around him, but he himself remains firm in his trust. He has lost everything, except the knowledge of the divine presence. The Biblical Job fears the distant, silent, God; Job of the Testament can love him: "I shall from love of God endure until the end." Thus Satan, who in the Biblical Job is but the initiator of the tension between Job and God, remains in the Testament a fighting antagonist throughout the drama, and his spirit imbues Elihu, the youngest of Job's "friends." Against the mighty but perishable realm of the Evil One, Job represents the eternal kingdom of God. K. Kohler seems justified in assigning the composition of the Testament to the community of the early Hasidim. It is indeed a hasidic interpretation of the Job problem, a reading that does not admit the communion between God and man to be disturbed by the sad and sorry state of this world.

On the day he [Job] became sick and knew that he would have to leave his bodily abode, he called his seven sons and his three daughters together and spoke to them as follows:

Form a circle around me, children, and hear, and I shall relate to you what the Lord did for me and all that happened to me. For I am Job your father. Know ye then my children, that you are the generation of a chosen one [Abraham] and take heed of your noble birth.

For I am of the sons of Esau. My brother is Nahor, and your mother is Dinah. By her have I become your father. For my first wife died with my other ten children in bitter death. Hear now, children, and I will reveal unto you what happened to me.

I was a very rich man living in the East in the land Ausitis [Utz], and before the Lord had named me Job, I was called Jobab.

The beginning of my trial was thus. Near my house there was the idol of one worshipped by the people; and I saw constantly burnt offerings brought to him as a god.

Then I pondered and said to myself: "Is this he who made heaven and earth, the sea and us all? How will I know the truth?"

In that night as I lay asleep, a voice came and called: "Jobab! Jobab! rise up, and I will tell thee who is the one whom thou wishest to know. This, however, to whom the people bring burnt offerings and libations, is not God, but this is the power and work of the Seducer [Satan] by which he beguiles the people."

When I heard this, I fell upon the earth and I prostrated myself saying: "O my Lord who speakest for the salvation of my soul, I pray thee, if this is the idol of Satan, I pray thee, let me go hence and destroy it and purify this spot. For there is none that can forbid me doing this, as I am the king of this land, so that those that live in it will no longer be led astray."

The voice that spoke out of the flame answered to me: "Thou canst purify this spot. But behold, I announce to thee what the Lord ordered me to tell thee. For I am the archangel of God." And I said: "Whatever shall be told to his servant, I shall hear." And the archangel said to me: "Thus speaketh the Lord: If thou undertakest to destroy, and takest away the image of Satan, he will set himself with wrath to wage war against thee, and he will display against thee all his malice. He will bring upon thee many and severe plagues, and take from thee all that thou hast. He will take away thine children, and will inflict many evils upon thee. Then thou must wrestle like an athlete and sustain pain, sure of thy reward, and overcome trials and afflictions.

"But when thou endurest, I shall make thy name renowned throughout all generations of the earth until to the end of the world. I shall restore thee to all that thou hadst had, and the double part of what thou shalt lose will be given to thee in order that thou mayest know that God does not consider the person but giveth to each who deserveth the good. And also to thee shall it be given, and thou shalt put on a crown of amarant. And at the resurrection thou shalt awaken for eternal life. Then shalt thou know that the Lord is just, and true and mighty."

Whereupon, my children, I replied: "I shall from love of God endure until death all that will come upon me, and I shall not shrink back." Then the angel put his seal upon me and left me.

After this I rose up in the night and took fifty slaves and went to the temple of the idol and destroyed it to the ground.

I went back to my house and gave orders that the door should be firmly locked; saying to my doorkeepers: "If somebody shall ask for me, bring no report to me, but tell him: He investigates urgent affairs; he is inside."

Then Satan disguised himself as a beggar and knocked heavily at the door, saying to the doorkeeper:

"Report to Job and say that I desire to meet him."

[Having failed to get Job into his hand, Satan secured from God the power to take away Job's wealth with which he supported "the poor that came from all the lands." "The four doors of my house were opened" and the poor "could take whatever they needed." After the feasts held by his children, Job offered sacrifices and gifts to the poor, in case the children have sinned "in a haughty spirit"; he said: "May my children never think evil towards God in their hearts."]

While I lived in this manner, the Seducer could not bear to see the good I did, and he demanded the warfare of God against me. And he came upon me cruelly. First he burnt up the large number of sheep, then the camels, then he burnt up the cattle and all my herds; or they were captured not only by enemies but also by such as had received benefits from me. And the shepherds came and announced that to me. But when I heard it, I gave praise to God and did not blaspheme.

When the Seducer learned of my fortitude, he plotted new things against me. He disguised himself as King of Persia and besieged my city, and after he had led off all that were therein, he spoke to them in malice, saying in boastful language: "This man Job who has obtained all the goods of the earth and left nothing for others, he has destroyed and torn down the temple of god. Therefore shall I repay to him what he has done to the house of the great god. Now come with me and we shall pillage all that is left in his house."

The [men of the city] answered and said to him: "He has seven sons and three daughters. Take heed lest they flee into other lands and they may become our tyrants and then come over us with force and kill us." And he said: "Be not at all afraid. His flocks and his wealth have I destroyed by fire, and the rest have I captured, and behold his children shall I kill." Having spoken thus, he went and threw the house upon my children and killed them.

My fellow-citizens, seeing that what was said by him had become true, came and pursued me and robbed me of all that was in my house. I saw with mine own eyes the pillage of my house, and men without culture and without honor sat at my table and on my couches, and I could not remonstrate against them. For I was exhausted like a woman with her loins let loose from multitude of pains, remembering chiefly that this warfare had been predicted to me by the Lord through His angel. I became like one who, when seeing the rough sea and the adverse winds, while the lading of the vessel in mid-ocean is too heavy, casts the burden into the sea, saying: "I wish to destroy all this only in order to come safely into the city so that I may take as profit the rescued ship and the best of my things." Thus did I manage my own affairs.

But there came another messenger and announced to me the ruin of my own children, and I was shaken with terror. And I tore my clothes and said: "The Lord hath given, the Lord hath taken. As it hath deemed best to the Lord, thus it hath come to be. May the name of the Lord be blessed."

When Satan saw that he could not put me to despair, he went and asked my body of the Lord in order to inflict plague on me, for the Evil One could not bear my patience. Then the Lord delivered me into his hands to use my body as he wanted, but He gave him no power over my soul.

Satan came to me as I was sitting on my throne still mourning over my children. He resembled a great hurricane and turned over my throne and threw me upon the ground; I continued lying on the floor for three hours. Then he smote me with a hard plague from the top of my head to the toes of my feet. Thereupon I left the city in great terror and woe and sat down upon a dunghill, my body being worm-eaten. [. . .]

Thus I endured for seven years, sitting on a dunghill outside of the city while being plague-stricken. I saw with mine own eyes my longed-for children [carried by angels to heaven]. My humbled wife who had been brought to her bridal chamber in such great luxuriousness and with spearmen as bodyguards, I saw do a water-carrier's work like a slave in the house of a common man in order to win some bread and bring it to me.

[When she was no longer permitted to bring him food, Satan sold her three loaves of bread for the hair of her head. The Seducer "troubled her heart greatly" and she lost her faith.]

Then my wife came near me, and crying aloud and weeping she said "Job! Job! how long wilt thou sit upon the dunghill outside of the city, pondering yet for a while and expecting to obtain your hoped-for salvation!" I have been wandering from place to place, roaming about as a hired servant, behold thy memory has already died away from earth. My sons and the daughters that I carried on my bosom and the labors and pains that I sustained have been for nothing? And thou sittest in the malodorous state of soreness and worms, passing the nights in the cold air. I have undergone all trials and troubles and pains, day and night until I succeeded in bringing bread to thee. [. . .] Who would then not be astonished saying: "Is this Sitis, the wife of Job, who had fourteen curtains to cover her inner sitting room, and doors within doors so that he was greatly honored who would be brought near her, and now behold, she barters off her hair for bread!

"Who had camels laden with goods, and they were brought into remote lands to the poor, and now she sells her hair for bread!

"Behold her who had seven tables immovably set in her house at which each poor man and each stranger ate, and now she sells her hair for bread.

"Behold her who had the basin wherewith to wash her feet made of gold and silver, and now she walks upon the ground and sells her hair for bread!

"Behold her who had her garments made of byssus interwoven with gold, and now she exchanges her hair for bread!

"Behold her who had couches of gold and of silver, and now she sells her hair for bread!"

In short then, Job, after the many things that have been said to me, I now say in one word to thee: "Since the feebleness of my heart has crushed my bones, rise then and take these loaves of bread and enjoy them, and then speak some word against the Lord and die! For I too, would exchange the torpor of death for the sustenance of my body."

But I replied to her: "Behold I have been for these seven years plague-stricken, and I have stood the worms of my body, and I was not weighed down in my soul by all these pains. And as to the word which thou sayest: 'Speak some word against God and die!,' together with thee I will sustain the evil which thou seest, and let us endure the ruin of all that we have. Yet thou desirest that we should say some word against God and that He should be exchanged for the great Pluto.

"Why dost thou not remember those great goods which we possessed? If these goods come from the lands of the Lord, should not we also endure evils and be high-minded in everything until the Lord will have mercy again and show pity to us? Dost thou not see the Seducer stand behind thee and confound thy thoughts in order that thou shouldst beguile me?"

Then he turned to Satan and said: "Why dost thou not come openly to me? Stop hiding thyself, thou wretched one. Does the lion show his strength in the weasel cage? Or does the bird fly in the basket? I now tell thee: Go away and wage thy war against me."

Satan went off from behind my wife, placed himself before me crying and he said: "Behold, Job, I yield and give way to thee who art but flesh while I am a spirit. Thou art plague-stricken, but I am in great trouble. For I am like a wrestler contesting with a wrestler who has, in a singlehanded combat, torn down his antagonist and covered him with dust and broken every limb of his, whereas the other one who lies beneath, having displayed his bravery, gives forth sounds of triumph testifying to his own superior excellence. Thus thou, O Job, art beneath and stricken with plague and pain, and yet thou hast carried the victory in the wrestling match with me, and behold, I yield to thee." Then he left me abashed. Now my children, do you also show a firm heart in all the evil that happens to you, for greater than all things is firmness of heart.

At this time the kings heard what had happened to me and they rose and came to me, each from his land to visit me and to comfort me. When they came near me, they cried with a loud voice and each tore his clothes. After they had prostrated themselves, touching the earth with their heads, they sat down next to me for seven days and seven nights, and none spoke a word. They were four in numbers: Eliphaz, the king of Teman, and Baldad, and Sophar, and Elihu. And when they had taken their seat, they conversed about what had happened to me.

Now when for the first time they had come to me and I had shown them my precious stones, they were astonished and said: "If of us three kings all our possessions would be brought together into one, it would not come up to the precious stones of Jobab's kingdom. For thou art of greater nobility, than all the people of the East." When therefore, they now came to the land of Ausitis to visit me, they asked in the city: "Where is Jobab, the ruler of this whole land?" And they told them concerning me: "He sitteth upon the dunghill outside of the city; for he has not entered the city for seven years." [. . .]

The kings drew nigh and Eliphaz began and said: "Art thou, indeed, Job, our fellow-king? Art thou the one who owned the great glory? Art thou he who once shone like the sun of day upon the whole earth? Art thou he who once resembled the moon and the stars effulgent throughout the night?" I answered him and said: "I am," and thereupon all wept and lamented, and they sang a royal song of lamentation, their whole army joining them in a chorus.

And again Eliphaz said to me: "Art thou he who had ordered seven thousand sheep to be given for the clothing of the poor? Whither, then hath gone the glory of thy throne?

"Art thou he who had ordered three thousand cattle to

do the ploughing of the field for the poor? Whither, then hath thy glory gone!" [. . .]

And when Eliphaz had for a long time cried and lamented, while all the others joined him, so that the commotion was very great, I said to them: "Be silent and I will show you my throne, and the glory of its splendor: My glory will be everlasting. The whole world shall perish, and its glory shall vanish, and all those who hold fast to it, will remain beneath, but my throne is in the upper world, and its glory and splendor will be to the right of the Savior in the heavens. My throne exists in the life of the "holy ones" and its glory in the imperishable world. For rivers will be dried up and their arrogance shall go down to the depth of the abyss, but the streams of the land in which my throne is erected, shall not dry up, but shall remain unbroken in strength.

"The kings perish and the rulers vanish, and their glory and pride is as the shadow in a looking glass, but my kingdom lasts forever and ever, and its glory and beauty is in the chariot of my Father."

When I spoke thus to them, Eliphaz became angry and said to the other friends: "For what purpose is it that we have come here with our hosts to comfort him? Behold, he upbraids us. Therefore let us return to our countries. This man sits here in misery wormeaten amidst an unbearable state of putrefaction, and yet he challenges us saying: 'Kingdoms shall perish and their rulers, but my Kingdom, says he, shall last forever.'" Eliphaz, then, rose in great commotion, and, turning away from them in great fury, said: "I go hence. We have indeed come to comfort him, but he declares war to us in view of our armies."

But then Baldad seized him by the hand and said: "Not thus ought one to speak to an afflicted man, and especially to one stricken down with so many plagues. Behold, we, being in good health, dared not approach him on account of the offensive odor, except with the help of plenty of fragrant aroma. But thou, Eliphaz, art forgetful of all this. Let me speak plainly. Let us be magnanimous and learn what is the cause.

Must he in remembering his former days of happiness not become mad in his mind? Who should not be altogether perplexed seeing himself thus lapse into misfortune and plagues? But let me step near him that I may find by what cause is he thus?"

And Baldad rose and approached me saying: "Art thou Job?" and he said: "Is thy heart still in good keeping?" And I said: "I did not hold fast to the earthly things, since the earth with all that inhabit it is unstable. But my heart holds fast to the heaven, because there is no trouble in heaven."

Then Baldad rejoined and said: "We know that the earth is unstable, for it changes according to season. At times it is in a state of peace, and at times it is in a state of war. But of the heaven we hear that it is perfectly steady. But art thou truly in a state of calmness? Therefore let me ask and speak, and when thou answerest me to my first word, I shall have a second question to ask, and if again thou answerest in well-set words, it will be manifest that thy heart has not been unbalanced."

And he said: "Upon what dost thou set thy hope?" And I said: "Upon the living God." And he said to me: "Who deprived thee of all thou didst possess? And who inflicted thee with these plagues?" And I said: "God." And he said: "If thou still placest thy hope upon God, how can He do wrong in judgment, having brought upon thee these plagues and misfortunes, and having taken from thee all thy possessions? And since He has taken these, it is clear that He has given thee nothing. No king will disgrace his soldier who has served him well as body-guard?" I answered saying: "Who understands the depths of the Lord and of His wisdom to be able to accuse God of injustice?" [. . .]

Then Sophar rejoined and said: "We do not inquire after our own affairs, but we desire to know whether thou art in a sound state, and behold, we see that thy reason has not been shaken. What now dost thou wish that we should do for thee? Behold, we have come here and brought the physicians of three kings, and if thou wishest, thou mayest be cured by them." But I answered and said: "My cure and my restoration cometh from God, the Maker of physicians."

And when I spoke thus to them, behold, there my wife Sitis came running, dressed in rags, from the service of the master by whom she was employed as slave; though she had been forbidden to leave, lest the kings, on seeing her, might take her as captive. When she came, she threw herself prostrate to their feet, crying and saying: "Remember, Eliphaz and ye other friends, what I was once with you, and how I have changed, how I am now dressed to meet you." Then the kings broke forth in great weeping and, being in double perplexity, they kept silent. But Eliphaz took his purple mantle and cast it about her to wrap herself up with it.

But she asked him saying: "I ask as favor of you, my Lords, that you order your soldiers that they should dig among the ruins of our house which fell upon my children, so that their bones could be brought in a perfect state to the tombs. For we have, owing to our misfortune, no power at all, and so we may at least see their bones. For have I like a brute the motherly feeling of wild beasts that my ten children should have perished on one day and not to one of them could I give a decent burial?"

Then the kings gave order that the ruins of my house should be dug up. But I prohibited it, saying: "Do not go to the trouble in vain; for my children will not be found, for they are in the keeping of their Maker and Ruler."

The kings answered and said: "Who will gainsay that he is out of his mind and raves? For while we desire to bring the bones of his children back, he forbids us to do so saying: 'They have been taken and placed in the keeping of their Maker.' Therefore prove unto us the truth." But I said to them: "Raise me that I may stand up." They lifted me, holding up my arms from both sides. I stood upright, pronounced first the praise of God, and after the prayer I said to them: "Look with your eyes to the East." And they looked and saw my children with crowns near the glory of the King, the Ruler of heaven.

When my wife Sitis saw this, she fell to the ground and prostrated herself before God, saying: "Now I know that my memory remains with the Lord." After she had spoken this, and the evening came, she went to the city, back to the master whom she served as slave, and lay herself down at the manger of the cattle and died there from exhaustion.

When her despotic master searched for her and did not find her, he came to the fold of his herds, and there he saw her stretched out upon the manger dead, while all the animals around were crying about her. And all who saw her wept and lamented, and the cry extended throughout the whole city. Then the people brought her down and wrapt her up and buried her by the house which had fallen upon her children. The poor of the city made a great mourning for her and said: "Behold this Sitis whose like in nobility and in glory is not found in any woman. Alas! she was not found worthy of a proper tomb!" The dirge for her you will find in the record.

But Eliphaz and those that were with him were astonished at these things, and they sat down with me and replying to me, spoke in boastful words concerning me for twenty-seven days. They repeated it again and again that I suffered deservedly thus for having committed many sins, and that there was no hope left for me; I retorted to these men in zest of contention myself. And they rose in anger, ready to part in wrathful spirit.

But Elihu conjured them to stay yet a little while until he would have shown them what it was. "For," said he, "so many days did you pass, allowing Job to boast that he is just. But I shall no longer suffer it. For from the beginning did I continue crying over him, remembering his former happiness. But now he speaks boastfully and in overbearing pride, he says that he has his throne in the heavens. Therefore, hear me, and I will tell you what is the cause of his destiny." Then, imbued with the spirit of Satan, Elihu spoke hard words which are written down in the records left of Elihu. After he had ended, God appeared to me in a storm and in clouds, and spoke, blaming

Elihu and showing me that he who had spoken was not a man, but a wild beast.

[When the three friends finally realized their error, God pardoned them "through His servant Job." However, "He did not deign to pardon Elihu" for "he has loved the beauty of the serpent." A hymn by Eliphaz concludes the story of the friends.]

> Righteous is the Lord, and His judgments are true,
> With Him there is no preference of person,
> for He judgeth all alike.
> Behold, the Lord cometh!
> Behold, the holy ones have been prepared!
> The crowns and the prizes of the victors precede them!
> Let the saints rejoice, and let their hearts exult in gladness;
> for they shall receive the glory which is in store for them.
> Our sins are forgiven,
> our injustice has been cleansed,
> but Elihu hath no remembrance among the living.

After Eliphaz had finished the hymn, we rose and went back to the city, each to the house where they lived. [Here is the part missing which told of Job's restoration.]

And the people made a feast for me in gratitude and delight of God, and all my friends came back to me. [. . .]

Then the Lord blessed all that was left to me, and after a few days I became rich again in merchandise, in flocks and all things which I had lost, and I received all in double number again. Then I also took as wife your mother and became the father of you ten in place of the ten children that had died.

And now, my children, let me admonish you: "Behold I die. You will take my place. Do not forsake the Lord. Be charitable towards the poor; do not disregard the feeble. Take not unto yourselves wives from strangers.

"Behold, my children, I shall divide among you what I possess, so that each may have control over his own and have full power to do good with his share." After he had spoken thus, he brought all his goods and divided them among his seven sons, but he gave nothing of his goods to his daughters.

Then they said to their father: "Our lord and father!
Are we not also thy children? Why, then, dost thou not also
give us a share of thy possessions?" Then said Job to his daughters: "Do not become angry my daughters. I have not forgotten you. Behold, I have preserved for you a possession
better than that which your brothers have taken." [Job gave
them three-stringed magic girdles by means of which his own
leprosy was cured. As soon as his daughters put these girdles
around their bodies they were transfigured and, in the voices
of angels, sang hymns echoing the mysteries of heaven].

And Job lay down from sickness on his couch, yet without pain and suffering, because his pain did not take strong
hold of him on account of the charm of the girdle which he
had wound around himself. After three days Job saw the holy
angels come for his soul. Instantly he rose, took the cithara
and gave it to his daughter Day [Yemima]. And to Kassia
[Perfume] he gave a censer with perfume and to Amalthea's
Horn [Keren Happukh] he gave a timbrel in order that they
might bless the holy angels who came for his soul. They took
these, and sang, and played on the psaltery and praised and
glorified God in the holy dialect.

After this came He who sitteth upon the great chariot
and kissed Job, while his three daughters looked on, but the
others saw it not. He took the soul of Job and soared upward,
taking the soul by the arm and carrying her upon the chariot,
and He went towards the East. His body, however, was
brought to the grave, while the three daughters marched
ahead, having put on their girdles and singing hymns in
praise of God.

Then held Nahor his brother and his seven sons, with
the rest of the people and the poor, the orphans and the
feeble ones, a great mourning over him saying: "Woe unto us,
for today has been taken from us the strength of the feeble,
the light of the blind, the father of the orphans. The receiver
of strangers has been taken off, the leader of the erring, the
cover of the naked, the shield of the widows. Who would not
mourn for the man of God!"

And as they were mourning in this and in that form, they would not suffer him to be put into the grave. After three days, however, he was finally put into the grave like one in sweet slumber, and he received the name of the good who will remain renowned throughout all generations of the world.

He left seven sons and three daughters, and there were no daughters found on earth, as fair as the daughters of Job. The name of Job was formerly Jobab, and he was called Job by the Lord. He had lived before his plague eighty five years, and after the plague he took the double share of all; hence also his years he doubled, which is one hundred and seventy years. Thus he lived altogether two hundred and fifty-five years. And he saw sons of his sons unto the fourth generation. It is written that he will rise up with those whom the Lord will reawaken. To our Lord be glory. Amen.

VI. Interpreting Jewish Faith to the World

Hellenist Exposition of Scripture

FROM PHILO'S COMMENTARIES

A note on Philo. From the Stoics, Philo (see introductory note to "The Order of the Essenes") learned the method of allegory (a term derived from Greek rhetoric) by which a text, the literal meaning of which no longer satisfies, is interpreted to imply a deeper, or more universal, philosophical or religious meaning. The text then no longer concerns itself with concrete, temporal, historically limited inquiries but with abstract, eternal, universally valid issues. By using this method, which Philo brought to systematic perfection, he rediscovered in Scripture ideas of Platonic philosophy. The Bible, as he interpreted it, tells not the story of three patriarchs, historic ancestors of a historic nation, but of three men who symbolically represent three types of man's relationship to God; Abraham is the symbol of man who knows God through learning, Isaac through inspiration, Jacob through ascetic life. These three types unite in the "most pure mind" and "lover of virtue," symbolized by Moses.

The Stoics, who inherited allegory from pre-Platonic philosophers, used this method in an effort to harmonize the Greek myths—which were no longer believed—with their own philosophy. Philo employed allegory in order to teach the Bible as being the authentic document of the correspondence of Hebraic and Greek wisdom.

The following selections, taken from his commentaries (written in Greek), are examples of Philo's thinking and his method of Biblical interpretation.

On hiding from the presence of God

"And Adam and his wife hid themselves from the pres-

ence of the Lord God amongst the trees of the garden"
(Gen. 3:8). Here Scripture acquaints us with the principle
that the wicked are homeless.[1] For if virtue constitutes the
true city of the wise, then he who cannot participate in virtue
is an exile from that city. And the wicked cannot participate
in virtue, and so they are exiled, they are fugitives. But he who
flees from virtue, at once hides himself from God.

For if the wise are visible to God—since they are his
friends—the wicked are apparently all hidden and concealed
from him, since they are enemies of right reason. Scripture
testifies that the wicked man has no home and no habitation,
in the allusion to Esau in his "hairy mantle" (Gen. 25:25) and
guise of sinfulness, for it is said: "Esau was a cunning hunter,
a man of the field" (Gen. 25:27). For wickedness bound on
the hunt for passions, and foolishly hastening in pursuit of
boorishness,[2] cannot live in the city of virtue. Jacob, on the
other hand, who is full of wisdom, is a citizen of virtue and
dwells in virtue, for of him it is said: "And Jacob was a quiet
man, dwelling in tents" (Gen. 25:27). And this is also the
reason why it is said: "And it came to pass, because the midwives feared God, that they made themselves houses" (Exod.
1:21).[3] For such souls as seek out the hidden secrets of God
—and that means "bringing the male children to the birth"
(Exod. 1:17)—build up the works of virtue in which they
choose to dwell. Thus it is shown in what sense the wicked
are without a home and without a habitation, since they are
exiled from the precincts of virtue, while the good have received wisdom as their house and as their city.

Now we shall investigate in what sense it can be said of a
person that he is hiding from God. It is impossible to understand these words we have before us in Scripture, unless we
give them an allegorical interpretation. For God fills and penetrates everything; he has left nothing empty and void of his
presence. How then could anyone be in a place where God is
not? Another passage testifies to this: "The Lord, He is God
in heaven above, and upon the earth beneath; there is none
else" (Deut. 4:39). And further on: "Behold, I will stand before thee" (Exod. 17:6). For before anything was created,

there was God, and he is found everywhere, so that no one can hide from him. Why should this fill us with wonder? We could not escape from the elements of all things created, even if we had cause to wish to hide from them. Just try to flee from water and air, from the sky or from the whole of the world! We are, of necessity, caught in their compass, for no one can flee from the world. But if we cannot hide from parts of the world, and from the world itself, how then could we hide from the presence of God? Never! So what is meant by the expression "hid themselves"? The wicked believe that God is in a certain place, that he does not encompass, but that he is encompassed. And so they think they can hide, because the Creator of all life is not in that part of the world which they have selected for their hiding place.

Thus we have shown in what way the wicked are fugitives and hide from God. Now we shall see where they hide. "Amongst the trees of the garden" (Gen. 3:8) is what we read, that is, in the center of the mind, which is, so to speak, in the middle of the garden, that is, of the whole soul. He who flees from God, flees into himself. For there are two kinds of mind, the mind of the universe, and that is God, and the mind of individual man. And the one flees from his own mind to the mind of the universe—for whoever leaves his own mind, avows therewith that the works of the mortal mind are as nothing, and ascribes everything to God. But the other flees from God, and declares that not God is the cause of anything at all, but that he himself is the cause of all that comes to pass. Thus there are many who believe that all the things in the world go their own course by themselves, without a guide, and that it is the spirit of man that has invented the arts, crafts, laws, customs, state institutions, and the rights of the individual and the community, both in regard to men and to beasts, that are without reason. But you, O my soul, see the difference between these two points of view. For the one leaves the perishable mortal mind, which has been created, and chooses for its true aid the primordial and immortal mind of the universe. But the other, which sets aside God, foolishly courts as its ally the human mind, which is not even able to help itself.

Revelation in the Sinai desert

Having related in the preceding treatises the lives of those whom Moses judged to be men of wisdom, who are set before us in the Sacred Books as founders of our nation and in themselves unwritten laws, I shall now proceed in due course to give full descriptions of the written laws. And if some allegorical interpretation should appear to underlie them, I shall not fail to state it. For knowledge loves to learn and advance to full understanding and its way is to seek the hidden meaning rather than the obvious.

To the question why he [Moses] promulgated his laws in the depths of the desert instead of in cities we may answer in the first place that most cities are full of countless evils, both acts of impiety towards God and wrongdoing between man and man. For everything is debased, the genuine overpowered by the spurious, the true by the specious, which is intrinsically false but creates impressions whose plausibility serves but to delude. So too in cities there arises that most insidious of foes, Pride [or, vanity], admired and worshipped by some who add dignity to vain ideas by means of gold crowns and purple robes and a great establishment of servants and cars, on which these so-called blissful and happy people ride aloft, drawn sometimes by mules and horses, sometimes by men, who bear the heavy burden on their shoulders, yet suffer in soul rather than in body under the weight of extravagant arrogance.

Pride is also the creator of many other evils, boastfulness, haughtiness, inequality, and these are the sources of wars, both civil and foreign, suffering no place to remain in peace whether public or private, whether on sea or on land. Yet why dwell on offences between man and man? Pride also brings divine things into utter contempt, even though they are supposed to receive the highest honors. But what honor can there be if truth be not there as well, truth honorable both in name and function, just as falsehood is naturally dishonorable? This contempt for things divine is manifest to those of keener vision. For men have employed sculpture and painting to fashion innumerable forms which they have enclosed in shrines and temples and after building altars have assigned celestial and divine honors to idols of stone and wood and suchlike images, all of them lifeless things. Such persons are happily compared in the sacred Scriptures to the children of a harlot; for as they in their ignorance of their one natural father ascribe their paternity to all their mother's lovers, so too throughout the cities those who do not know the true, the really existent God have deified hosts of others who are falsely so called. Then as some honor one, some another god, diversity of opinion as to which was best waxed strong and engendered disputes in every other matter also. This was the primary consideration which made him prefer to legislate away from cities.

He [Moses] had also a second object in mind. He who is about to receive the holy laws must first cleanse his soul and purge away the deep-set stains which it has contracted through contact with the motley promiscuous horde of men in cities. And to this he cannot attain except by dwelling apart, nor that at once, but only long afterwards, and not till the marks which his old transgressions have imprinted on him have gradually grown faint, melted away and disappeared. In this way, too, good physicians preserve their sick folk: they think it unadvisable to give them food or drink until they have removed the causes of their maladies. While these still remain, nourishment is useless, indeed harmful, and acts as fuel to the distemper. Naturally therefore he first led them away from the highly mischievous associations of cities into the desert, to clear the sins out of their souls, and then began to set the nourishment before their minds—and what should this nourishment be but laws and words of God?

He had a third reason as follows: Just as men when setting out on a long voyage do not begin to provide sails and rudders and tillers when they have embarked and left the harbor, but equip themselves with enough of the gear needed for the voyage while they are still staying on shore, so Moses did not think it good that they should just take their portions and settle in cities and then go in quest of laws to regulate their civic life, but rather should first provide themselves with the rules for that life and gain practice in all that would surely enable the communities to steer their course in safety, and then settle down to follow from their use, in harmony and fellowship of spirit and rendering to every man his due.

Some, too, give a fourth reason which is not out of keeping with the truth but agrees very closely with it. As it was necessary to establish a belief in their minds that the laws were not the inventions of a man but quite clearly the oracles of God, he led the nation a great distance away from cities into the depths of a desert, barren not only of cultivated fruits but also of water fit for drinking, in order that, if after lacking the necessaries of life and expecting to perish from hunger and thirst they suddenly found abundance of sustenance self-produced—when heaven rained the food called manna[4] and the shower of quails from the air to add relish to their food—when the bitter water grew sweet and fit for drinking and springs gushed out of the steep rock—they should no longer wonder whether the laws were actually the pronouncements of God, since they had been given the clearest evidence of the truth in the supplies which they had so unexpectedly received in their destitution. For He who gave abundance of the means of life also bestowed the wherewithal of a good life; for mere life they needed food and drink which they found without making provision; for the good life they needed laws and ordinances which would bring improvement to their souls.

We may properly ask why, when all these many thousands were collected in one spot, He thought good in proclaiming His ten oracles to address each not as to several persons but as to one, [e.g.] "Thou shalt not commit adultery," "Thou shalt not kill," "Thou shalt not steal," and so too with the rest. One answer which must be given is that He wishes to teach the readers of the sacred Scriptures a most excellent lesson, namely that each single person, when he is law-abiding and obedient to God, is equal in worth to a whole nation, even the most populous, or rather to all nations, and if we may go still farther, even to the whole world. And therefore elsewhere, when He praises a certain just man, He says, "I am thy God," though He was also the God of the world. And thus we see that all the rank and file who are posted in the same line and give a like satisfaction to their commander, have an equal share of approbation and honor.

A second reason is that a speaker who harangues a multitude in general does not necessarily talk to any one person, whereas if he addresses his commands or prohibitions as though to each individual separately, the practical instructions given in the course of his speech are at once held to apply to the whole body in common also. If the exhortations are received as a personal message, the hearer is more ready to obey, but if collectively with others, he is deaf to them, since he takes the multitude as a cover for disobedience.

A third reason is that He wills that no king or despot swollen with arrogance and contempt should despise an insignificant private person but should study in the school of the divine laws and abate his supercilious airs, and through the reasonableness or rather the assured truth of their arguments unlearn his self-conceit. For if the Uncreated, the Incorruptible, the Eternal, Who needs nothing and is the maker of all, the Benefactor and King of kings and God of gods could not brook to despise even the humblest, but deigned to banquet him on holy oracles and statutes, as though he should be the sole guest, as though for him alone the feast was prepared to give good cheer to a soul instructed in the holy secrets and accepted for admission to the greatest mysteries, what right have I, the mortal, to bear myself proud-necked, puffed-up and loud-voiced, towards my fellows, who, though their fortunes be unequal, have equal rights of kinship because they can claim to be children of the one common mother of mankind, nature? So then, though I be invested with the sovereignty of earth and sea, I will make myself affable and easy of access to the poorest, to the meanest, to the lonely who have none close at hand to help them, to orphans who have lost both parents, to wives on whom widowhood has fallen, to old men either childless from the first or bereaved by the early death of those whom they begot. For as I am a man, I shall not deem it right to adopt the lofty grandeur of the pompous stage, but make nature my home and not overstep her limits. I will inure my mind to have the feelings of a human being, not only because the lot both of the prosperous and the unfortunate may change to the reverse we know not when, but also because it is right that even if good fortune remains securely established, a man should not forget what he is. Such was the reason, as it seems to me, why he willed to word the series of his oracles in the singular form, and delivers them as though to one alone.

The Sabbath

On this day we are commanded to abstain from all work, not because the law inculcates slackness; on the contrary it always inures men to endure hardship and incites them to labor, and spurns those who would idle their time away, and accordingly is plain in its directions to work the full six days. Its object is rather to give men relaxation from continuous and unending toil and by refreshing their bodies with a regularly calculated system of remissions, to send them out renewed to their old activities. For a breathing space enables not merely ordinary people but athletes also to collect their strength and with a stronger force behind them to undertake promptly and patiently each of the tasks set before them.

Further, when He forbids bodily labor on the seventh day, He permits the exercise of the higher activities, namely, those employed in the study of the principles of virtue's lore. For the law bids us take the time for studying philosophy and thereby improve the soul and the dominant mind. So each seventh day there stand wide open in every city thousands of schools of good sense, temperance, courage, justice and the other virtues in which the scholars sit in order quietly with ears alert and with full attention, so much do they thirst for the draught which the teacher's words supply, while one of special experience rises and sets forth what is the best and sure to be profitable and will make the whole of life grow to something better.

But among the vast number of particular truths and

principles there studied, there stand out practically high above the others two main heads: one of duty to God as shewn by piety and holiness, one of duty to men as shewn by humanity and justice, each of them splitting up into multiform branches, all highly laudable. These things shew clearly that Moses does not allow any of those who used his sacred instruction to remain inactive at any season. But since we consist of body and soul, he assigned to the body its proper tasks and similarly to the soul what falls to its share, and his earnest desire was, that the two should be waiting to relieve each other. Thus while the body is working, the soul enjoys a respite, but when the body takes its rest, the soul resumes its work, and thus the best forms of life, the theoretical and the practical, take their turn in replacing each other. The practical life has six as its number allotted for ministering to the body. The theoretical has seven for knowledge and perfection of the mind.

The Emperor's Statue

FROM PHILO: LEGACY TO GAIUS

The tranquil government of Augustus and Tiberius was followed by the rule of the mentally unbalanced Gaius Caligula (37–41). To please the self-deifying emperor and also to harm the large Jewish community in Alexandria, the Roman prefect, Flaccus, ordered the erection of the emperor's statues in the synagogues. The Jews resisted this idolatry, and a pogrom—the first in history—ensued. In the year 40 the Alexandrian Jews sent a deputation, headed by Philo, to Rome. The Greeks, too, sent a delegation, led by the Jew-baiter Apion. At the same time the emperor ordered his image set up in the Temple in Jerusalem, instructing the legate of Syria, Petronius, to effect the command. Agrippa I, grandson of King Herod, whom Caligula had appointed king over a part of the land of Israel, decided to write a letter to the emperor, his childhood friend, to plead for the revocation of the order so offensive to Jewish monotheist thinking. This epistle, reproduced on the following pages, is recorded by Philo, who also wrote a vivid account of the (unsuccessful) embassy to Caligula (*Legacy to Gaius*). The death of Caligula

(41) made his order obsolete. His successor Claudius restored peace in Jerusalem and in Alexandria.

Having taken tablets, Agrippa wrote to Gaius in the following manner:

O master, fear and shame have taken from me all courage to come into your presence to address you; since fear teaches me to dread your threats; and shame, out of respect for the greatness of your power and dignity, keeps me silent. But a letter will show my request, which I now here offer to you as my earnest petition.

In all men, O emperor! a love of their country is innate, and an eager fondness for their national customs and laws. Concerning these matters there is no need that I should give you information, since you have a heartfelt love of your own country, and a deep-seated respect for your national customs. [. . .]

I am, as you know, a Jew; Jerusalem is my country, in which there is erected the holy temple of the most high God. I have kings for my grandfathers and for my ancestors,[5] the greater part of whom have been called high priests, looking upon their royal power as inferior to their office as priests; thinking that the high priesthood is as much superior to the power of a king, as God is superior to man; for that the one is occupied in rendering service to God, and the other has only the care of governing them.

Accordingly, I, being one of this nation, and being attached to this country and to such a temple, address to you this petition on behalf of them all; on behalf of the nation, that it may not be looked upon by you in a light contrary to the true one; since it is a most pious and holy nation, and one from the beginning most loyally disposed to your family.

For in all the particulars in which men are enjoined by the laws, and in which they have it in their power to show their piety and loyalty, my nation is inferior to none whatever in Asia or in Europe, whether it be in respect of prayers, or of the supply of sacred offerings [. . .] by which means they show their loyalty and fidelity more surely than by their mouth and tongue, providing it by the designs of their honest hearts, not indeed saying that they are friends to Caesar, but being so in reality.

Concerning the holy city I must now say what is necessary. Jerusalem, as I have already stated, is my native city, and the metropolis, not only of the one country of Judaea, but also of many, by reason of the colonies which it has sent out from time to time into the bordering districts of Egypt, Phoenicia, Syria in general, and especially that part of it which is called Coele-Syria, and also with those more distant regions of Pamphylia, Cilicia, the greater part of Asia Minor as far as Bithynia and the furthermost corners of Pontus. And in the same manner into Europe, into Thessaly, Boeotia, Macedonia, Aetolia, Attica, Argos, Corinth and all the most fertile and wealthiest districts of Peloponnesus. Not only are the continents full of Jewish colonies, but also all the most celebrated islands are so too; such as Euboea and Cyprus and Crete.

I say nothing of the countries beyond the Euphrates, for all of them except a very small portion, and Babylon, and all the satrapies around, which have any advantages whatever of soil or climate, have Jews settled in them. So that if my native land is, as it reasonably may be, looked upon as entitled to a share in your favor, it is not one city only that would then be benefited by you, but ten thousand of them in every region of the habitable world, in Europe, in Asia, and in Africa, on the continent, in the islands, on the coasts and in the inland parts. It corresponds well to the greatness of your good fortune, that, by conferring benefits on one city, you should also benefit ten thousand others, so that your renown may be celebrated in every part of the habitable world, and many praises of you may be combined with thanksgiving. [. . .]

I indeed am perfectly aware that I belong to the class which is in subjection to a lord and master, and also that I am admitted to the honor of being one of your companions, being inferior to you in respect of my birthright and natural rank, and inferior to no one whomsoever, not to say the most eminent of all men, in good will and loyalty towards you, both because that is my natural disposition, and also in consequence of the number of benefits with which you have enriched me;[6] so that if I in consequence had felt confidence to implore you myself on behalf of my country, if not to grant to it the Roman constitution, at least to confer freedom and a remission of taxes on it, I should not have thought that I had any reason to fear your displeasure for preferring such a petition to you, and for requesting that most desirable of all things, your favor, which it can do you no harm to grant, and which is the most advantageous of all things for my country to receive.

For what can possibly be a more desirable blessing for a subject nation than the good will of its sovereign? It was at Jerusalem, O emperor! that your most desirable succession to the empire was first announced; the news of your advancement spread from the holy city all over the continent on each side, and was received with great gladness. On this account that city deserves to meet with favor at your hands; for, as in families the eldest children receive the highest honors as their birthright, because they were the first to give the name of father and mother to their parents, so, in like manner, since this is first of all the cities in the east to salute you as emperor, it ought to receive greater benefit from you than any other; or if not greater, at all events as great as any other city.

Having now advanced these pleas on the ground of justice, and made these petitions on behalf of my native country, I now come at last to my supplication on behalf of the Temple. O my lord and master, Gaius! this Temple has never, from the time of its original foundation until now, admitted any form made by hands, because it has been the abode of God. Now, pictures and images are only imitations of those gods who are perceptible to the outward senses; but it was not considered by our ancestors to be consistent with the reverence due to God to make any image or representation of the invisible God. [. . .]

On which account, no one, whether Greek or barbarian, satrap, or king, or implacable enemy; no sedition, no war, no capture, no destruction, no occurrence that has ever taken place, has ever threatened this Temple, with such innovation as to place in it any image, or statue, or any work of any kind made with hands; for, though enemies have displayed their hostility to the inhabitants of the country, still, either reverence or fear has possessed them sufficiently to prevent them from abrogating any of the laws which were established at the beginning, as tending to the honor of the Creator and Father of the universe; for they knew that it is these and similar actions which bring after them the irremediable calamities of heaven-sent afflictions. [. . .]

But why need I invoke the assistance of foreign witnesses when I have plenty with whom I can furnish you from among your own countrymen and friends? Marcus Agrippa,[7] your own grandfather on the mother's side, the moment that he arrived in Judaea, when Herod, my grandfather, was king of the country, thought fit to go up from the seacoast to the metropolis, which was inland. And when he had beheld the Temple, and the decorations of the priests, and the piety and holiness of the people of the country, he marveled, looking upon the whole matter as one of great solemnity and entitled to great respect, and thinking that he had beheld what was too magnificent to be described. And he could talk of nothing else to his companions but the magnificence of the Temple and every thing connected with it.

Therefore, every day that he remained in the city, by reason of his friendship for Herod, he went to that sacred place, being delighted with the spectacle of the building, and of the sacrifices, and all the ceremonies connected with the worship of God, and the regularity which was observed, and the dignity and honor paid to the high priest, and his grandeur when arrayed in his sacred vestments and when about to begin the sacrifices.[8] And after he had adorned the Temple with all the offerings in his power to contribute, and had conferred many benefits on the inhabitants, doing them many important services, and having said to Herod many friendly things, and having been replied to in corresponding terms, he was conducted back again to the seacoast, and to the

harbor, and that not by one city only but by the whole country, having branches strewed in his road, and being greatly
admired and respected for his piety.

What again did your other grandfather, the emperor
Tiberius[9] do? Does not he appear to have adopted an exactly
similar line of conduct? At all events, during the three and
twenty years that he was emperor, he preserved the form of
worship in the Temple as it had been handed down from the
earliest times, without abrogating or altering the slightest
particular of it.

Moreover, I have it in my power to relate one act of ambition on his part, though I suffered an infinite number of
evils when he was alive; but nevertheless the truth is considered dear, and much to be honored by you. Pilate[10] was one
of the emperor's lieutenants, having been appointed governor
of Judaea. He, not more with the object of doing honor to
Tiberius than with that of vexing the multitude, dedicated
some gilt shields in the palace of Herod, in the holy city; which
had no form nor any other forbidden thing represented on
them except some necessary inscription which mentioned
these two facts, the name of the person who had placed them
there, and the person in whose honor they were so placed
there. But when the multitude heard what had been done,
and when the circumstance became notorious, then the
people, putting forward the four sons of the king [Herod], who
were in no respect inferior to the kings themselves, in fortune
or in rank, and his other descendants, and those magistrates
who were among them at the time, entreated him to alter and
to rectify the innovation which he had committed in respect
of the shields; and not to make any alteration in their national
customs, which had hitherto been preserved without any in-
terruption, without being in the least degree changed by any
king or emperor.

But when he steadfastly refused this petition (for he was
a man of a very inflexible disposition, and very merciless as
well as very obstinate), they cried out: "Do not cause a sedition; do not make war upon us; do not destroy the peace

which exists. The honor of the emperor is not identical with dishonor to the ancient laws; let it not be to you a pretence for heaping insult on our nation. Tiberius is not desirous that any of our laws or customs shall be destroyed. And if you yourself say that he is, show us either some command from him, or some letter, or something of the kind, that we, who have been sent to you as envoys, may cease to trouble you, and may address our supplications to your master."

But this last sentence exasperated him in the greatest possible degree, as he feared lest they might in reality go on an embassy to the emperor, and might impeach him with respect to other particulars of his government, in respect of his corruption, and his acts of insolence, and his rapine, and his habit of insulting people, and his cruelty, and his continual murders of people untried and uncondemned, and his never-ending, gratuitous and most grievous inhumanity. Therefore, being exceedingly angry, and being at all times a man of most ferocious passions, he was in great perplexity, neither venturing to take down what he had once set up, nor wishing to do any thing which could be acceptable to his subjects, and at the same time being sufficiently acquainted with the firmness of Tiberius on these points.

Those who were in power in our nation, seeing this, and perceiving that he was inclined to change his mind as to what he had done, but that he was not willing to be thought to do so, wrote a most supplicatory letter to Tiberius. And he, when he had read it, what did he say of Pilate, and what threats did he utter against him! But it is beside our purpose at present to relate to you how very angry he was, although he was not very liable to sudden anger; the facts speak for themselves. Immediately, without putting any thing off till the next day, he wrote a letter, reproaching and reviling him in the most bitter manner for his act of unprecedented audacity and wickedness, and commanding him immediately to take down the shields and to convey them away from the metropolis of Judaea to Caesarea,[11] [. . .] in order that they might be set up in the temple of Augustus. And accordingly, they were set up in that edifice. And in this way he provided for two matters: both for the honor due to the emperor, and for the preservation of the ancient customs of the city.[12]

Now the things set up on that occasion were shields, on which there was no representation of any living thing whatever engraved. But now the thing proposed to be erected is a colossal statue. Moreover, then the erection was in the dwelling house of the governor; but they say, that which is now contemplated is to be in the inmost part of the Temple, in the very holy of holies itself, into which, once in the year, the high priest enters, on the day called the great fast,[13] to offer incense, and on no other day, being then about in accordance with our national law also to offer up prayers for a fertile and ample supply of blessings, and for peace to all mankind. [. . .] Great are the precautions taken by our lawgiver with respect to the holy of holies, as he determined to preserve it alone inaccessible to and untouched by any human being.

How many deaths then do you not suppose that the people, who have been taught to regard this place with such holy reverence, would willingly endure rather than see a statue introduced into it? I verily believe that they would rather slay all their whole families, with their wives and children, and themselves last of all, in the ruins of their houses and families, and Tiberius knew this well. And what did your great-grandfather, the most excellent of all emperors that ever lived upon the earth, he who was the first to have the appellation of Augustus given him, on account of his virtue and good fortune; he who diffused peace in every direction over earth and sea, to the very furthest extremities of the world? Did not he, when he had heard a report of the peculiar characteristics of our Temple, and that there is in it no image or representation made by hands, no visible likeness of Him who is invisible, not attempt at any imitation of his nature, did not he, I say, marvel at and honor it? For as he was imbued with something more than a mere smattering of philosophy, inasmuch as he had deeply feasted on it, and continued to feast on it every day, he partly retraced in his recollection all the precepts of philosophy which his mind had previously learnt, and partly also he kept his learning alive by the conversation of the literary men who were always about him; for at his banquets and entertainments, the greatest part of the time was devoted to learned conversation, in order that not only his friends' bodies but their minds also might be nourished.

And though I might be able to establish this fact, and demonstrate to you the feelings of Augustus, your great-grandfather, by an abundance of proofs, I will be content with two. In the first place, he sent commandments to all the governors of the different provinces throughout Asia, because he heard that the sacred first fruits were neglected, enjoining them to permit the Jews alone to assemble together in the synagogues,[14] for that these assemblies were not revels, which from drunkenness and the intoxication proceeded to violence, so as to disturb the peaceful condition of the country, but were rather schools of temperance and justice, as the men who met in them were students of virtue, and contributed the first fruits every year, sending commissioners to convey the holy things to the Temple in Jerusalem.

In the next place, he commanded that no one should hinder the Jews, either on their way to the synagogues, or when bringing their contributions, or when proceeding in obedience to their national laws to Jerusalem, for these things were expressly enjoined, if not in so many words, at all events in effect. [. . .] He [also] commanded perfect sacrifices of whole burnt offerings to be offered up to the most high God every day, out of his own revenues, which are performed up to the present time, and the victims are two sheep and a bull, with which Caesar honored the altar of God, well knowing that there is in the Temple no image erected, either in open sight or in any secret part of it.[15] But that great ruler, who was inferior to no one in philosophy, considered within himself, that it is necessary in terrestrial things, that an especial holy place should be set apart for the invisible God, who will not permit any visible representation of himself to be made, by which to arrive at a participation in favorable hopes and the enjoyment of perfect blessings.

And your grandmother, Julia Augusta,[16] following the

example of so great a guide in the paths of piety, did also adorn the Temple with some golden vials and censers, and with a great number of other offerings, of the most costly and magnificent description; and what was her object in doing this, when there is no statue erected within the Temple? For the minds of women are, in some degree, weaker than those of men, and are not so well able to comprehend a thing which is appreciable only by the intellect, without any aid of objects addressed to the outward senses; but she, as she surpassed all her sex in other particulars, so also was she superior to them in this, by reason of the pure learning and wisdom which had been implanted in her, both by nature and by study; so that, having a masculine intellect, she was so sharp-sighted and profound, that she comprehended what is appreciable only by the intellect, even more than those things which are perceptible by the outward senses, and looked upon the latter as only shadows of the former.

Therefore, O master, having all these examples most nearly connected with yourself and your family, of our purposes and customs, derived from those from whom you are sprung, of whom you are born, and by whom you have been brought up, I implore you to preserve those principles which each of those persons whom I have mentioned did preserve; they who were themselves possessed of imperial power do, by their laws, exhort you, the emperor; they who were august, speak to you who are also Augustus; your grandfathers and ancestors speak to their descendant; numbers of authorities address one individual, all but saying, in express words: Do not you destroy those things in our councils which remain, and which have been preserved as permanent laws to this very day; for even if no mischief were to ensue from the abrogation of them, still, at all events, the result would be a feeling of uncertainty respecting the future, and such uncertainty is full of fear, even to the most sanguine and confident, if they are not despisers of divine things.

If I were to enumerate the benefits which I myself have received at your hands, the day would be too short for me; besides the fact that it is not proper for one who has undertaken to speak on one subject to branch off to a digression about some other matter. Even if I should be silent, the facts themselves speak and utter a distinct voice. You released me when I was bound in chains and iron.[17] Who is there who is ignorant of this? But do not, after having done so, O emperor, bind me in bonds of still greater bitterness: for the chains from which you released me surrounded a part of my body, but those which I am now anticipating are the chains of the soul, which are likely to oppress it wholly and in every part; you abated from me a fear of death, continually suspended over my head; you received me when I was almost dead through fear; you raised me up as it were from the dead. Continue your favor, O master, that your Agrippa may not be driven wholly to forsake life; for I shall appear (if you do not do so) to have been released from bondage, not for the purpose of being saved, but for that of being made to perish in a more conspicuous manner. [. . .]

I am willing to descend from this spendid position in which you have placed me; I do not deprecate a return to the condition in which I was a short time ago; I will give up everything; I look upon everything as of less importance than the one point of preserving the ancient customs and laws of my nation unaltered; for if they are violated, what could I say, either to my fellow countrymen or to any other men? It would follow of necessity that I must be looked upon as one of two things, either as a betrayer of my people, or as one who is no longer accounted a friend by you. And what could be a greater misery than either of these two things? For if I am still reckoned among the company of your friends, I shall then receive the imputation of treason against my own nation, if neither my country is preserved free from all misfortune, nor even the Temple left inviolate. [. . .]

Having written this letter and sealed it, he sent it to Gaius, and then shutting himself up he remained in his own house, full of agony, confusion, disorder and anxiety, as to what was the best way of approaching and addressing the emperor; for he and his people had incurred no slight danger, but they had reason to apprehend expulsion from their country, slavery and utter destruction, as impending not only over those who were dwelling in the holy land, but over all the Jews in every part of the world.

But the emperor, having taken the letter and read it, and having considered every suggestion which was contained in it, was very angry, because his intentions had not been executed; and yet, at the same time, he was moved by the appeals to his justice and by the supplications which were thus addressed to him, and in some respects he was pleased with Agrippa, and in some he blamed him.

He blamed him for his excessive desire to please his fellow countrymen, who were the only men who had resisted his orders and shown any unwillingness to submit to his deification; but he praised him for concealing and disguising none of his feelings, which conduct he said was a proof of a liberal and noble disposition. Therefore being somewhat appeased, at least as far as appearance went, he condescended to return a somewhat favorable answer, granting to Agrippa that highest and greatest of all favors, the consent that this erection of his statue should not take place; and he commanded letters to be written to Publius Petronius the governor of Syria, enjoining him not to allow any alterations or innovations to be made with respect to the temple of the Jews. Nevertheless, though he did grant him the favor, he did not grant it without any alloy, but he mingled with it a grievous terror; for he added to the letter the following:

"If any people in the bordering countries, with the exception of the metropolis itself, wishing to erect altars or temples, nay, images or statues, in honor of me and of my family are hindered from doing so, I charge you at once to punish those who attempt to hinder them, or else to bring them before the tribunal."

Now this was nothing else but a beginning of seditions and civil wars, and an indirect way of annulling the gift which he appeared to be granting. For some men, more out of a desire of mortifying the Jews than from any feelings of loyalty towards Gaius, were inclined to fill the whole country with erections of one kind or another. But they who beheld the violation of their national customs practised before their eyes were resolved above all things not to endure such an injury unresistingly. But Gaius, judging those who were thus excited to disobedience to be worthy of the most severe punishment possible, a second time ordered his statue to be erected in the Temple. However, by the providence and care of God, who beholds all things and governs all things in accordance with justice, not one of the neighboring nations made any movement at all; so that there was no occasion for these commands being carried into effect, and these inexorably appointed calamities all terminated in only a moderate degree of blame.

I Take Refuge

THE PRAYER OF ASENATH

A Hellenistic Midrash tells of the conversion of beautiful Asenath, daughter of Potiphar, Pharaoh's chief counselor, who fell in love with Biblical Joseph. She renounced her family's idols, gave to the poor her costly robes and jewelry, acknowledged the God of mercy and compassion and prayed. Having thus become a proselyte, Joseph married her and both received Pharaoh's blessing. The story has all the signs of Hellenistic propaganda for the Jewish faith. Rabbinic and patristic sources do not mention this Midrash, but the original Greek rendition has been preserved, as also have been a Syriac, Armenian and Slavonic translation. Asenath's prayer is here reproduced.

I take refuge with Thee, O Lord.
As the little child flees in fear to the father,
and the father takes it to his bosom,
so do Thou stretch forth Thy hands as a loving father
and save me from the enemy who pursues me as a lion,
from Satan, the father of the Egyptian gods,
who desires to devour me
because I have despised his children, the Egyptian gods.
Deliver me from his hands,
lest he cast me into the fire;

lest the monster of the deep eat me up,
and I perish forever.
Save me;
for my father and mother deny me
and I have no hope nor refuge but Thy mercy,
O Lover of men,
Helper of the broken-hearted.
There is no father so good and sweet as Thou, O Lord.
All the houses my father gives me as possessions are for a time
        and perishable;
but the houses of Thy possession, O Lord,
are indestructible and last forever.

Inspired Reason

FROM THE FOURTH BOOK OF MACCABEES

Basing his material on Second Maccabees, an author writing in Greek
at the beginning of the Christian era, composed a treatise, known as the
Fourth Book of Maccabees, in which he tried to demonstrate "the power of
inspired reason over the passions and over pain." He believed that adherence
to Torah would lead to attainment of the central virtues of Stoic philosophy.
The treatise is a good example of the symbiosis of Hellenist and Jewish
thought. Our selection is its concluding chapter.

O Israelites, children born of the seed of Abraham, obey
this Law, and be righteous in all ways, recognizing that Inspired Reason is lord over the passions, and over pains, not
only from within, but from without ourselves; by which means
those men, delivering up their bodies to the torture for righteousness' sake, not only won the admiration of mankind, but
were deemed worthy of a divine inheritance. And through
them the nation obtained peace and restoring the observance
of the Law in our country has captured the city from the
enemy.

Vengeance has pursued the tyrant Antiochus [Epiph-
anes] upon earth, and in death he suffers punishment. For

when he failed utterly to constrain the people of Jerusalem to live like heathens and abandon the customs of our fathers, he thereupon left Jerusalem and marched away against the Persians.

Now these are the words that the mother of the seven sons, the righteous woman, spoke to her children:

"I was a pure maiden, and I strayed not from my father's house, and I kept guard over the rib that was builded into Eve. No seducer of the desert, no deceiver in the field, corrupted me; nor did the false, beguiling Serpent sully the purity of my maidenhood; I lived with my husband all the days of my youth; but when these my sons were grown up, their father died.

"Happy was he; for he lived a life blessed with children, and he never knew the pain of their loss. Who, while he was yet with us, taught you the Law and the prophets. He read to us of Abel who was slain by Cain, and of Isaac who was offered as a burnt offering, and of Joseph in the prison. And he spake to us of Phinehas, the zealous priest, and he taught you the song of Hananiah, Azariah, and Mishael in the fire. And he glorified also Daniel in the den of lions, and blessed him; and he called to your minds the saying of Isaiah, 'Yea even though thou pass through the fire, the flame shall not hurt thee' (Isa. 43:2). He sang to us the words of David the psalmist, 'Many are the afflictions of the just' (Ps. 34:20). He quoted to us the proverb of Solomon, 'He is a tree of life to all them that do his will.' (Prov. 3:18). He confirmed the words of Ezekiel, 'Shall these dry bones live?' (Ezek. 37:3). For he forgot not the song that Moses taught, which teaches, 'I will slay and I will make alive. This is your life and the blessedness of your days.'" (Deut. 32:39; 30:20).

Ah, cruel was the day, and yet not cruel, when the cruel tyrant of the Greeks set the fire blazing for his barbarous braziers, and with his passions boiling brought to the catapult and back again to his tortures the seven sons of the daughter of Abraham, and blinded the eyeballs of their eyes, and cut out their tongues, and slew them with many kinds of torment. For which cause the judgment of God pursued, and shall pursue,

the accursed wretch. But the sons of Abraham with their victorious mother are gathered together unto the place of their
ancestors, having received pure and immortal souls from God,
to whom be glory for ever and ever. Amen.

In Defense of Judaism

FROM FLAVIUS JOSEPHUS: AGAINST APION

After completing his major works, *The Jewish War* and *The Jewish
Antiquities*, Flavius Josephus wrote (about A.D. 96) a short book, *Against
Apion* (*Contra Apionem*). The title refers to a first-century grammarian and
anti-Jewish author of Alexandria. The attacks by Apion and other pagan
writers directed against Josephus' historiography and the Jewish religion in
general caused Josephus to write this presentation of his religious beliefs and
to state his position in the intellectual world around him. He reveals a detailed knowledge of Greek literature and an understanding of the contribution
of the Greek philosophers to human thought, but criticizes the Greeks for
neglecting the records of their history, for ignoring religion in their legislation,
and for the immorality of their gods. In discussing ancient writers, Josephus
quotes works now lost and surviving only in these quotations.

In his passionately eloquent exposition, Josephus pictures ancient Israel
not as a state (the fall of which he described in his works) but as a religious
society. Israel is a people with a political, historical past. Its true task, however, is to maintain an extraterritorial society dedicated to religious life and
fellowship and cultivating a universally applicable faith.

Introduction

Now as Apollonius Molon,[18] Lysimachus[19] and some
others, partly from ignorance, but chiefly from ill will, have
written treatises about our lawgiver Moses and our laws, which
are neither fair nor true, calumniating Moses as an imposter
and deceiver, and asserting that our laws teach us wickedness
and not virtue, I intend to state briefly, to the best of my
ability, our constitution as a whole and its details. For I think
it will then be plain that the laws we have are most excellently
adapted for the advancement of piety, and for the interests
of society, and for general philanthropy, as also for justice,

for sustaining labors with fortitude, and for contempt of death. [. . .]

I would say this first, that those who were lovers of order and laws—one law for all—and who first introduced them, when men were living without law and order, may well have this testimony, that they were better than other men in mildness and natural virtue. And certainly such persons endeavor to have every thing they introduce believed to be very ancient, that they may not be thought to imitate others, but may rather seem themselves to have suggested an orderly way of life to others. Since, then, this is the case, the excellence of a legislator is seen in seeing what is best, and in persuading those who are to use the laws he ordains to have a good opinion of them, and the excellence of a people is seen in their abiding by the laws, and making no changes in them either in prosperity or adversity.

The work of Moses

Now, I say that our legislator is the most ancient of all the legislators who are anywhere recorded. For Lycurgus and Solon, and Zaleucus, the legislator of the Locrians, and all those legislators who are admired by the Greeks, seem to be of yesterday if compared with our legislator, indeed the very word "law" was not so much as known in old times among the Greeks.[20] Homer bears me out in this, for he never uses the word law in all his poems. Indeed there was in his time no such thing, but the multitude was governed by undefined opinions and by the orders of their kings. They continued also a long time after Homer in the use of these unwritten customs, although they frequently changed them to suit a particular emergency. But our legislator, who was of so much greater antiquity than the rest (as even those who speak against us upon all occasions admit), exhibited himself to the people as their best guide and counsellor; he included in his legislation the whole conduct of life, and persuaded his people to accept it, and brought it to pass that those who were acquainted with his laws did most carefully observe them.

[. . .] When [our legislator] had first persuaded himself that his actions and designs were governed by God's will, he thought it his duty to impress that notion above all things upon the multitude; for those who believe that God surveys their lives cannot bear the thought of sin. Such was our legislator, who was no imposter, or deceiver, as his revilers say unjustly, but such a one as they boast Minos [of Crete] to have been among the Greeks, and other legislators after him. For some of them maintained that they had their laws from God, and Minos referred the oracular origin of his laws to Apollo and his oracle at Delphi, whether they thought they were really so derived, or that they could so more easily persuade the people to obey them. And as to who made the best laws, and who had the truest of God, it is easy to determine this by comparing the laws themselves together, for it is time that we come to that point.

Theocracy

There are innumerable differences in detail in the customs and laws that prevail among all mankind; for some legislators have permitted their governments to be monarchies, others oligarchies, and others democracies. But our legislator had no regard to any of these things, but ordained our government to be what, by a strained expression, may be termed a theocracy, ascribing the sovereignty and authority to God. He persuaded all to look to Him as the author of all good things that were enjoyed either in common by all mankind, or by each individual privately, and of all that they themselves obtained by prayer in their greatest straits. He informed them also that it was impossible to escape God's observation, either in any of their outward actions, or in any of their inward thoughts. Moreover, he represented God as One, unbegotten,[21] and immutable through all eternity, surpassing all mortal conception in beauty, and though known to us by His power, yet unknown to us as to His essence. I do not now say that the wisest of the Greeks were taught these notions of God by principles that Moses supplied them with; but they have borne emphatic witness that these notions are good and agreeable to the nature and majesty of God.

Greek philosophy versus Jewish religion

For Pythagoras, Anaxagoras, Plato, the Stoics that succeeded them, and almost all other philosophers, seem to have had similar notions about the nature of God. But these men disclosed those true notions to the few, because the body of the people were prepossessed by other opinions, while our legislator, who made his actions square with his laws, not only prevailed upon his contemporaries to agree to his notions, but so firmly imprinted this faith in God upon all their posterity, that it could never be moved. And the reason why our lawgiver in his legislation far exceeded all other legislators in usefulness to all, is that he did not make religion a part of virtue, but had the insight to make the various virtues parts of religion; I mean justice, fortitude, self-control, and the mutual harmony in all things of the members of the community with one another.[22] All our actions and studies and words have a connection with piety towards God; for our lawgiver has left none of these things indefinite or undetermined.

There are two ways of arriving at any discipline or moral conduct of life; the one is by instruction in words, the other by exercises in practice. Now all other lawgivers separated these two ways in their codes, and choosing the one of those methods which best pleased them, neglected the other. Thus did the Lacedaemonians and Cretans teach by exercises in practice, and not by words; while the Athenians and almost all the other Greeks made laws about what was to be done or left undone, but neglected exercising people thereto in practice.

But our legislator very carefully joined these two methods of instruction together. He neither left these exercises in practice to go on without verbal instruction, nor did he permit the hearing of the Law to proceed without exercises in practice. Beginning immediately with the earliest infancy, and the partaking of every one's food, he left nothing of the very smallest consequence to be done at the pleasure and caprice of the persons themselves; he made fixed rules and laws what sorts of food they should abstain from, and what sorts they should make use of, as also what intercourse they should have with others; what diligence they should use in their occupations, and what times of rest should be interposed; that, by living under those laws as under a father and master, we might be guilty of no sin either from wilfulness or ignorance.

Knowledge and conduct of life

He did not suffer the pretext of ignorance to be valid. He showed the Law to be the best and most necessary of instructions, for he ordained the people to leave off all their other occupations, and assemble together to hear the Law and to be perfectly instructed in it, not once or twice or on several occasions, but every week; a thing which all other legislators seem to have neglected.

Indeed most of mankind are so far from living according to their own laws, that they hardly know them. Only when they have sinned do they learn from others that they have transgressed the law. Even those who are in the highest and most important offices confess they are not acquainted with their laws, and are obliged to take experts in those laws for their assessors in the administration of public affairs. But if anyone only were to ask anyone of our people about our laws, he could more easily tell them all than he could tell his own name. Because of our having learned them as soon as ever we became sensible of anything, we have them as it were engraven on our souls. Transgressors are but few; it is impossible, when any do offend to escape punishment by excuses.

And it is this very thing that principally creates such wonderful oneness of mind among us. For our having one and the same religious belief, and our having no difference from one another in our course of life and manners, brings about among us the most excellent accord in human character. Among us alone will no one hear any discourses about God that contradict one another, which are yet frequent among other nations (and this is true not only among ordinary persons, according to one's personal disposition, but some of the philosophers also have been bold enough to indulge in such speculations; some attempting to argue against the existence of God,[23] others taking away His providence over mankind).[24]

Nor will anyone perceive amongst us any difference in the conduct of our lives. The actions of all among us are common, and we have one doctrine about God, which chimes in with our law and affirms that He surveys all things. And as to the conduct of our lives, that we consider that all things ought to have piety for their end, anybody may hear even from our women and dependents [. . .].

Government

As we are ourselves persuaded that our Law was made in accordance with the will of God, it would be impious for us not to observe the same. For what is there in it that anybody would change, or what could one invent better, or what could one borrow from other people's laws more excellent? Would any have the entire framework of our constitution altered? And what could be a better or more righteous policy than ours which makes us esteem God the head of the universe, which commits to the priests generally the administration of the principal affairs, and entrusts the rule over the other priests to the supreme high priest? Nor did our legislator, at their first appointment, advance these priests to that dignity for their riches, or for any other fortuitous advantages, but he entrusted the managment of divine worship mainly to those who exceeded others in powers of persuasion and in self-control. These men had the strict care of the Law, and had the rest of the people's conduct committed to them: for the priests were ordained to be overseers of everything, and to be judges in doubtful cases, and to be the punishers of condemned persons.

What form of government then can be more saintly than this? What more worthy worship can be paid to God than we pay, where the entire body of the people are prepared for religion, where an extraordinary degree of care is required in the priests, and where the whole polity is so ordered as if it were some sacred ceremony? For what foreigners, when they solemnize such festivals, and call them mysteries and initiations, are not able to observe even for a few days, we observe with much pleasure and unshaken resolution during our whole lives.

What are the things then that we are commanded or forbidden? They are simple and well known.

God

The first command is concerning God; it affirms that God is almighty and perfect and blessed, self-sufficing and sufficient for all; He is the beginning, the middle and the end of all things. He is manifest in His works and benefits, and more manifest than any other being; but His form and magnitude is most obscure. All materials, let them be ever so costly, are unworthy to compose an image of Him, and all arts are inartistic to express the notion of Him. We cannot see anything like Him, nor is it agreeable to piety to conjecture about Him. We see His works, the light, the heaven, the earth, the sun and moon, the waters, the generations of animals and the growth of fruits. God did not make these things with hands nor with labor, nor did He need the assistance of any to co-operate with Him.[25] His will resolved they should be made and be good also, and they were made and became good immediately. All men ought to follow and worship Him in the exercise of virtue; for this way of worship of God is the most saintly.

There is also but one temple for one God (for like ever loveth like), common to all men, because God is common to all. His priests are continually occupied by His worship, led by him who is head of the line. His office is to offer sacrifices to God with his fellow-priests, to see that the laws are observed, to determine controversies, and to punish those convicted of wrong-doing. He that does not submit to him is subject to the same punishment as for impiety towards God Himself.

When we offer sacrifices to Him, we do not take this as an occasion for drunken self-indulgence (for such excesses are against the will of God) but for sobriety, orderliness, and readiness for our other occupations. At these sacrifices we ought first to pray for the welfare of all, and after that for our own (for we are made for fellowship with one another), and he

who prefers the common good to his own private good is especially acceptable to God. And let our prayers and supplications
be made to God, not so much that He would give us what is
good, (for He has already given that of His own accord, and
distributed it alike to all,) as that we may duly receive it, and
having received it, keep it. The law has also appointed several
purifications at our sacrifices, whereby we are cleansed after a
funeral, after any nocturnal pollution, and after union with
our wives, and after some other occasions [. . .].

The family

What are our marriage laws? The Law recognizes no connection of the sexes but the natural connection between a
man and his wife, and that only for the procreation of children; it abhors sodomy, and death is the punishment for that
crime. The law commands us also, when we marry, not to have
regard to dowry, nor to take a woman by violence, nor to persuade her by deceit and guile, but to demand her in marriage
of him who has power to give her away and is fit to do so because of his nearness of kin. For the legislator says that a
woman is inferior to her husband in all things. Let her, therefore, be obedient to him; not that he should ill-treat her, but
that she may be directed; for God has given the authority to
the husband. A husband is to lie only with his wife, and to
seduce another man's wife is a wicked thing, which, if any
one ventures upon, death is inevitably his punishment, as it
is also his who forces a virgin betrothed to another man.

The Law, moreover, enjoins us to bring up all our offspring, and forbids women to cause abortion of what is begotten, or to destroy the foetus in any other way, for she will
be an infanticide who thus destroys life and diminishes the human race. If any one, therefore, commits adultery or seduc-
tion, he cannot be considered pure. Why, even after the
regular union of man and wife, the Law enjoins that they shall
both wash themselves [. . .].

Moreover the Law does not permit us to feast at the
births of our children, and so make excuses for drinking to
excess, but it ordains that the very beginning of life should

be sober. It also commands us to bring our children up in learning, and to make them conversant with the laws and acquainted with the acts of their forefathers, that they may imitate them, and, being grounded in them, may neither transgress them nor have any excuse for ignorance of them.

Our Law also provides for the decent burial of the dead, but without any extravagant expense at their funerals or the erection of conspicuous monuments. It orders that the nearest relations should perform their obsequies. It also ordains that all who pass by when any one is buried should accompany the funeral and join in the lamentation. It also orders that the house and its inhabitants should be purified after the funeral is over [. . .].

The Law also ordains, that parents should be honored next after God himself, and orders the son who does not requite them for the benefits he has received from them, but comes short on any occasion, to be handed over to justice and stoned. It also says that young men should pay due respect to every elder, because God is the eldest of all beings. It does not give permission to conceal anything from our friends, for that is not friendship which will not trust them. It also forbids the revelation of their secrets, if subsequent enmity arise between them. If any judge take bribes, his punishment is death.[26] He that neglects one that begs for aid, when he is able to relieve him, is liable to be called to account. What one has not entrusted to another, cannot be required back again. No one is to touch another's goods. He that lends money must not receive interest. These, and many more of the like sort are the rules that unite us in the bonds of society with one another.

Aliens and humanity at large

It will also be worth our while to see what equity our legislator would have us exercise in our treatment of aliens. For it will then appear that he made the best provision he possibly could, that we should neither infringe our own polity, nor show a grudging spirit to those who would cultivate a friendship with us. Thus our legislator receives in a friendly manner all those who wish to come and live under our laws, esteeming relationship to lie not only in family ties but also in similarity of life and manners. But he does not allow those who come to us only to sojourn for a time to be admitted into communion with us.

There are, however, various things which our legislator ordered us as obligatory on us to impart to all men; as to give fire, water, and food, to all that require them, to show them the way, and not to let any corpse lie unburied. He also would have us treat those accounted our enemies with moderation. For he does not allow us to set their country on fire, nor does he permit us to cut down their fruit trees; he also forbids us to strip those that have been slain in war. He has also provided for such as are taken captive, that they may not be ill-treated, especially women. Indeed, he has taught us gentleness and humanity so effectually, that he has not neglected the care of brute beasts, permitting no other than the regular use of them, and forbidding any other. If any of them flee to our houses like suppliants, we are forbidden to slay them. Nor may we kill the dams with their young ones; and we are obliged, even in an enemy's country, to spare and not kill those animals that labor for mankind. Thus has our lawgiver contrived to teach us merciful conduct every way, using such laws to instruct us therein, while those who break these laws are to be punished without excuse.

Reward, punishment and obedience to the Law

Most offences with us are capital, as if any one is guilty of adultery, if any forces a virgin, if any one is so impudent as to attempt to commit sodomy with a male, or if the person solicited submits to be so used. The Law is also equally inexorable for slaves. If any one cheats another in measures or weights, or makes a knavish bargain and sale to cheat another, or if any one steal what belongs to another, and takes what he never deposited, all these have punishments allotted them which are not on the same scale as with other nations, but more severe. And as to misbehavior to parents, or impiety to God, for the very intention the offender is put to death immediately.

For those, on the other hand, who act according to the

laws the reward is not silver nor gold, nor again a crown of wild olive or parsley, nor any such public mark of commendation. Each one, having his own conscience bearing him witness, believes (on the word of the legislator, confirmed by the sure testimony of God) that to those that observe laws, even though they should be obliged to die willingly for them, God has granted that they shall come into being again, and after their vicissitudes have a better life than they had before. I should have hesitated to write thus at this time, were it not well known to all from their actions, that many of our people have frequently bravely resolved to endure any suffering rather than speak one word against the law. [. . .]

I venture to say, that no one can tell of so many, nay, of more than one or two, that have abandoned our laws, or feared death, I do not mean that easiest of deaths which happens in battles, but that which comes with bodily tortures, and seems to be the hardest death of all. Indeed I think those that have conquered us have put us to such deaths, not from their hatred to us when they had got us in their power, but rather from their desire to see a wonderful sight, namely, that there are men in the world, who believe the only evil is being compelled to do or to speak any thing contrary to their laws!

Nor ought men to wonder at us, if we are more courageous in dying for our laws than all other men are. For other men do not easily submit to what seem the easiest of our practices, I mean such things as working with our hands, and simple diet, and being contented to eat and drink and lie with our wives by rule, as also in respect to luxury, and again in the constant observance of our days of rest. For those that can use their swords in war, and can put their enemies to flight when they attack them, cannot bear to submit to rules about their mode of everyday living; whereas our being accustomed willingly to submit to laws in these cases makes us readier to show our fortitude upon other occasions.

Criticism of Greek institutions

[. . .] It is the custom of our country to keep our own laws, and not to advance criticism of the laws of others; our legislator has expressly forbidden us to jeer or rail at gods recognized by others, out of respect to the very name of God. But as our antagonists think to run us down by a comparison of their religion and ours, it is not possible to keep silence, especially as what I shall now say to confute these men will not be an invention of mine, but has been already said by many of the highest reputation.

For who among those that have been admired among the Greeks for wisdom has not greatly censured not only the most famous poets, but also the most esteemed legislators, for spreading originally among the masses such notions concerning the gods as that they may be allowed to be as numerous as they themselves have a mind to declare, and that they are begotten by one another, and that in all kinds of ways. They also classify them in their places and ways of living, as one would classify various kinds of animals, placing some under the earth, others in the sea, the oldest of them all being bound in Tartarus. In the case of those gods to whom they have allotted heaven, they have set over them one who in name is their father, but in his actions a tyrant and despot; so that his wife and brother and daughter, whom he brought forth from his own head, made a conspiracy against him to seize upon him and confine him, as he had himself seized upon and confined his own father.

[. . .] Now what sensible person would not be provoked at such stories, to rebuke those that made them up, and to condemn the great silliness of those that believe them? They have even deified Terror and Fear, and even Madness and Fraud, and other of the vilest passions. And they have persuaded cities to offer sacrifices to the better sort of these gods. Thus they have been absolutely forced to esteem some gods as the givers of good things, and to call others averters of evil. These last they endeavor to move, as they would the vilest of men, by gifts and presents, expecting to receive some great mischief from them unless they bribe them as it were by such offerings.

[. . .] Nothing that I have said was unknown to those who were real philosophers among the Greeks, nor were they ignorant of the frigid pretensions of allegories. So they justly despised them and agreed with us in forming true and becoming notions of God. From this standpoint Plato would not admit into his republic any poet, and dismisses even Homer himself with panegyric, after placing a garland on his head and pouring ointment upon him, that he should not destroy right notions about God with his fables.[27] Plato also especially imitated our legislator in that he enjoined his citizens to pay to nothing more attention than to this, that every one of them should learn their laws accurately; as also that they should not have foreigners mixing with their own people at random, but that the republic should be pure, and consist only of those who obeyed the laws.

Apollonius Molon failed to consider this, when he accused us of not admitting those who have their own preconceptions about God, and having no fellowship with those who choose to observe a different way of living to ourselves. For this method is not peculiar to us, but common to all men, not to Greeks only, but also to men of the greatest reputation among the Greeks. The Lacedaemonians continually expelled foreigners and would not suffer their own citizens to travel abroad, suspecting that both these things would tend to the detriment of their laws. And perhaps there may be some reason to blame the rigid severity of the Lacedaemonians, for they gave no one the privilege of citizenship or indeed leave to live among them; whereas we, though we do not think fit to imitate the ways of others, yet willingly admit those that desire to share ours. And I think I may reckon this a proof both of our humanity and magnanimity.

But I shall say no more about the Lacedaemonians. And as to the Athenians, who glory in having made their city common to all men, Apollonius did not know what their behavior was either, for they punished without mercy those who did but speak one word about the gods contrary to their laws. On what other account was Socrates put to death? Certainly he neither betrayed their city to its enemies, nor was he guilty of any sacrilege; but it was because he swore by novel oaths, and affirmed either in earnest, or, as some say, only in jest, that a demon used to intimate to him what he should or should not do, that he was condemned to die by drinking hemlock. His accuser also complained that he corrupted the young men, because he induced them to despise the policy and laws of their city. Such was the punishment of Socrates, though a citizen of Athens.

And Anaxagoras of Clazomenae[28] was within a few votes of being condemned to death, because he said the sun, which the Athenians thought a god, was a red-hot mass of fire. They also made public proclamation, that they would give a talent to any one who would kill Diagoras of Melos,[29] because he was said to have laughed at their mysteries. Protagoras[30] also, who was thought to have written something about the gods that was not admitted by the Athenians, would have been arrested and put to death, if he had not fled quickly. Nor need we at all wonder that they thus treated such considerable men, seeing that they did not even spare women. For indeed they slew a certain priestess, because she was accused by somebody of initiating people into the worship of foreign gods; this was forbidden by their laws, and capital punishment was decreed to any who introduced a foreign god. But it is manifest that those who made such a law did not believe the gods of other nations to be really gods, else they would not have grudged themselves the advantage of having more gods than they already had. Such was the happy administration of the affairs of the Athenians.

The Scythians and the Persians

The Scythians also take a pleasure in killing men, and differ little from brute beasts, yet they think it reasonable to have their institutions upheld and they put to death Anacharsis,[31] a person greatly admired for his wisdom by the Greeks, because on his return home to them he appeared full of Greek customs. One may also find many to have been punished among the Persians on the very same account. But it is plain that Apollonius was greatly pleased with the laws of the Persians and admired them, doubtless because the Greeks had a taste of their courage and held similar opinions about the

gods! This similarity of opinion in religious matters was exhibited in their burning temples, and their courage in coming
and almost entirely enslaving the Greeks. And Apollonius imitated all the Persian practices, forcing other men's wives and
castrating their sons.

Judaism

Now with us it is a capital crime, if any one thus ill-treats
even a brute beast. And neither the fear of our conquerors, nor
the desire of imitating what other nations hold in esteem, has
been able to draw us away from our own laws. Nor have we
exercised our courage in undertaking wars to increase our
wealth, but only to continue in the observation of our laws.
For though we bear other losses with patience, yet when any
persons would compel us to violate our laws, we then choose
to go to war, even against tremendous odds, and bear the
greatest calamities to the last with much fortitude. [. . .]
It will be found that our laws have always inspired imitation and still more admiration in all other men. For the
earliest Greek philosophers, though to all appearance they
observed the laws of their own countries, yet in their actions
and philosophical notions followed our legislator, instructing
men to live simply and to have friendly communications with
one another. Moreover, multitudes have had a great inclination now for a long time to follow our religious observances;
there is not one city of the Greeks or barbarians, nor any nation, where our custom of resting on the seventh day has not
reached, and by whom our fasts and lighting of lamps and
many of our prohibitions in the matter of food are not observed. They also endeavor to imitate our mutual concord with
one another, the charitable distribution of our goods, our diligence in the crafts, and our fortitude in undergoing the dis-
tresses in behalf of our laws. And what is most wonderful, our
Law has no bait of pleasure to allure men to it, but only gains
ground on its own merits; and as God himself pervades all the
world, so has the Law passed through all the world. [. . .]
Even if we were unable ourselves to understand the excellence
of our laws, yet would the number of those who desire to

imitate them induce us to pride ourselves upon them. [. . .]

As to our laws themselves, more words are unnecessary. They can be seen for themselves, and evidently do not teach impiety, but the truest piety in the world; not calling men to misanthropy, but encouraging people to share what they have with one another freely; being enemies to injustice and eager for righteousness, anxious to banish idleness and extravagant living, teaching men to be content with what they have, and to work with determination; forbidding men to make war from a desire of greed, but making men bold in defending the laws; inexorable in punishing malefactors, admitting no sophistry of words, but ever established themselves by actions. Actions we adduce as surer proofs than what is written only.

And so I boldly say that we have become the teachers of other men in a great number of most excellent ideas. What is more excellent than inviolable piety? What is more just than obedience to the laws? What is more beneficial than mutual love and concord, neither to be divided by calamities, nor to become injurious and seditious in prosperity; to despise death when we are in war, and to apply ourselves in peace to crafts and agriculture; and to be persuaded that God surveys and directs everything everywhere? If these precepts had either been written before by others, or more exactly observed, we should have owed them thanks as their disciples, but if it is plain that we have made more use of them than any other men, and if we have proved that the original invention of them is our own, let the Apions and Molons and all others who delight in lies and abuse stand confuted.

VII. After the Fall of Jerusalem

The Heroes of Masada

FROM FLAVIUS JOSEPHUS: THE JEWISH WAR

When Rome conquered Judaea and Jerusalem fell (A.D. 70), there still remained three fortresses, strongly defended by the remnants of the Jewish rebels (*sicarii*). The last of them, Masada, defended by Eleazar, stubbornly resisted the concentrated Roman attack. The mighty fortress of Masada, overlooking the southwest shore of the Dead Sea, had been fortified by Jonathan, brother of Judah the Maccabee, and perfected under Herod the Great. The rock of Masada was high and steep. After overcoming serious strategic difficulties, the Romans built a solid bank for the operation of the battering ram. Eleazar, descendant of Judah the Galilean (leader of the Jewish rebels in the period of Herod), and his men had resolved "never to serve the Romans nor any master other than God, who alone is the true and just lord of mankind." Unable to offer further resistance, Eleazar bid his men to commit mass suicide and preserve their freedom, rather than "taste slavery." Some were ready to follow Eleazar, other, "of softer mold," were moved by pity for their wives and children and refused. Eleazar, therefore, renewed his proposal in a second speech, presented below.

The fall of Masada (April 73) ended the seven years' Judaeo-Roman war. The account of the defense of Masada and its fall is given by Flavius Josephus in the seventh book of his *The Jewish War*.

Thus spoke Eleazar:

Truly I was greatly mistaken in thinking that I was aiding brave men in their struggles for freedom—men determined to live with honor or to die. But you are, it seems, no better than the common herd in virtue or in courage, since you are afraid even of that death which will deliver you from the direst evils, though you ought neither to delay nor wait for a counsellor. For from of old and the first dawn of reason, have our nation's laws and divine revelation, confirmed by the deeds and noble spirit of our forefathers, continued to teach us that life, not death, is a misfortune to men.

For it is death that sets the soul at liberty, and permits it to depart to its proper and pure abode, where it will be free from every misery. But so long as it is imprisoned in a mortal body and infected with its pains, it is, to speak most truly, dead; for association with what is mortal befits not that which is divine. Great, it is true, is the power of the soul, even while imprisoned in the body, its sensible instrument, that invisibly, it moves and advances in its actions beyond the range of mortal nature. But it is not until, freed from that weight which hangs suspended from it and drags it down to earth, the soul has reassumed its proper sphere that it enjoys a blessed strength and a power wholly unrestricted, remaining, as does God himself, invisible to human eyes.

For certainly it is not seen when it is in the body. It enters unperceived and unseen still withdraws, its own nature one and uncorruptible, though a cause of change to the body. Because whatever the soul has touched lives and flourishes, whatever it is removed from withers and dies; so much is there in it of immortality.

[Here follows a reference to sleep, during which the soul "converses with God because of its relationship to Him," and a discourse on the Indian view of death as the release of the soul from the body. "Should we hold baser notions than the Indians?"]

But even had we from the first been educated in opposite principles and taught that to live is the supreme good and death a calamity, the occasion still is one that calls upon us to bear death cheerfully, since we die by the will of God and out of necessity. For long ago, so it seems, God issued against the entire Jewish nation a common decree—that we were to be deprived of life if we did not use it rightly. Do not ascribe the blame to yourselves, nor the credit to the Romans, that this war with them has involved us all in ruin. It is not their might that has caused these things to pass, a more powerful agent has intervened to give them the semblance of victory.

[Here follow examples of persecutions of Jews outside Judaea and not occasioned by the Romans.]

Perhaps, however, it was because they were in a foreign land and unable to offer any opposition to their enemies that these were killed. But had not all those of us who waged war against the Romans in our own country sufficient reason to entertain hopes of certain victory? We had arms, walls, fortresses well nigh impregnable, and a spirit not to be shaken by any perils in the cause of liberty. But these advantages helped us only for a brief season, and only served to buoy us up with hopes, proving in the end to be the source of greater misfortunes. For, as if provided not for the security of those who had prepared them but for the more glorious triumph of our foes, all has been taken, all has fallen into the hands of our enemies. Those who perished in battle we cannot but count happy, for they died defending, not betraying, liberty. But the multitudes who have been subjected to the Romans—who would not pity them? Who would not make haste to die, ere he suffered the same fate as they? Some have expired upon the rack, some under the torture of fire and from scourges. Some, half-devoured by wild beasts, have, after affording derision and merriment to their foes, been preserved alive to furnish these beasts with a second repast. But those men are to be deemed most miserable who, still living, often pray for death, yet cannot obtain it.

And where is now that great city, the metropolis of the entire Jewish nation, protected by so many walls, secured by so many forts and by the vastness of its towers, which could hardly contain its implements of war and had so many myriads of men to fight for it? What has become of that city of ours which, so it was believed, God himself had founded? Uprooted from its foundations, it has been swept away and its sole preserved memorial is the camp of its destroyers still planted upon its ruins! Hapless old men are sitting among the ashes of the Temple, and a few women, reserved by our enemies for the basest of injuries.

Who of us, then, casting these things in his mind, shall bear to see the sun, even could he live unendangered? Who is so much his country's foe, so unmanly, so fond of life, not to regret that he is still alive? How I would that we had all been dead ere we had seen that holy city overthrown by hostile hands, our holy Temple so profanely uprooted! But since we were beguiled by a not ignoble hope that we might possibly be able to avenge her on her foes, and that hope is now forever vanished, leaving us alone in our distress, let us hasten to die honorably. Let us take pity on ourselves, our children, and our wives while it is still in our power to show them pity. For we were born to die, as were those whom we have begotten; and this even the fortunate cannot escape. But insult and servitude and the sight of our wives being led to infamy with their children, these, among men, are not natural or necessary evils; though those who do not prefer death, when death is in their power, must suffer even these because of their cowardice.

Elated with courage, we revolted against the Romans, and when bidden to assent to an offer of safety, would not listen to them. Who then, if they take us alive, does not anticipate their fury? Wretched will be the young, whose strong bodies can sustain many tortures, wretched, too, the old, whose age cannot endure afflictions! One man will see his wife dragged away by violence, another hear the voice of his child crying to a father whose hands are bound. But ours are still free and grasp the sword. While they are so free, let them do us honorable service. Let us die unenslaved by our foes, and, in a state of freedom, depart, together with our wives and children, from this life. That is what our laws command us to do, what our wives and children implore of us. God himself has brought this upon us, and the contrary is what the Romans, who fear lest any of us die before they capture us, desire. Instead of giving them their hoped-for pleasure in the possession of our persons, let us hasten, then to leave them in awe at our death and admiration at our fortitude.

While still anxious to inspire them with courage, Eleazar was cut short by his hearers, who, filled with uncontrollable ardor, were all in haste to commit the deed. [. . .] Natural passion and love were still alive in every breast, but the belief that what they had resolved to do was best for those dearest to them vanquished everything. They clasped and fondly embraced their wives and took their children in their arms, clinging to them and weeping as they kissed them for the last time. At the same time, and as if executing the deed with the hands of strangers, they carried out what they had resolved to do, deriving consolation in the exigency of slaying them from contemplation of the miseries they would endure if they fell into the hands of their enemies. Nor did anyone waver in the execution of this terrible task; all, in the end, perpetrated the deed upon their closest kin. Oh, wretched victims of necessity, to whom it seemed the lesser evil to slay with their own hands their wives and children!

Unable thereupon, to endure their anguish at the deed they had committed, and deeming it a wrong to the slain to survive them even for a moment, they hurriedly made a heap of all their effects, set it on fire, then chose by lot ten of their number to slay the rest. Stretched at the side of his fallen wife and children, with his arms about them, each then offered his throat to those who were to execute the rueful office. The latter, after slaying all without flinching, adopted [for their own death] the same lot-drawing procedure. The one to whose lot it fell to kill the other nine was, after so doing, to destroy himself on the bodies of his companions. None lacked the courage to equal the others in either execution or suffering. Eventually, the nine bared their throats. The last survivor examined all the bodies to see whether in so widespread a slaughter any perchance were left who still required his hand. On ascertaining that all were dead, he set fire to the palace, then drove his sword in one collected effort through his body, and fell by the side of his family.

They died believing that not a single soul among them was left alive to be subject to the Romans. But five children, an elderly woman, and still another woman, related to Eleazar and in sagacity and wisdom superior to most of her sex, escaped by hiding in the subterranean aqueducts when the rest were intent on slaughter. Including women and children, nine hundred and sixty perished on this occasion. [. . .]

The Romans, still expecting opposition, were in arms at daybreak. Having planked bridges from the mounds to the fortress, they advanced to the assault. When they saw no enemy but [only] fearful solitude on every side, flames within, and silence, they were at a loss to conjecture what had happened. In an effort to call forth some of those within, they shouted, as if at the discharge of a missile. On hearing the noise, the women emerged from their retreat and told the Romans what had occurred, one of them describing fully both what was said and how the deed was perpetrated. But the Romans, unable to credit so desperate an act, did not accept her account. In an attempt to quelch the flames, they quickly opened a passage through them, and reached the palace. Here they encountered the mounds of the slain. Instead of rejoicing at the death of their foes, they admired the courage of their resolve and the intrepid contempt of death so many had shown by such a deed as this.

The Vision of a New Era

FROM THE FOURTH BOOK OF EZRA

The fall of Jerusalem in the year A.D. 70 gave rise to the question: How could it come to be that ungodly Rome ("Babylon" in our text) triumphed over Zion, the city chosen by God and recipient of Messianic promises? Why had the Kingdom of God, envisaged as imminent by Daniel, failed to be established? The answer is revealed to the apocalyptic writer, hiding behind the name of the post-Exilic leader, Ezra. The catastrophe that befell Jerusalem is but a symbol of the state of the world at large, he postulates. The era which began with the fall of the first man is an era of evil and is to come to an end. The present rule of wickedness is a sign that the end is near. Thus the visionary's pessimism engulfs the whole historic existence of mankind. Daniel's vision is reinterpreted, with the "fourth kingdom" taken to refer to Rome. The divine plan calls for a new world. The Messiah, a transcendental figure, will appear and inaugurate a New Jerusalem. This new era of bliss on earth is not to endure; after four hundred years all humanity—including the Messiah—will die and the world will be "turned into the primeval silence seven days" (i.e., years). Only then will a universal resurrection take place and all men stand in judgment before the "splendor of the brightness of the Most High." And only in a "world to come" will the failure of Creation and of human history be rectified. Notwithstanding this failure, God says to the visionary, "Thou comest far short of being able to love my creation more than I."

The designation of this apocalypse as the "fourth" Ezra is to distinguish it from the Biblical Book of Ezra, the Book of Nehemiah, called in the Septuagint the "Second Ezra," and from the apocryphal book of Ezra. The Hebrew, or Aramaic, original is lost, and so is the Greek translation. Our knowledge of the book is based on the Syriac, Latin and other translations made from the Greek. Some of the ideas and terms of the book reappear in the New Testament Book of Revelation. The fourth of the seven visions of the book, the "Vision of the Disconsolate Women," which is among the selections here reproduced, finds its parallel in midrashic literature.

Introduction

In the thirtieth year after the downfall of the City,[1] I, Salathiel—who am also Ezra[2]—was in Babylon, and as I lay upon my bed I was disquieted . . . and my mind was preoccupied with my thoughts; because I saw Zion's desolation on the one hand matched with the abundant wealth of Babylon's[3] inhabitants on the other. And my spirit was stirred profoundly, and in my agitation I began to address the Most High.

Whence the evil?

And I said: O Lord my Lord, was it not Thou who in the beginning, when Thou didst form the earth—and that Thyself alone—didst speak and commandedst the dust, so that it gave Thee Adam,[4] a lifeless body? But yet it was both itself the formation of Thy hands and Thou breathedst into him the breath of life, so that he was made living before Thee. And Thou didst lead him into Paradise, which Thy right hand did plant before ever the earth came forward; and to him Thou commandedst one only commandment of Thine, but he transgressed it. Forthwith Thou appointedst death for him and for his generations, and from him were born nations and tribes, peoples and clans innumerable. And every nation walked after their own will, and behaved wickedly before Thee, and were ungodly—but Thou didst not hinder them.

Nevertheless again in due time Thou broughtest the Flood upon the earth and upon the inhabitants of the world, and destroyedst them. And their fate was one and the same; as death overtook Adam, so the Flood overwhelmed these. Nevertheless one of them Thou didst spare—Noah with his household and with him all the righteous his descendants.

And it came to pass that when the inhabitants upon the earth began to multiply, and there were born children also and peoples and nations many, that they began to practice ungodliness more than former generations. And it came to pass that when they practiced ungodliness before Thee, Thou didst choose Thee one from among them whose name was Abraham: him Thou didst love, and unto him only didst Thou reveal the end of the times secretly by night; and with him Thou didst make an everlasting covenant, and didst promise him that Thou wouldst never forsake his seed. And Thou gavest him Isaac, and to Isaac Thou gavest Jacob and Esau. And Thou didst set apart Jacob for Thyself, but Esau Thou didst hate; and Jacob became a great host. And it came to pass that when Thou leadest forth his seed out of Egypt, and didst bring them to the Mount Sinai,

Thou didst bow down the heavens,
didst make the earth quake
and convulsedst the world—
Thou didst cause the deeps to tremble
and didst alarm the spheres.
And Thy glory went through the four gates of fire, earthquake,
      wind, and cold,
To give the law to Jacob's seed
and the Commandment to the generation of Israel.

And yet Thou didst not take away from them the evil heart, that Thy Law might bring forth fruit in them. For the first Adam, clothing himself with the evil heart, transgressed and was overcome; and likewise also all who were born of him.[5] Thus the infirmity became inveterate; the Law indeed was in the heart of the people, but in conjunction with the evil germ; so what was good departed, and the evil remained.

So the times passed away and the years came to an end; and then Thou didst raise up for Thyself a servant whose name was David; and Thou commandedst him to build the City which is called after Thy name, and to offer Thee oblations therein of Thine own. And after this had been done many years, the inhabitants of the City committed sin, in all things doing even as Adam and all his generations had done: for they also had clothed themselves with the evil heart: and so Thou gavest Thy city over into the hands of Thine enemies.

Then I said in my heart: Are their deeds any better that inhabit Babylon? Has He for this rejected Zion? It came to pass when I came hither and saw ungodly deeds innumerable, and myself saw many sinners these thirty years, that my heart was perturbed. For I have seen

how Thou dost suffer the sinners
and dost spare the ungodly,
how Thou hast destroyed thy people
and preserved Thine enemies;

and hast not made known at all unto any how this course of Thine shall be abandoned. Have the deeds of Babylon been better than those of Zion? Has any other nation known Thee beside Israel? Or what tribes have so believed Thy covenants as those of Jacob?—whose reward nevertheless hath not appeared nor their labor borne fruit! For I have gone hither and thither through the nations and seen them in prosperity, although unmindful of Thy commandments.

Now, therefore, weigh Thou our iniquities, and those of the inhabitants of the world, in the balance and so shall be found which way the turn of the scale inclines. Or when was it that the inhabitants of the earth did not sin before Thee? Or what nation hath so kept Thy precepts? Individual men of note indeed Thou mayst find to have kept Thy precepts; but nations Thou shalt not find.

The divine reply

Thereupon the angel answered me who had been sent to

me, and whose name was Uriel;[6] and he said to me: Thy heart
hath utterly failed thee regarding this world; and thinkest thou
to comprehend the way of the Most High?

Then said I: Yes, my Lord.

And he answered me, and said: Three ways have I been
sent to show thee, and three similitudes to set before thee: if
thou canst declare me one of these I also will show thee the
way thou desirest to see, and teach thee whence comes the evil
heart.

And I said: Speak on, my Lord.

Then he said unto me:

Come, weigh me the weight of the fire;
Or measure me the measure of the wind,
Or recall me the day that is past.

Then answered I and said: Who of the earth-born could
do so that thou shouldst ask me about such matters?

And he said to me: Had I asked thee
How many dwellings are in the heart of the sea?
Or how many springs in the source of the deep?
Or how many ways above the firmament?
Or where are the portals of Hades?
Or where the paths of Paradise?
Perchance thou wouldst have said to me:
Into the deep I have not descended,
nor as yet gone down into Hades;
Neither to heaven have I ever ascended,
nor entered Paradise.

But now I have only asked thee of the fire, the wind, and
the day that is past—things without which thou canst not be;
and yet thou hast vouchsafed me no answer about them!

He said moreover unto me: What belongs to thee—the
things that have intermingled with thy growth—thou art in-
capable of understanding; how then should thy vessel[7] be able
to comprehend the way of the Most High? For the way of the
Most High has been formed without measure, how, then,
should it be possible for a mortal in a corruptible world to
understand the ways of the Incorruptible?

And when I heard these things I fell upon my face and said unto him: It would have been better that we had never been created than having come into the world to live in sins and suffer, and not to know why we suffer.[8]

And he answered me and said: Once upon a time the woods of the trees of the field went forth, and took counsel, and said: Come, let us go and make war against the sea, that it may retire before us, and we will make us more woods. In like manner also the waves of the sea took counsel, and said: Come, let us go up and wage war against the wood of the field, that there also we may win us more territory.

The counsel of the wood was in vain, for the fire came and consumed it; likewise, also, the counsel of the waves of the sea, for the sand stood up and stopped them. If thou, now, hadst been judge between them whom wouldst thou have justified or whom condemned? I answered and said: Both have taken a foolish counsel; for to the wood the land has been assigned, and to the sea a place to bear its waves.

Then he answered me and said: Thou hast judged aright; but why hast thou not given judgment in thine own case? For just as the earth has been assigned to the wood, and the place of the sea to bear its waves; even so the dwellers upon earth can understand only what is upon the earth, and they who are above the heavens that which is above the heavenly height.

The New Age

Then answered I and said: I beseech thee, O Lord, wherefore have I been endowed with an understanding to discern? For I meant not to ask about the ways above but of those things we daily experience;
Why is Israel to the heathen given over for reproach,
thy beloved people to godless tribes given up?
The Law of our fathers has been brought to destruction,
the written covenants exist no more;
We vanish from the world as locusts,
our life is as a breath.
We indeed are not worthy to obtain mercy; but what will He

do for His own name whereby we are called? It is about these things that I have asked.

Then he answered me and said: If thou survive thou shalt see, and if thou livest long thou shalt marvel; for the age is hastening to its end. Because it is unable to bear the things promised in their season to the righteous; for this age is full of sorrow and impotence.

For the evil concerning which thou askest me is sown, but the ingathering of it has not yet come. Unless, therefore, that which is sown be reaped, and unless the place where the evil is sown shall have passed away, the field where the good is sown cannot come. For a grain of evil seed was sown in the heart of Adam from the beginning, and how much fruit of ungodliness has it produced unto this time, and shall yet produce until the threshing-floor come!

Reckon up, now, in thine own mind: if a grain of evil seed has produced so much fruit of ungodliness, when once the ears of the good seed shall have been sown without number, how great a floor shall they be destined to fill?

Then I answered and said: How long and when shall these things be coming to pass? For our years are few and evil.

And he answered me and said: Thy haste may not exceed that of the Most High; for thou art hastening for thine own self, but the Exalted One on behalf of many.

Were not these questions of thine asked by the souls of the righteous in their chambers?[9] How long are we to remain here? When cometh the fruit upon the threshing-floor of our reward?

And to them the archangel Jeremiel[10] made reply, and said: Even when the number of those like yourself is fulfilled![11]
For he has weighed the age in the balance,
And with measure has measured the times,
And by number has numbered the seasons:
Neither will he move nor stir things,
till the measure appointed be fulfilled.[12]

Then I answered and said: O Lord my Lord, but behold

we are all full of ungodliness. Is it, perchance, on our account
that the threshing-floor of the righteous is kept back—on account of the sins of the dwellers upon earth?

So he answered me and said: Go and ask the woman who
is pregnant, when she has completed her nine months, if her
womb can keep the birth any longer within her?

Then said I: No, Lord, it cannot. And he said to me: The
netherworld and the chambers of souls are like the womb: for
just as she who is in travail makes haste to escape the anguish
of the travail; even so do these places hasten to deliver what
has been entrusted to them from the beginning. Then to thee
it shall be showed concerning those things that thou desirest
to see.

The end will come soon

Then I answered and said: If I have found favor in thy
sight, and if it be possible, and if I be sufficient, show me this
also: whether there be more to come than is past, or whether
the more part is already gone by us? For what is gone by I
know, but what is to come I know not.

And he said to me: Stand to the right, and I will explain
the meaning of a similitude unto thee.

So I stood, and saw, and lo! a blazing furnace passed by
before me; and it happened that when the flame had gone by
I looked and lo! the smoke remained still.

Thereupon there passed by before me a cloud full of
water, and sent down much rain with a storm; and when the
rainstorm was past the drops remained therein still.

Then said he unto me: Consider for thyself; for as the
rain is more than the drops, and as the fire is greater than the
smoke, so has the measure of what is past exceeded by far; but
there are still left over—the drops and the smoke!

The signs which precede the end

Then I made supplication, and said: Thinkest thou that
I shall live in those days?

He answered me, and said: As for the signs concerning
which thou askest me, I may tell thee of them in part; but

concerning thy life I have not been sent to speak to thee, nor have I any knowledge thereof.

Concerning the signs, however:

Behold, the days come when the inhabitants of earth shall be seized with great panic,
And the way of truth shall be hidden,
and the land be barren of faith.

And iniquity shall be increased above that which thou thyself now seest or that thou hast heard of long ago. And the land that thou seest now to bear rule shall be a pathless waste; and men shall see it forsaken: if the Most High grant thee to live, thou shalt see it after the third period in confusion.

Then shall the sun suddenly shine forth by night
and the moon by day:
And blood shall trickle forth from wood,
and the stone utter its voice:
The peoples shall be in commotion,
the outgoings of the stars shall change.

And one whom the dwellers upon earth do not look for shall wield sovereignty,[13] and the birds shall take to general flight,
and the sea shall cast forth its fish.
And one whom the many do not know will make his voice heard by night; and all shall hear his voice.
And the earth o'er wide regions shall open,
and fire burst forth for a long period:
The wild beasts shall desert their haunts;
    and women bear monsters.
Salt water shall be found in the sweet;
friends shall attack one another suddenly.
Then shall intelligence hide itself,
and wisdom withdraw to its chamber—
by many shall be sought and not found.

And unrighteousness and incontinency shall be multiplied upon the earth. One land shall also ask another and say: Is Righteousness—that doeth the right—passed through thee? And it shall answer, No.

And it shall be
In that time men shall hope and not obtain,
shall labor and not prosper.

Such are the signs I am permitted to tell thee; but if thou wilt pray again, and weep as now, and fast seven days, thou shalt hear again greater things than these.

Conclusion

Then I awoke, and my body trembled greatly; my soul also was wearied even unto fainting. But the angel who came and spake with me took hold of me, strengthened me, and set me up upon my feet.

The Vision of the Disconsolate Woman

FROM THE FOURTH BOOK OF EZRA

And when I spake thus[14] in my heart I lifted up my eyes, and saw a woman upon the right; and lo! she was mourning and weeping with a loud voice, and was much grieved in mind, and her clothes were rent and there were ashes upon her head. Then I dismissed my thoughts in which I had been preoccupied, and turned to her and said: Wherefore weepst thou? And why art thou grieved in thy mind? And she said unto me: Suffer me, my lord, to indulge my sorrow and continue my grief, for I am embittered in soul and deeply afflicted.

And I said unto her: What has befallen thee? tell me.

She said unto me: I, thy servant, was barren, and bore no child, though I had a husband thirty years. Both hourly and daily during these thirty years I besought the Most High night and day.

And it came to pass after thirty years
God heard thy handmaid
and looked upon my affliction;
He considered my distress,
and gave me a son.

And I rejoiced in him greatly, I and my husband and all my fellow townsfolk, and we gave great glory unto the Mighty One. And I reared him with great travail. So when he was grown up, I came to take him a wife, and made a feast day.

And it came to pass when my son entered into his wedding chamber, he fell down and died. Then I removed the lights, and all my fellow townsfolk rose up to comfort me; but I remained quiet until the night of the next day. And it came to pass when they were all quiet and desisted from consoling, as I remained quiet, I rose up by night, and fled, and came to this field, as thou seest. And I purpose never again to return to the city, but here to stay and neither eat nor drink, but continually to mourn and to fast till I die.

Then I left the thoughts in which I was still occupied, and answered her in anger, and said: O thou above all other women most foolish! Seest thou not our mourning, and what has befallen us? How Zion, the mother of us all, is in great grief and deep affliction? It is right now to mourn, seeing that we all mourn, and to grieve, seeing that we are all grief-stricken; thou, however, art grief-stricken for one son. But ask the earth, and she shall tell thee, that it is she who ought to mourn the fall of so many that have sprung into being upon her. Yea, from the beginning all who have been born, and others who are to come—lo! they go almost all into perdition, and the multitude of them comes to destruction. Who, then, should mourn the more? Ought not she that has lost so great a multitude? or thou who grieved but for one? But if thou sayest to me: My lamentation is not like the earth's, for I have lost the fruit of my womb
which I bare with pains
and brought forth with sorrows—
but as regards the earth, it is according to the course of nature; the multitude present in it is gone as it came: then I say to thee: Just as thou hast borne offspring with sorrow, even so also the earth has borne her fruit, namely man, from the beginning unto him that made her.
Now, therefore, keep thy sorrow within,
and bear gallantly the misfortunes that have befallen thee.

For if thou wilt acknowledge God's decree to be just, thou shalt receive thy son again in due time, and shalt be praised among women. Therefore go into the city to thy husband. And she said unto me: I will not do so: I will not enter the city, but here will I die. So I proceeded to speak further unto her, and said: No, woman! no, woman! do not do so;

but suffer thyself to be prevailed upon by reason of Zion's
      misfortunes,
be consoled by reason of Jerusalem's sorrow.
For thou seest how
our sanctuary is laid waste,
our altar thrown down;
our Temple destroyed,
our harp laid low;
our song is silenced,
our rejoicing ceased;
the light of our lamp is extinguished,
the ark of our covenant spoiled;
our holy things are defiled,
the name that is called upon us is profaned [. . .]
and what is more than all—
Zion's seal is now sealed up dishonored,
and given up into the hands of them that hate us.
Do thou, then, shake off thy great grief,
abandon thy much sorrow,
That the Mighty One may again forgive thee,
and the Most High give thee rest,
a respite from thy troubles!

And it came to pass, while I was talking to her, lo! her countenance on a sudden shone exceedingly, and her aspect became brilliant as lightning, so that I was too much afraid to approach her, and my heart was terrified exceedingly: and while I was debating what this might mean, she suddenly uttered a loud and fearful cry, so that the earth shook at the noise. And when I looked, lo! the woman was no longer visible to me, but there was a City builded, and a place showed itself of large foundations. Then

I was afraid, and cried with a loud voice, and said: Where is
Uriel, the angel who came unto me at the first? For he it is
who has caused me to fall into this great bewilderment;
and so my prayer is made futile,
and my request disappointed!

And while I was speaking thus, lo! the angel came to
me, who had come to me at the first; and when he saw that I
lay on the ground as one dead, my understanding being confused, he grasped my right hand and strengthened me, and
set me on my feet, and said to me:
What aileth thee?
Why art thou so disquieted?
Wherefore is thy understanding confused,
and the thoughts of thy heart?
And I said: Because thou hast forsaken me! Yet I did as thou
commandedst, and went into the field, and lo! I have seen—
and yet see—that which I am unable to express.

And he said unto me: Stand up like a man, and I will
advise thee. Then said I: Speak on, my lord; only forsake me
not, lest I die to no purpose.
For I have seen what I did not know and heard what I do not
          understand.
Or is my mind deceived,
And my soul in a dream?
Now, therefore, I beseech thee to show thy servant concerning
          this perplexity!
          And he answered me, and said:
Hear me, and I will teach thee,
and tell thee concerning the things thou art afraid of;
for the Most High hath revealed many secrets unto thee.
For he hath seen thy righteous conduct,
how thou hast sorrowed continually for thy people,
and mourned greatly on account of Zion—
The matter, therefore, is as follows. The woman who appeared to thee a little while ago, whom thou sawest mourning
and begannest to comfort: whereas now thou seest no likeness
of a woman any more, but a builded City hath appeared unto

thee: and whereas she told thee of the misfortune of her son—
this is the interpretation.

This woman, whom thou sawest, is Zion, whom thou
now beholdest as a builded City. And whereas she said unto
thee that she was barren thirty years: the reason is that there
were three years[15] in the world before any offering was offered
there [in Zion]. And it came to pass after three years that
Solomon built the City, and offered offerings: then it was
that the barren bare a son. And whereas she told thee that she
reared him with travail: that was the divine dwelling in Jerusalem. And whereas she said unto thee: My son entering into his
marriage-chamber died, and that misfortune befell her—this
was the fall of Jerusalem that has come to pass. And lo! thou
hast seen the heavenly pattern of her,[16] how she mourned her
son, and thou didst begin to comfort her for what had
befallen.

Now, the Most High seeing
that thou art grieved deeply
and art distressed wholeheartedly on account of her;
hath showed thee the brilliance of her glory,
and her majestic beauty.

Therefore I bade thee come into the field where no
foundation of any building is, for in the place where the City
of the Most High was about to be revealed no building-work
of man could endure.

Therefore be not thou afraid, and let not thy heart be
terrified; but go in and see the brightness and vastness of the
building, as far as it is possible for thee with the sight of thine
eyes to see!
Then shalt thou hear as much as the hearing of thine can hear.
For thou art blessed above many,
and art named before the Most High as but few!

And he departed from me. And I went forth and walked
in the field greatly magnifying and praising the Most High on
account of the marvelous acts which he performs in due season; and because he governs the times, and the things which
come to pass in due time.

The Consolation of Zion

FROM THE APOCALYPSE OF BARUCH

This apocalypse is attributed to the prophet Jeremiah's disciple Baruch, who, after the destruction of Jerusalem, is bidden to "remain amid the desolation of Zion" and be shown the end of days. The historical background, time of composition of the work, and the major themes are, in broad outline, the same as the time, situation, and teachings of the Fourth Ezra. Different is Baruch's belief in free will as opposed to the Fourth Ezra's emphasis on the fateful sin of Adam. In contradistinction to Ezra's vision of the rule of God over the entire world, Baruch pictures the Messianic kingdom as an earthly one, without, however, losing sight of the universally human aspects of Jewish eschatology. In the end, this "world of corruption will vanish," and after a period of judgment, the Lord "will renew His creation," "gather the dispersed," and "renew Zion in glory." As Joseph Klausner has pointed out, some of Baruch's Messianic vision resembles the views in the early parts of the Talmud and Midrash.

Originally written in Hebrew, the book was translated into Greek. Both original and translation disappeared. Only a Syriac version, done from the Greek, survived.

To those among the Jews whom the destruction of Jerusalem and the Temple led to the depths of despair, apocalyptic writings such as Fourth Ezra and Baruch opened new vistas of a new creation, a supernatural order of things, a new Jerusalem, an eternal world.

And I, Baruch [. . .] came to my people, and I called my first-born son and my friends, and seven of the elders of the people, and I said unto them:

Behold, I go unto my fathers
According to the way of all the earth.

But withdraw ye not from the way of the law,
But guard and admonish the people which remain,
Lest they withdraw from the commandments of the Mighty
    One.

For ye see that He whom we serve is just,
And our Creator is no respecter of persons.

And see ye what hath befallen Zion,
And what hath happened to Jerusalem.

For the judgment of the Mighty One shall be made known,
And His ways, which, though past finding out, are right.

For if ye endure and persevere in His fear,
And do not forget His law,
The times shall change over you for good,
And ye shall see the consolation of Zion.

Because whatever is now is nothing,
But that which shall be is very great.
For everything that is corruptible shall pass away,
And everything that dies shall depart,
And all the present time shall be forgotten,
Nor shall there be any remembrance of the present time,
    which is defiled with evils.
For that which runs now runs unto vanity,
And that which prospers shall quickly fall and be humiliated.

For that which is to be shall be the object of desire,
And for that which comes afterwards shall we hope;
For it is a time that passes not away,
And the hour comes which abides for ever.

And the new world comes which does not turn to corruption
    those who depart to its blessedness,
And has no mercy on those who depart to torment,
And leads not to perdition those who live in it.

For these are they who shall inherit that time which has been
    spoken of,
And theirs is the inheritance of the promised time.

These are they who have acquired for themselves treasures of
    wisdom,
And with them are found stores of understanding,
And from mercy have they not withdrawn,

And the truth of the law have they preserved.

For to them shall be given the world to come,
But the dwelling of the rest who are many shall be in the fire.

Do ye therefore so far as ye are able instruct the people,
for that labor is ours. For if ye teach them, ye will quicken
them.

And my son and the elders of the people answered and
said unto me: Has the Mighty One humiliated us to such a
degree as to take thee from us quickly?

And truly we shall be in darkness,
And there shall be no light to the people who are left.
For where again shall we seek the law,
Or who will distinguish for us between death and life?

And I said unto them: The throne of the Mighty One I can-
not resist;
Nevertheless, there shall not be wanting to Israel a wise man
Nor a son of the law to the race of Jacob.

But only prepare ye your hearts, that ye may obey the law,
And be subject to those who in fear are wise and under-
standing;
And prepare your souls that ye may not depart from them.

For if ye do these things,
Good tidings shall come unto you.

The Ten Martyrs

FROM THE TALMUD AND MIDRASH

Two generations after the fall of Jerusalem, Judaea again rose against
Rome. The rebellion, led by Bar Kokhba (132–135), which ended in a Roman
victory, was followed by a period of persecution. Talmudic tradition preserves
the memory of ten chief scholars who suffered martyrdom rather than bow to
the imperial decree that forbade the study of the Torah, ordination of dis-

ciples, and the observance of certain laws. In defying the empire of Rome, the martyrs died for the "sanctification of the Name" and as exponents of the Kingdom of God. It was Rabbi Akiba's death especially that served as an example to later-day Jewish martyrs. The story of the Ten Martyrs became one of the motifs in medieval Jewish liturgy. The dramatic account of martyrdom is recited in the service of the Day of Atonement.

Simon ben Gamliel and Ishmael

It is written: "And a stranger shalt thou not wrong, neither shalt thou oppress him. Ye shall not afflict any widow, or fatherless child. If thou afflict them in any wise—for if they cry at all unto Me, I will surely hear their cry" (Exod. 22:20-22).

Rabbi Ishmael and Rabbi Simon were on the way to their execution.

Rabbi Simon said to Rabbi Ishmael: Rabbi, my heart is consumed, for I do not know why I am to be executed.

Rabbi Ishmael said to Rabbi Simon: Perhaps a man once came to you to hear judgment, or to consult you about something, and you let him wait until you had emptied your goblet, or fastened your sandals, or put on your cloak? The Torah says: "If thou afflict them in any wise" (Exod. 22:22). It counts the same whether you afflict them greatly or only a little!

Then the other said to him: You have consoled me, Rabbi!

A highborn Roman matron fastened her gaze upon Ishmael, for he was a man of great beauty, and in this he was like Joseph, the son of Jacob. She said to the executioners: Tell him to raise his head, so that I can see him; I shall grant him his life.

But he did not heed her request. When she repeated the same thing a second and a third time, Ishmael answered: Shall I forfeit my life in the world to come for an hour of pleasures such as those!

When the godless woman heard this answer, she said to the executioners: Flay him!

They went to work. They began at his chin and flayed the skin of the righteous from his face. When they came to his forehead, to the place where the phylacteries are fastened, Ishmael uttered a piercing scream that shook the earth, and cried: Lord of the universe, will you not have mercy upon me?

A voice from heaven answered him: If you accept the suffering to which you have been sentenced, it is well; if not, I shall let the world lapse back into chaos.

Then Ishmael willingly suffered martyrdom.

Akiba

"And thou shalt love the Lord thy God with all thy heart, and with all thy soul, and with all thy might" (Deut. 6:5).

Rabbi Akiba taught: "With all thy soul"—that means: You shall love God even in that hour in which he takes your soul from you.[17]

When Akiba was led off to be executed—it was the hour in which "Hear, O Israel" is recited—they gashed his flesh with iron combs, but he willingly took the punishment of heaven upon himself. When he avowed his faith, he drew out the last word, which testifies that God is One, and the breath of life left him while he was saying the word "One."

Then a voice sounded from heaven: Hail to you, Akiba, whose last breath was spent upon the word "One."

The angels said to God: Such is the Torah, and such is its reward? Is it not written: "To die by Thy hand, O Lord"—"thy hand" (Ps. 17:14), but not the hand of man?

Then He answered them: "Their portion is . . . life!" (*ibid.*).

And a voice rang out: Blessed be you, Akiba, you who have been elected to life in the world to come!

"Gather My saints, those that have made a covenant with Me by sacrifice" (Ps. 50:5). The "saints"—those are the righteous whom every age brings forth. "Those that have made a covenant" are, above all, the three in the fiery furnace—Hananiah, Mishael, and Azariah. And the "sacrifice" refers to Akiba and his friends, who were willing to let themselves be slaughtered for the sake of the Torah.

Judah ben Baba

The memory of the man whose name is Judah ben Baba is held in high honor. Once the wicked empire of Rome had a devastating law proclaimed, to the effect that ordination of scholars would no longer be permitted. The master who laid his hands upon his disciple and ordained him was to be executed, likewise the disciple who submitted to the laying on of hands on the part of his master. A city in which such an act took place was to be destroyed, and everything within the bounds of the place in which it occurred, torn down.

What did Rabbi Judah ben Baba do? He went to a place flanked on two sides by high mountains, and equally distant from two great cities, between [. . .] Usha and Shefaram. There he himself ordained five to teacherhood—Meir, Judah, Simon, Jose, and Eleazar ben Shammua; and some say that Nehemiah was also included.

When their enemies discovered them, Judah ben Baba said to the five: My sons, flee!

They said: But master, what will become of you?

He replied: I shall lie here before them as if I were a stone that none cares to move.

It is told that the enemy did not leave that place until three hundred lances had pierced Rabbi Judah, and his body was like a sieve.

Hananyah ben Teradyon

About Hananyah ben Teradyon they relate that he was in the act of reading the Torah when the bailiffs came to fetch him. When they found him deep in his book, they said: Have you not been sentenced to be burned to death?

He answered them, saying: "The Rock, His work is perfect: for all His ways are justice" (Deut. 32:4).

Hananyah's wife asked him: What is to be my fate?

He answered her: Death by the sword.

Thereupon she said: "A God of faithfulness and without iniquity, just and right is He" (ibid.).

Hananyah's daughter asked him: And what has been decreed for me?

His answer was: Your father has been condemned to burn to death, your mother to be slain; you, however, will be forced to sit in a house of harlots.

Then she cried out: "The Lord of hosts, great in counsel, and mighty in work"! (Jer. 32:18-19).

How holy were these three people, the master, his wife, and his daughter—in the very hour when they had to submit to the judgment of heaven, they thought of three verses in the Scriptures that deal with justice and the judgment of God!

They relate:

When Hananyah was led away to be burned to death, his daughter wept. He asked her: My daughter, why do you weep?

She answered him: I weep for the Torah that is to be burned with you.

He answered: The Torah is fire, and no fire can burn fire itself.

They seized him and wrapped him in the scroll of the Torah, heaped faggots around him and lit the pyre. But they took woolen cloths, soaked them in water, and laid them on his heart, so that he should not die too quickly.

His disciples said: Rabbi, what do you see?

He replied: I see the parchment consumed by fire, but the letters of the Scriptures are flying aloft.

They continued: Rabbi, open your mouth wide, that the fire may enter more swiftly.

He said: It is better that only He who gave the soul should take it, rather than that men do anything to hasten it on its way.

Then the executioner said to Rabbi Hananyah: If I quicken the flames and take the cooling cloth from your heart—will you bring me into eternal life?

The martyr answered: That I will do.

The Roman went on: Swear it.

And Rabbi Hananyah gave him his oath. At once the executioner quickened the flames, took the woolen cloths from the teacher's heart, and soon after, his soul left his body. But the executioner threw himself into the fire.

Then a voice sounded from heaven, and called: Hananyah ben Teradyon and the Roman executioner are both chosen for the life in the world to come!

Concerning this event, Rabbi Judah the Prince once said with tears: One man can win eternal life in an hour, while another needs many years.

Hutzpit, the interpreter

Then Hutzpit, the interpreter, was to be put to death. He was a very old man—a hundred and thirty years old—beautiful in face and form, and like one of God's angels. They told the emperor of his great age and of his beauty, and begged him to show mercy to this one man.

The emperor turned to the condemned and asked him: What is your age?

Hutzpit replied: One hundred and thirty years less one day, and I beg of you to give me this one day.

The emperor said: What difference does it make whether you die today or tomorrow?

The old man answered: There are two commandments that I should like to carry out one more time. I want to recite "Hear, O Israel" this evening and tomorrow morning, so that once more I may avow the almighty and awful God as my king.

The emperor said: You people who are bold in your manners and bold of spirit, how long will you continue to cling to your God who has not the power to help you?

When Rabbi Hutzpit heard these words, he wept bitterly and clutched his clothes to rend them, because of his anguish in hearing the name of the Lord blasphemed in this way. He addressed the emperor: Woe to you, O prince! What will you do on the Day of Judgment, when the Lord punishes Rome and your gods!

Then the emperor said: How long am I to dally words with this old man? And he bade them slay him with the sword, stone him, and hang him.

Yeshebab, the Scribe

Concerning Yeshebab, the scribe, they relate that he was ninety on the day he was to be executed.

His disciples asked him: What is to become of us?

Their teacher answered: Cleave to one another, love peace and justice; perhaps there is hope.

They say that the day on which this holy man was killed, was the second day of the week, the day on which he usually fasted.

His pupils asked him whether he did not wish to strengthen himself with food before he died.

He answered them: Should the servant not be content to be like his master? Should I not be content to resemble my master Judah ben Baba? He died fasting, and so I too shall do.

And the godless Roman bade them kill the devout man just as he was about to recite "Hear, O Israel." At the words, "And the Lord spoke unto Moses" (Num. 15:37) he gave up the ghost.

A voice was heard and it cried: Blessed be you, Rabbi Yeshebab, who never for an instant faltered from the law of Moses!

Hanina ben Hakhinai

The day on which Hanina ben Hakhinai was to be executed, was the day of preparation for the Sabbath.

He began to pronounce the benediction ushering in the holy day, and got as far as the words, "And God . . . hallowed it—" (Gen. 2:3) but he had not finished speaking when he was killed.

A voice issued from heaven and cried: Happy are you, Hanina, son of Hakhinai, who were yourself a holy man, and whose soul flew on high at the word "hallowed"!

Judah ben Dama

Then it was the turn of the teacher, Judah ben Dama, to suffer punishment. But the day on which he was to be executed was the day before the Feast of Tabernacles, and so the devout man said to the emperor: By your life, wait a little until I have blessed this holiday and praised God, who gave us the Torah.

The ruler said: So even now you still cling to the belief that there is a God who gave you the Torah?

The son of Dama said: Yes.

The emperor scoffed and said: And what reward does your faith promise you?

Judah replied in the words of the psalmist: "Oh, how abundant is Thy goodness, which Thou hast laid up for them that fear Thee" (Ps. 31:20).

The emperor said: There are no fools greater than you who believe in a life after death.

To this Rabbi Judah replied: There are no fools greater than you who deny the living God. Oh, how shamed and dishonored you will be when you see us, God's people, walking in the light of life, while you thirst in the deepest abyss!

When he heard these words, the emperor's anger flared up. He commanded the teacher to be tied by the hair to a horse's tail and dragged through the streets of Rome, and after this he was to be torn to pieces besides.

Eleazar ben Shammua

Eleazar ben Shammua was the last to suffer death. He was a hundred and five years old, and no one had ever heard of his occupying himself with useless matters, or quarreling with his friends, even though his views differed from theirs. Eleazar ben Shammua was of a gentle and humble spirit, and had spent eighty years of his life fasting. The day on which he was to be executed was the Day of Atonement.

His disciples asked him: Tell us what your eyes behold!

He answered: [. . .] My sons, I see the soul of every righteous man cleansing itself in the well of Shiloah, so that it may be purified for entering the school of heaven, where Akiba will teach. And the angels bring golden chairs for the righteous, who seat themselves upon them in purity.

After these words, the emperor bade them execute this devout man.

A voice was heard: Hail to you, Eleazar ben Shammua, you who have been pure, and whose soul has risen from the body in a state of purity!

The captive children

Once it happened that four hundred boys and girls were captured for shameful purposes.

They realized why they were wanted and said:

If we drown in the sea, shall we have the life of the world to come?

The eldest of them expounded:

"The Lord said . . . I will bring them back from the depths of the sea" (Ps. 68:23).

"I will bring them back"—those who drown in the sea.

As soon as the girls heard this, they all leaped into the sea.

The boys argued:

If these, whose nature it is to succumb, do so,

how much more ought we to do so, whose nature it is not to succumb.

They too leaped into the sea.

And it is of them that Scripture says:

"For Thy sake are we killed all the day; we are accounted as sheep for the slaughter" (Ps. 44:23).

VIII. From the Ordinances of the Talmudic Masters

A note on the Mishnah. The Mishnah is the record of the Oral Law, which was believed to have been revealed on Mount Sinai together with the Written Law as contained in Scripture. This Oral Law, adhered to by the Pharisees and rejected by the Sadducees (who accepted as valid the Written Law only), was taught and interpreted in the academies of Palestine from about the second pre-Christian century onwards. After several attempts made in various generations of scholars to transcribe these traditions, such codification was achieved by Judah the Prince in Tiberias in about A.D. 200.

The Mishnah ("Repetition," teaching by repetition), is divided into six "orders" and sixty-three tractates. It covers the laws pertaining to all aspects of life: agriculture and business; property and labor; family; Sabbath and holy seasons; sacrifice, offerings, and prayer; purity and uncleanness; the administration of justice. Both laws of practical application and those no longer of practical value (e.g., the Temple regulations) were preserved. If traditions varied between the schools, the variant views were recorded. No dogmatic definition was intended; *Halakhah*, law, was thought of as a living organism that called for the human mind to cultivate it.

The masters represented in the Mishnah are called *Tannaim* (plural of *Tanna*, teacher). The language of the Mishnah is Hebrew, which, however, incorporated many Aramaic, Greek, and some Latin elements; the style is terse, precise.

Very few complete manuscripts of the Mishnah have survived; the work was first printed in Naples, in 1492.

The following are selections from the Tractate Berakhot ("Benedictions") and the Tractate Pesahim ("Passover"). Underlying the first selection is the thought that the Jew is to pronounce a blessing on every occasion of life. The second is the earliest record of the Seder, the home celebration on the eve of Passover that has taken the place of the ancient ritual of the sacrifice of the Paschal lamb.

The Order of Benedictions

FROM MISHNAH BERAKHOT

What benediction do they say over fruits? Over the fruit of trees a man says, "[Blessed art Thou Lord our God, King of the Universe] who createst the fruit of the tree," except over wine, for over wine a man says ". . . who createst the fruit of the vine."

Over the fruits of the earth a man says, ". . . who createst the fruit of the ground," except over bread, for over bread a man says ". . . who bringest forth bread from the earth." And over vegetables a man says, ". . . who createst the fruit of the ground"; but Rabbi Judah says, ". . . who createst divers kinds of herbs."

If over the fruits of trees he said the benediction, "[Blessed art thou . . .] who createst the fruit of the ground," he has fulfilled his obligation; but if over the fruits of the earth he said, ". . . who createst the fruit of the tree," he has not fulfilled his obligation. If over them all he said, "[Blessed art thou . . .] by whose word all things exist," he has fulfilled his obligation.

Over aught that does not grow from the earth he should say, ["Blessed art thou . . .] by whose word all things exist." Over soured wine or unripe fallen fruits or over locusts he should say, ". . . by whose word all things exist." Over milk, cheese, or eggs he should say, ". . . by whose word all things exist." Rabbi Judah says: Over aught that is of the nature of a curse [like spoilt fruit or locust] no benediction should be said.

When a man has before him many kinds [of food], Rabbi Judah says: If there is among them one of the seven kinds, [i.e., wheat, barley, grapes, figs, pomegranates, olive oil and (date) honey] he must say the benediction over that one. But the Sages say: He may say the benediction over which of them he will.

If he said the benediction over the wine before the meal he need not say it over the wine after the meal. If he said the benediction over the savory before the meal he need not say it over the savory after the meal. If he said it over the bread he need not say it over the savory; but if he said it over the savory he is not exempt from saying it over the bread. The School of Shammai say: Or over aught that was cooked in the pot.

If men sit [apart] to eat, each should say the benediction for himself; if they reclined [around the table together] one should say the benediction for all. If wine is brought to them during the meal each should say the benediction for himself; but if after the meal, one should say the benediction for all, and he, too, should say the benediction over the burning spices even though they are brought in only after the meal is over.

If salted relish was first brought before him together with bread he should say the benediction over the salted relish and he need not say it over the bread, since the bread is but an accompaniment. This is the general rule: where there is a main food and aught that is but an accompaniment to it, the benediction should be said over the main food and it need not be said over the accompaniment.

If a man ate figs, grapes or pomegranates, he should say the three benedictions after them.[1] So Rabban Gamaliel. But the sages say: One benediction, the substance of the three. Rabbi Akiba says: Even if he ate but boiled vegetables for his meal he must say the three benedictions after them. If he drank water to quench his thirst he should say, "[Blessed art thou . . .] by whose word all things exist." Rabbi Tarfon says: [He should say,] ". . . who createst many living beings and their wants (for all the means thou hast created wherewith to sustain the life of each of them. Blessed be He who is the life of all worlds)."

If a man saw a place where miracles had been wrought for Israel he should say, "Blessed is he that wrought miracles for our fathers in this place." [If he saw] a place from which idolatry had been rooted out he should say, "Blessed is he that rooted out idolatry from our land."

[If he saw] shooting stars, earthquakes, lightnings, thunders and storms he should say, "Blessed is He whose power and might fill the world." [If he saw] mountains, hills, seas, rivers and deserts he should say, "Blessed is the author of creation." Rabbi Judah says: If a man saw the Great Sea[2] he should say, "Blessed is he that made the Great Sea," but only if he sees it at intervals of time. For rain and good tidings he should say, "Blessed is He, the good and the doer of good." For bad tidings he should say, "Blessed is He, the true Judge."

If a man built a house or bought new vessels he should say, "Blessed is He that hath given us life [and hath preserved us and enabled us to reach this season]." A man should say the benediction for misfortune regardless of [any consequent] good, and for good fortune regardless of [any consequent] evil. If a man cries out [to God] over what is past, his prayer is vain. Thus if his wife was with child and he said, "May it be Thy will that my wife shall bear a male," this prayer is vain. If he was returning from a journey and heard a sound of lamentation in the city and said, "May it be Thy will that they [which make lamentation] be not of my house," this prayer is vain.

He that enters into a town should pray twice: once on his coming in and once on his going forth. Ben Azzai says: Four times: twice on his coming in and twice on his going forth, offering thanks for what is past and making supplication for what is still to come.

Man is bound to bless [God] for the evil even as he blesses [God] for the good, for it is written, "And thou shalt love the Lord thy God with all thy heart and with all thy soul and with all thy might" (Deut. 6:5). "With all thy heart" means with both thine impulses, thy good impulse and thine evil impulse; "and with all thy soul" means even if He takes away thy soul; "and with all thy might"—with all thy wealth. Another explanation is: "With all thy might [meodekha]"—for whichever measure [middah] He measures out to thee, do thou give Him thanks [modeh] exceedingly [bimeod meod].

A man should not behave himself unseemly while opposite the Eastern Gate [of the Temple] since it faces toward the Holy of Holies. He may not enter into the Temple Mount with his staff or his sandal or his wallet, or with the dust upon his feet, nor may he make of it a short bypath; still less may he spit there.

At the close of every benediction in the Temple they used to say "[Blessed be the God of Israel], for everlasting"; but after the heretics[3] had taught corruptly and said that there is but one world, it was ordained that they should say, "From everlasting to everlasting."

And it was ordained that a man should salute his fellow with [the use of] the Name [of God]; for it is written, "And, behold, Boaz came from Bethlehem, and said unto the reapers, The Lord be with you. And they answered him, The Lord bless thee" (Ruth 2:4). And it is written: "The Lord is with thee, thou mighty man of valor" (Judg. 6:12). And it is written: "And despise not thy mother when she is old" (Prov. 23:22). And it is written: "It is time to work for the Lord: they have made void the Law" (Ps. 119:126). Rabbi Nathan explains: They have made void thy law because it was a time to work for the Lord.[4]

The Seder Ceremony

FROM MISHNAH PESAHIM

On the eve of Passover, when the late afternoon approaches,[5] a man must eat naught until nightfall. Even the poorest in Israel must not eat unless he sits down to table, and they must not give them less than four cups of wine to drink even if it is from the [Paupers'] Dish.[6]

After they have mixed him[7] his first cup, the School of Shammai say: He says the benediction first over the [holy] day and then the benediction over the wine. And the School of

Hillel say: He says the benediction first over the wine and then the benediction over the day.

When [food] is brought before him he eats it seasoned with lettuce, until he is come to the bread condiment [the bitter herbs]; they bring before him unleavened bread and lettuce, and the *haroseth*,[8] although *haroseth* is not a religious obligation. Rabbi Eliezer ben Rabbi Zadok says: It is a religious obligation. And in the Holy City they used to bring before him the complete Passover-offering.

They then mix him the second cup. And here the son asks his father (and if the son has not enough understanding his father instructs him [how to ask]): "Why is this night different from other nights? For on other nights we eat sea- soned food once, but this night twice; on other nights we eat leavened or unleavened bread, but this night all is unleavened;[9] on other nights we eat flesh roast, stewed, or cooked, but this night all is roast."[10] And according to the understanding of the son his father instructs him. He begins with the disgrace[11] and ends with the glory; and he expounds from "A wandering Aramean was my father" (Deut. 26:5), until he finishes the whole section.

Rabban Gamaliel[12] used to say: Whosoever has not said [the verses[13] concerning] these three things at Passover has not fulfilled his obligation. And these are they: Passover, un- leavened bread, and bitter herbs: "Passover"—because God passed over the houses of our fathers in Egypt; "unleavened bread"—because our fathers were redeemed from Egypt; "bit- ter herbs"—because the Egyptians embittered the lives of our fathers in Egypt.

In every generation a man must so regard himself as if he came forth himself out of Egypt, for it is written: "And thou shalt tell thy son in that day saying, It is because of that which the Lord did for me when I came forth out of Egypt" (Exod. 13:8). Therefore are we bound to give thanks, to praise, to glorify, to honor, to exalt, to extol, and to bless him who wrought all these wonders for our fathers and for us. He brought us out from bondage to freedom, from sorrow to gladness, and from mourning to a Festival day, and from darkness to great light, and from servitude to redemption; so let us say before him the Hallelujah.[14]

How far do they recite [the Hallel]? The School of Shammai say: To "A joyful mother of children."[15] and the School of Hillel say: To "A flintstone into a springing well."[16] And this is concluded with the [benediction recounting] Redemption.

Rabbi Tarfon says: "He that redeemed us and redeemed our fathers from Egypt and brought us to this night to eat therein unleavened bread and bitter herbs." But there is no concluding benediction.

Rabbi Akiba adds: "Therefore, O Lord our God and the God of our fathers, bring us in peace to the other set feasts and festivals which are coming to meet us, while we rejoice in the building-up of Thy city and are joyful in Thy worship; and may we eat there of the sacrifices and of the Passover-offerings whose blood has reached with acceptance the wall of Thy altar, and let us praise Thee for our redemption and for the ransoming of our soul. Blessed art Thou, O Lord, who hast redeemed Israel!"

After they have mixed for him the third cup he says the benediction over his meal. [Over] a fourth [cup] he completes the "Hallel" and says after it the benediction over song. If he is minded to drink [more] between these cups he may drink; only between the third and the fourth cups he may not drink.

After the Passover meal they should not disperse to join in revelry.[17] [. . .]

IX. Beliefs and Opinions of the Talmudic Masters

Hillel the Elder

FROM THE TALMUD AND MIDRASH

Jewish tradition credits Hillel with reconstructing the Torah, which Ezra the Scribe helped make the constitution of Judaea and which had been "forgotten" in the course of the rapid advance of the Hasmonean rule and the spread of Hellenism. Hillel's activity falls in the historic period marked by Herod's pro-Roman policy, the rivalries between the Pharisees and Sadducees, the deterioration of the official priesthood, the segregation of the Essene or Dead Sea sect in the Jordan region. It was a period of tensions, disappointments, and Messianic expectations, so vividly expressed in some of the apocryphal writings. Born around 60 B.C. in Babylonia, Hillel came to Jerusalem in about 40 B.C., studied in the schools of Shemaiah and Abtalion, and, roughly, between 30 B.C. and A.D. 10 taught in Jerusalem.

Hillel supplemented the body of teachings known from a scrupulously guarded tradition by a system of interpretation which allowed the student to derive the teachings from the written word of the Torah. This emphasis on "learning" made the Torah a living concern of an ever widening group of disciples and of the people at large. The commandments are many, Hillel taught, but they can be reduced to one: loving kindness. In *hesed*, loving concern, man emulates God. By a number of legislative measures, Hillel helped the poor and underprivileged classes. His ideal was the true and just community (as against the state), for which he found a model in the early hasidic groups (from which possibly the Essenes derived). He welcomed proselytes and accorded them equality of rights. His attitude of peacefulness, mercy, and forgiveness is in contrast to the stringency and harshness of his colleague, Shammai. Both Hillel and Shammai headed schools that bear their names; in most instances, however, the opinion of the School of Hillel prevailed. Hillel's work made possible the reconstruction of Judaism after the fall of Jerusalem His youngest disciple, Johanan ben Zakkai, assumed the leadership of the remnant.

The stories about Hillel and the sayings attributed to him are scattered in the vast literature of Talmud and Midrash.

The re-established Torah

In ancient days when the Torah was forgotten from Israel,
Ezra came up from Babylon[1] and re-established it.
Then it was again forgotten
until Hillel the Babylonian came up and re-established it.

Education

It was said of Hillel
that he had not neglected any of the words of the Wise but
        had learned them all;
he had studied all manners of speech,
even the utterance of mountains, hills and valleys,
the utterance of trees and plants,
the utterance of beasts and animals,
tales of spirits, popular stories and parables,
everything he had learned.

Disciples

"Raise many disciples." [2]
The School of Shammai says:
One ought teach only a student who is wise, humble, of a
        good family and rich.
The School of Hillel says:
One ought to teach every man;
for there were many transgressors in Israel who came close to
        the study of the Torah
and from them issued righteous men, pious and worthy.

On disseminating knowledge

When there are those who want to gather, you scatter [the
        seed of teaching];

when there are those who scatter, you gather.
[That is to say:]
If you see a generation to which the Torah is dear, you spread
    [its knowledge];
but if you see a generation to which the Torah is not dear, you
    gather it and keep it to yourself.

Peace

Be of the disciples of Aaron [the priest],
loving peace, pursuing peace.
Be one who loves his fellow-creatures
and draws them near to the Torah.

How did Hillel bring his fellow-man near to the Torah?
One day Hillel stood in the gate of Jerusalem and met people
    going out to work.
He asked: How much will you earn today?
One said, A denarius; the other said, Two denarii.
He asked them: What will you do with the money?
They gave answer: We will pay for the necessities of life.
Then he said to them:
Why don't you rather come with me and gain knowledge of
    the Torah,
that you may gain life in this world
and life in the world to come?
Thus Hillel was wont to do all his days and has brought many
    under the wings of heaven.[3]

The ignorant cannot be a hasid

The uneducated knows not fear of sin;
the ignorant cannot be a pious man.
The timid is not apt to learn,
the impatient is not fit to teach.
He whose whole time is absorbed in business will not attain
    wisdom.
In a place where [a man is needed and] there are no men,
    strive to be a man.

Torah

The more flesh, the more worms;
the more possessions, the more worry;
the more women, the more witchcraft;
the more maidservants, the more immorality;
the more menservants, the more thieving.
[But:]
The more Torah, the more life;
the more study and contemplation, the more wisdom;
the more counsel, the more discernment;
the more charity, the more peace.

Do not separate yourself from the community.
Trust not in yourself until the day of your death;
judge not your fellow-man until you have come to his place;
say not of a thing which cannot be understood that it will be
      understood in the end;
say not: When I have leisure I will study:
perchance you will never have leisure.

With people

Do not appear naked [among the dressed]
neither dressed [among the naked];
do not appear standing [among those who sit]
neither sitting [among those who stand];
do not appear laughing [among those who weep]
neither weeping [among those who laugh].
The rule is: Do not deviate from the usage of men.

Teachings

If I am not for myself—who is for me?
and being for mine own self—what am I?
and if not now—when?

A good name, once acquired, is your own possession;
he who has knowledge of the Torah has life in the world to
      come.

A name made famous is a name lost.
Knowledge that does not grow will shrink.
He who refuses to teach faces death.
He who uses the crown of learning for material gains vanishes.

Hillel saw a skull floating on the face of the water.
He said to it:
Because you have drowned others, they have drowned you;
but those that drowned you will, at the last, themselves be
    drowned.[4]

My humiliation is my exaltation;
my exaltation is my humiliation.

The human body

Once when Hillel was taking leave of his disciples, they
said to him: Master, whither are you going?

He replied: To do a pious deed. They said: What may
that be? He replied: To take a bath. They said: Is that a pious
deed?

He replied: Yes; if in the theaters and circuses the images
of the king must be kept clean by the man to whom they have
been entrusted, how much more is it a duty of man to care
for the body, since man has been created in the divine image
and likeness.

[In a parallel situation, Hillel answered the disciples'
question:]
I am going to do a kindness to the guest in the house.
When the disciples asked whether he had a guest every day,
    he answered:
Is not my poor soul a guest in the body? Today it is here,
    tomorrow it is gone.

Beautiful bride

What is being sung while one dances before the bride?
The School of Shammai says: The bride is described as she is.
The School of Hillel says: One [always] sings: Beautiful and
    graceful bride!

Based on this the sages say: A man's heart should always be outgoing in dealing with people.

Disaster

It once came to pass that Hillel the Elder was returning from a journey when he heard screams from the direction of the city.

He said: I am confident that this does not come from my house.

Concerning him, Scripture says:

"He shall not be afraid of evil tidings; his heart is steadfast, trusting in the Lord" (Ps. 112:7).

The poor man

There was a man of a wealthy family who had become poor.

Hillel provided him with a horse to ride upon and with a servant to run before him.

One day he could not find a servant, so he himself ran before him for three miles.

The wager

Two men made a wager with each other: he who would go and make Hillel angry would receive four hundred *zuz*.

One of them said: I will go and make him angry.

That day was Sabbath eve, and Hillel was washing his head.

The men went, passed by the door of his house, and cried: Is Hillel here? Is Hillel here?

Hillel wrapped himself up and came out to meet him: My son what do you wish?

—I have a question to ask.

He said to him: Ask my son, ask.

—Why are the heads of the Babylonians round?

Hillel answered: My son, you have asked an important question:—Because they have no skilled midwives.

The man went out, waited a while and returned.

[The scene is twice more repeated, the important questions being: Why are the eyes of the Palmyreans bleared?

Why are the feet of the Africans wide? Hillel answered
and the man promised to come with more problems.
Seeing that it was impossible to exhaust the master's
patience, he asked him:]
Are you the Hillel whom they call the prince of Israel?
Yes, answered Hillel.
The man said: If that is you, I wish, there may not be many
like you in Israel. Why, my son? asked Hillel. Because
I have lost four hundred *zuz* through you.
Said Hillel: Watch out; I may cause you to lose much money
but I will not easily lose my patience.

The entire Torah on one foot

A certain heathen came to Shammai and said to him:
Convert me provided that you teach me the entire Torah
while I stand on one foot.
Shammai drove him away with the builder's cubit which was
in his hand.
He went to Hillel who said to him:
What is hateful to you, do not do to your neighbor:[5]
that is the entire Torah;
the rest is commentary;
go and learn it.

Every day

It was told of Shammai the Elder: Whenever he found
a fine portion he said: This will be for the Sabbath. If later he
found a finer one, he put aside the second for the Sabbath
and ate the first; thus, whatever he ate, was meant for the
honor of the Sabbath.

But Hillel the Elder had a different way, for all his works
were for the sake of heaven; he used to say: "Blessed be the
Lord, day by day He beareth our burden" (Ps. 68:20).

Man

Our masters taught:
For two and half years the Schools of Schammai and Hillel
have maintained a dispute;

the former said: It would have been better if man had not
　　been created;
the School of Hillel said: It is better for man to have been
　　created than not to have been created.
They took a vote and came to this decision:
It would have been better had man not been created;
yet, since he had been created, let him pay close attention to
　　his actions, those past and those before him.

The rival schools

The words of both schools are the words of the living God,
but the law follows the ruling of the School of Hillel
because the Hillelites were gentle and modest,
and studied both their own opinions and the opinions of the
　　other school,
and humbly mentioned the words of the other school before
　　theirs.
The preference accorded to the School of Hillel teaches you
that he who humbles himself the Lord raises up,
and he who exalts himself the Lord humbles;
greatness flees him who seeks greatness;
greatness may follow him who flees from greatness.
He who [impatiently] tries to force time, is thrown back by
　　time;
he who [patiently] yields to time, finds time standing by him.

The heavenly voice

One day some wise men were assembled in the upper chamber
　　of one Gurya's house in Jericho;
a heavenly voice was granted them that announced:
There is among you one man who would deserve that the
　　Divine Presence rest upon him, but his generation is
　　not worthy of it.
Thereupon all the eyes were fixed upon Hillel the Elder.
And when he died, they lamented over him:
"The pious man, the humble man, the disciple of Ezra [is no
　　more]."

The Ways of Good Life

FROM THE TALMUD TRACTATE BERAKHOT

A note on the Talmud. The academies of Palestine and Babylonia took the Mishnah as the basic text to be studied, compared with other collections of traditions, and interpreted to apply to new conditions. The record of these deliberations is called Gemara ("Completion"), which together with the Mishnah constitutes the Talmud ("Study"). The relevant material from the Palestinian schools was compiled around A.D. 400, and is known as the Palestinian (or Jerusalem) Talmud. A century later the material of the schools in Babylonia was gathered and edited, to form the Babylonian Talmud. The latter, due to its greater richness, became the body of writings studied in the traditional houses of learning throughout the centuries.

While the Mishnah is a code of laws, the Talmud is a cyclopedia ranging over the entire realm of human life. Non-legal subjects, theology, history, ethics, life of the sages, legends, folklore (material referred to as Haggadah, or Agada, narrative, as distinguished from Halakhah, law) fill about one-third of the Babylonian Talmud (which contains some 2,500,000 words), and about 15 per cent of the Palestinian Talmud (which contains some 750,000 words.) The masters of the Talmud are called Amoraim (plural of Amora, speaker). The language varies between Aramaic (Western Aramaic in the Palestinian, Eastern Aramaic in the Babylonian Talmud) and Hebrew.

The most important manuscript of the Palestinian Talmud is in Leyden in the Netherlands. The best manuscript of the Babylonian Talmud is in Munich, written in 1343. The first complete printed edition appeared in Venice 1520 to 1523 f. The commentaries on the Talmud are a library in themselves.

The following is a selection of haggadic passages culled from one of the tractates, Berakhot ("Benedictions").

Every day

[Towards the end of his career, Moses said:]
"Keep silence and hear, O Israel; this day thou art become a
     people unto the Lord thy God" (Deut. 27:9).
But was the Torah given to Israel on that day?

Was not that day at the end of the forty years in the
    wilderness?
But—this is to teach you that every day the Torah is dear to
    those who study it,
as on the day it was given from Mount Sinai.

The gist of it

Which is the small section on which all the principles of the
    Torah depend?
—"In all thy ways know Him
And He will direct thy paths" (Prov. 3:6).

The gates of Torah

Learn with all your heart, and with all your soul,
to know My ways,
to watch at the gates of My Torah.
Keep My Torah in your heart,
may the fear of Me be before your eyes;
guard your mouth from all sin,
purify and sanctify yourself from faults and transgressions,
and I will be with you in every place.

My neighbor

The masters of Jabneh[6] were wont to say:
I am [God's] creature, and my fellow man is [God's] creature.
My work is in the city and his work is in the country.
I rise early to go to my work,
and he rises early to go to his work.
As he cannot excel in my work,
so do I not excel in his work.
And should you say, I do more, and he does less—
We have learned:[7]
"The one more, the other less—if only his heart is directed to
    heaven."

Brothers

Let man ever be subtle in the fear of God,

giving a soft answer that turneth away wrath.[8]
Let him increase the peace with his brothers, with his relatives,
    and with all men,
even with the heathen in the market place,
that he may be beloved above and desired below,
and well received by all his fellow creatures.

The final goal

The goal of wisdom is repentance and good works.
So that a man may not study the Torah and learn the
    Tradition
and then set foot on his father, or his mother,
or his master, or on him who is greater than he in wisdom and
    in rank.
Thus it is said:
"The fear of the Lord is the beginning of wisdom;
a good understanding have all they that do thereafter"
    (Ps. 111:10).

Chastisements of love

If a man sees chastisements coming upon him, let him search
    his conduct.
If he has searched his conduct and found nothing, let him
    attribute it to his idleness in Torah.
And if he has done this and found nothing,
surely they are chastisements of [God's] love [for man].
As it is said: "For whom the Lord loveth He correcteth"
    (Prov. 3:12).

Old men

Have care for an old man who has forgotten his learning under
    duress.
For it was said:
Both the whole tablets [of the Law] and the fragments of the
    tablets were placed in the Ark of the Covenant.

Animals first

It is forbidden for a man to eat before having fed his beast.

For it is said: "And I will give grass in the field for thy cattle" and [only] afterwards: "And thou shalt eat and be satisfied" (Deut. 11:15).

Sinners

Some outlaws lived in the neighborhood of Rabbi Meir, and caused him much trouble.
Because of this he prayed that they might die.
Whereupon Beruriah, his wife, said to him:
What are you thinking of?
Is it because it is written: "Let sins cease out of the earth" (Ps. 104:35)?
but does it say "sinners"?
"Sins" is what is written!
And more than this:
Look at the end of the verse: "And let the wicked be no more."
When sin will cease there will be no more wicked.
Rather pray for them, that they may repent and be wicked no more.
Rabbi Meir prayed for them,
and they repented.

Far and near

In that place where the penitents stand, the perfectly right-eous cannot stand,
as it is written:
"Peace, peace, to him that is far off and to him that is near (Isa. 57:19)"—
first to him who was far off,
then to him who is near!

Let a man ever say:
All that the Compassionate One does is for good.

Let a man's words ever be few before the Holy One, blessed be he.
For it is said:

"Be not rash with thy mouth, and let not thy heart be hasty to
    utter a word before God; for God is in heaven, and
    thou upon earth; therefore let thy words be few"
    (Eccles. 5:1).

Beauty

Rabbi Eliezer fell ill and Rabbi Johanan went in to visit him.
He saw Rabbi Eliezer lying in a dark [windowless] room.
Rabbi Johanan bared his arm and the room lit up.
He saw that Rabbi Eliezer was crying. He said to him: Why
    are you crying?
Is it for the Torah in which you have not learned enough?
We have learned: The one more, the other less—if only his
    heart is directed to heaven.[9]
If because of sustenance you lack—
not every man merits two tables.[10]
If because of [the lack of] children?
see, this is the bone of my tenth son.[11]
Rabbi Eliezer replied to him:
I am crying over this beauty of yours, which is to wither in the
    dust.
He said to him:
You are right to cry over that.
And they wept together.

The blessing

When Rabbi Johanan ben Zakkai fell ill, his disciples went in
    to visit him [. . .]. They spoke to him, saying: Mas-
    ter, give us your blessing.
He said to them: May it be His will that the fear of heaven be
    upon you like the fear of those who are of flesh and
    blood.
They asked: Only so much?
He answered them: Would that it were so much! For you
    must know that when a man wants to commit a trans-
    gression, he says: I hope no man sees me!

When Rabbi Eliezer fell ill, his disciples came to visit him.

They said to him:
Master, teach us the ways of life, that by following them, we
     may become worthy of life in the world to come.
He said to them:
Take heed of the honor of your colleagues,
Keep your children from superficiality, but have them sit at
     the feet of scholars;
and when you pray know before Whom you stand;
thus you will be worthy of the life in the world to come.

In farewell

When the masters departed from the school of Rabbi Ammi—
     some say from the school of Rabbi Hanina—they said
     to him:
May you see your world in your life,
may your aim be fulfilled in the life of the world to come,
your hope throughout the generations.
Let your heart meditate in understanding,
your mouth utter wisdom,
your tongue be abundant in songs of jubilation.
May your eyelids look straight before you,
your eyes glow with the light of the Torah,
your face shine with the radiance of heaven,
your lips proclaim knowledge,
your reins rejoice in uprightness,
your feet hasten to hear the words of the Ancient of Days.[12]

Creation and Man

FROM THE TALMUD AND MIDRASH

The first chapter of Genesis inspired some of the leading talmudic sages
to engage in esoteric cosmology. The Mishnah discouraged the expounding of
the mysteries of "The Work of Creation" except to a single student. But open
to all was meditation upon the majesty of the Creator, the beauty and pur-

posefulness of the world, which is but one continuous creation, and upon man's rightful place in the universe.

In its time

"He has made everything beautiful in its time" (Eccles. 3:11)
—in its due time was the world created.
The world was not fit to be created before then.
The Holy One, blessed be he, kept creating worlds and deso-
      lating them, creating worlds and desolating them,
until he created these [worlds of heaven and earth].
Then he said: "These please me; those did not please me."

In the beginning

"In the beginning God created" (Gen. 1:1).
It is not written, "The Lord created":[13]
First there rose within His mind the plan
of creating the world with the attribute of justice;
then He saw that thus the world could not endure,
and He set first the attribute of mercy and added it to the at-
      tribute of justice.
That is why [later] it is written:
"In the day that the Lord God made earth and heaven"
    (Gen. 2:4).

Between heaven and earth

You find that the Holy One, blessed be he, created heaven
      and earth with wisdom.
On the first day He created heaven and earth.
Five days were left: one day he created something on high, and
      something below, the next.
He created the firmament on high on the second day; on the
      third "Let the waters . . . be gathered together"
      below.
On the fourth day "Let there be lights" on high; on the fifth
    "Let the waters swarm" below.
Only the sixth day was left for something to be created on it.
The Holy One, blessed be he, said:
If I create something on high, the earth will be indignant,

if I create something below, heaven will be indignant.
What was it the Holy One, blessed be he, did?
He created man from that which is below, and the soul from
　　　that which is on high.

Origins

The first man, his dust was gathered together from all the
　　　world;
his body came from Babylon, his head from the land of Israel,
　　　and his limbs from the other countries.

In the past Adam was created from the earth and Eve was
　　　created from Adam; from then, "in our image, after
　　　our likeness" (Gen. 1:26):
Neither man without woman
nor woman without man,
nor the two of them without Divine Presence.[14]

The crown of creation

Man was created on the eve of Sabbath—and for what reason?
So that in case his heart grew proud, one might say to him:
Even the gnat was in creation before you were there!

Singularity[15]

Man was created single, to teach you
that whosoever wreck a single soul
Scripture considers to have wrecked a complete world,
and whosoever sustain a single soul
Scripture considers to have sustained a complete world.
Also: he was created single to keep peace among the human
　　　creatures:
that no man might say to his fellow,
my father was greater than your father.

For you[16]

In the hour when the Holy One, blessed be he, created the
　　　first man,

he took him and let him pass before all the trees of the garden
    of Eden,
and said to him:
See my works, how fine and excellent they are!
Now all that I have created for you have I created.
Think upon this, and do not corrupt and desolate my world;
for if you corrupt it, there is no one to set it right after you.

When iron was created, the trees began to tremble.
Said iron to them:
Why do you tremble? Let none of your wood enter me, and
    not one of you will be injured.

Grow!

There is no grass without its own guardian star in the
    firmament
which strikes it and says to it, Grow!

Evil desire

"And God saw everything that He had made, and behold, it
    was very good" (Gen. 1:31).
"Behold, it was very good"—that is the evil desire.[17]
But is the evil desire good?
Yet were it not for the evil desire,
men would not build homes, or take wives, or propagate, or
    engage in business.

. . . They said:
This being a time of Grace, let us pray for mercy for the evil
    desire.
They prayed and the evil desire was delivered to them.
The prophet [Zechariah] said to them:
Know, if you destroy this one, the world will come to an end.
They imprisoned it for three days:
then they sought a new-laid egg in all the land of Israel,
and not one could be found.

Coming and going

When a man comes into the world, his hands are clenched,

as though to say: All the entire world is mine; now I shall ac-
    quire it.
And when he goes out of the world, his hands are wide open,
as though to say: I have acquired nothing from this world.

Order

You will be called by your name,
you will be seated in your place,
you will be given what is yours.
No man touches what is meant for his fellow.
No kingdom touches its neighbor by so much as a hairs-
    breadth.

Everything is foreseen
and everything is laid bare
yet everything is in accordance with the will of man.

God-Man-World

FROM THE TALMUD AND MIDRASH

This selection of teachings, culled from the talmudic and midrashic
writings, should be read against the background of the apocalyptic writings. In
contradistinction to the pessimism of the apocalyptic writers, their disappointment with this world, and ardent, yet passive, expectation of a new aeon to
come, the talmudic masters courageously approached the issues of life, moving
about in a world governed by divine mercy, and by so doing they overcame the
tragedy of the fall of Jerusalem which, in the case of the apocalyptic, had
turned into a catastrophe.

Justice

"Shall not the Judge of all the earth do justly?" (Gen. 18:25).
[Abraham said to God:]
If it is the world you seek, there can be no [stern] justice;
and if it is [stern] justice you seek, there can be no world.
Why do you grasp the rope by both ends,
seeking both the world and [stern] justice?

Let one of them go,
for if you do not relent a little, the world cannot endure.

Sustenance

"And the people shall go out and gather a day's portion every
    day" (Exod. 16:4).[18]
He that created the day created the sustenance of the day.
A man who has something to eat today, and says, What shall
    I eat tomorrow—lo, he is lacking in faith.

Have you ever seen beast or fowl that have a trade, yet they
    sustain themselves without trouble, though they were
    created only to serve me—
and I was created to serve my Maker; how much more ought
    I to sustain myself without trouble—
but I have acted wickedly, and have spoiled my sustenance.

Ascent

The Torah leads to deliberation, deliberation leads to zeal,
    zeal leads to cleanness, cleanness leads to continence,
    continence leads to purity, purity leads to godliness,
    godliness leads to humility, humility leads to the fear
    of sin, the fear of sin leads to holiness, holiness leads
    to the Holy Spirit, the Holy Spirit leads to resurrection;
    but among all qualities, piety is the greatest.
Another opinion: Humility is the greatest among them all—
    as it is written: "The spirit of the Lord God is upon
    me; because the Lord hath anointed me to bring good
    tidings unto the humble" (Isa. 61:1).

The imitation of God

"To walk in all His ways" (Deut. 11:22):
those are the ways of the Holy One, blessed be he.
As it is said: "The Lord . . . merciful and gracious, long-
    suffering and abundant in goodness and truth; keeping
    mercy unto the thousandth generation, forgiving iniq-
    uity and transgression and sin . . ." (Exod. 34:6).[19]

This means: As the Omnipresent is called merciful and
        gracious,
you too must be merciful and gracious, and give freely to all.
As the Holy One, blessed be he, is called righteous,
you too must be righteous.
As the Holy One, blessed be he, is called kindly,
you too must be kindly.

It is written: "After the Lord your God shall ye walk"
        (Deut. 13:5).
What does this mean? Is it possible for man to walk after the
        Presence of God? What it means is that we shall walk
        after the attributes of the Holy One, blessed be he.
As he clothes the naked—for it is written, "And the Lord God
        made for Adam and his wife garments of skins, and
        clothed them" (Gen. 3:21)—thus you also shall do:
        you shall clothe the naked.
The Holy One, blessed be he, visited the sick, as it is written:
        "And the Lord appeared unto him by the terebinth of
        Mamre" (Gen. 18:1)—thus you also shall do: you shall
        visit the sick.
The Holy One, blessed be he, comforted those who mourned,
        as it is written: "And it came to pass after the death of
        Abraham, that God blessed Isaac his son" (Gen.
        25:11). Do likewise: comfort those who mourn.
The Holy One, blessed be he, buried the dead, as it is written:
        "And He buried him [Moses] in the valley in the land
        of Moab" (Deut. 34:6). Do likewise: bury the dead.

The Torah: It begins with the showing of mercy and it ends
        with the showing of mercy.
It begins with the showing of mercy, as it is written:
        "And the Lord God made for Adam and for his wife
        garments of skins, and clothed them."
It ends with the showing of mercy, as it is written: "And He
        buried him in the valley in the Land of Moab."

Four answers

Wisdom was asked: The sinner, what is his destiny?

She replied: "Evil pursueth sinners" (Prov. 13:21).
Prophecy was asked: The sinner, what is his destiny?
She replied: "The soul that sinneth, it shall die" (Ezek. 18:4).
The Torah was asked: The sinner, what is his destiny?
She replied: Let him bring a guilt offering, and atonement
    shall be made for him;
as it is written: "And it shall be accepted for him to make
    atonement for him" (Lev. 1:4).
The Holy One, blessed be he, was asked:
The sinner, what is his destiny?
He replied:
Let him turn in repentance, and atonement shall be made for
    him; as it is written:
"Good and upright is the Lord; therefore doth He instruct
    sinners in the way" (Ps. 25:8).

Of their own free will

"The Lord loveth the righteous" (Ps. 146:8).

Says the Holy One, blessed be he: They love me, and I
love them also. And why does the Holy One, blessed be he,
love the righteous? Because their righteousness is not a matter
of heritage or family.

You will find that the priests form a father's house and
the Levites form a father's house, for it is said: "O house of
Aaron, bless ye the Lord; O house of Levi, bless ye the Lord"
(Ps. 135:19-20). A man may wish to become a priest and yet
he cannot; he may wish to become a Levite and yet he cannot.
And why? Because his father was no priest, or no Levite.

But if a man, Jew or gentile, wishes to be righteous, he
can be this, because the righteous do not form a house. Therefore it is said: "Ye that fear the Lord, bless ye the Lord"
(Ps. 135:20). It is not said, *house* of those that fear the Lord,
but ye that fear the Lord, for they form no father's house.

Of their own free will, they have come forward and loved
the Holy One, blessed be he. And that is why he loves them.

The heart

A man of flesh and blood, if he has a vessel,

so long as the vessel is whole, he is happy with it;
broken, he does not wish it.
But not so the Holy One, blessed be he.
So long as the vessel is whole, he does not wish to see it;
broken, he wishes it.
And what is the favorite vessel of the Holy One, blessed be
    he?
The heart of man.
If the Holy One, blessed be he, sees a proud heart, he does not
    wish it;
as it is said: "Every one that is proud in heart is an abomina-
    tion to the Lord" (Prov. 16:5).
—Broken, he says: This is mine;
as it is said: "The Lord is nigh unto them that are of a broken
    heart" (Ps. 34:19).

Of every man whose spirit is haughty, the Holy One, blessed
    be he, says:
He and I cannot dwell together in the world.

Destiny

Everyone that humbles himself the Holy One, blessed be he,
    lifts up;
and everyone that lifts himself up the Holy One, blessed be
    he, humbles.
Everyone that pursues greatness, greatness flees;
and everyone that flees greatness, greatness pursues.
Everyone that pushes his hour ahead, his hour pushes him
    back;
and everyone that stands back for his hour, his hour stands by
    him.

Rain

Hanan the Hidden was the son of the daughter of Honi the
    Circle-Drawer.[20]
When the world was in need of rain, the masters would send
    the school children to him,
and they would clutch the hem of his cloak and say to him:

Father, give us rain.

He said to Him:

Master of the Universe, do it for the sake of these who do not
    know the difference between the Father who gives rain
    and a father who does not give rain.

Mercy not sacrifice

Once Rabban Johanan ben Zakkai[21] went forth from Jerusa-
    lem; and Joshua [his disciple] walked behind him.

When he beheld the sanctuary in ruins, Joshua said: Woe to
    us, that it has been destroyed! The place where Israel's
    iniquities found atonement!

Then the other said to him: My son, do not let it grieve you!
    We have atonement equal to that other. And what is
    that?

Deeds of loving-kindness,

as it is written: "For I desire mercy, and not sacrifice" (Hos.
    6:6).

Honor due to parents and to God

Great is the honoring of father and mother;

yes, the Holy One, blessed be he, even gave it precedence
    over the honor due to Him.

It is written,

"Honor thy father and thy mother" (Exod. 20:12),

and it is written,

"Honor the Lord with thy substance" (Prov. 3:9).

Wherewith can you honor Him?

With that wherewith He has endowed you:

You set aside the gleaning, the forgotten sheaf at the corner
    of the field;[22]

you set aside the heave offering, the first tithe, the second
    tithe,

the tithe for the poor, and the loaf;

you see to the booth, and the branch of the palm tree, the
    ram's horn, thy phylacteries and the fringes;[23]

you give food to the poor and the hungry, and you slake those
    who thirst.

If you have substance, you are bound to do all of this,
if you have none, you are not bound to do this.
But when it comes to the honoring of father and mother,
it is the same whether you have something to give or have
          nothing to give:
"Honor thy father and thy mother"—
even if you have to go begging at doors.

Rabbi Joseph,
when he heard the sound of his mother's steps, said:
I shall rise before the Divine Presence that is coming.

Captivity

If a man is in captivity with his father and his master,
he comes before his master,
his master comes before his father.
His mother comes before them all.

The law and more

It happened to Rabbah bar Hanan that some porters broke a
          barrel of his wine.
He took away their cloaks.[24]
They went and told Rav [the judge].
He said to Rabbah: Give them back their cloaks.
Rabbah asked him: Is that the law?
He replied: Yes: "That thou mayest walk in the way of good
          men" (Prov. 2:20).
He gave them back their cloaks.
The porters said to Rav: We are poor men, and have worked
          all day, and are in need, and have nothing.
Rav said to Rabbah: Go and pay them.
He asked him: Is that the law?
He replied: Yes: "And keep the paths of the righteous"
          (ibid.).[25]

Let everyone enter

Rabbi Judah the Prince[26] opened his granary in the years of
          drought. He said:

Let those who have studied the Torah enter, and those who
     have studied the Mishnah, those who have studied the
     Gemara, those who have studied the Halakhah, and
     those who have studied the Haggadah—but let no ig-
     noramus enter!
Jonathan ben Amram pressed forward and entered. He said:
     Master, feed me!
Rabbi Judah said to him: Have you studied the Torah, my
     son?
He said: No.
Have you studied the Mishnah?
He said: No.
If so, how can I feed you?
He said: Feed me as you would a dog or a crow.
Rabbi Judah fed him. After he had gone, Rabbi Judah sat
     regretting what he had done and said: Alas, for I have
     given my bread to an ignoramus.
Then Simon his son said to Rabbi Judah:
Perhaps that was Jonathan ben Amram, your disciple who has
     refused all his life to profit from the Torah.
They investigated, and found this to be so.
Then Rabbi Judah said: Let everyone enter.

The sufferings

The sufferings of Rabbi Judah the Prince came upon him with
     a certain event, and after a certain other event they
     went from him.
They came upon him with a certain event—how was that? A
     calf that was being led off to slaughter came and hid
     its head in the lap of Rabbi Judah's robe and wept.
     But he said: Go, that is what you were created for.
Then it was said: Because he did not have mercy, suffering
     shall come upon him.
After a certain other event they went from him: One day
     Rabbi Judah's serving maid was sweeping the house,
     and she wanted to sweep out and cast forth some young
     weasels. But he said: Let them be; it is written: "The
     Lord is good to all; and His tender mercies are over all

His works" (Ps. 145:9).

Then it was said: Because he has shown mercy, mercy shall also be shown to him.

Jesters

Rav Beroka of Be Hozae was often in the market at Be Lapat.[27]

There he would meet [the Prophet] Elijah.[28] Once he said to Elijah:

Is there anyone in this market who shall have the world to come?

Elijah said to him: No.

They were standing there when two men came along.

Elijah said to him: These shall have the world to come.

Rav Beroka went to them and said: What is your occupation?

They said to him:

We are jesters, and make the sad to laugh.

When we see two men quarreling,

we strive hard to make peace between them.

The guardian of chastity

The masters saw in a dream how a donkey-driver prayed and rain fell.

The masters sent for him, and he was brought before them.

They asked him: What is your trade?

He replied: I am a donkey-driver.

They asked him: What good thing have you done?

He replied:

Once I hired my donkey to a woman who was crying in the street.

I asked her: What is the matter?

She replied:

My husband is in prison, and I must do whatever I must in order to buy his freedom.

So I went and sold my donkey, and brought her the money; and I said to her:

Here it is; free your husband, and do not sin!

Then the masters said to him:

You are worthy to pray, and to be answered.

Demands

The woman demands with her heart
and the man demands with his mouth.
This is a good quality in women.

Blood

Someone came before Raba and said:
The chief of my town has ordered me:
Go and kill so and so; if you do not, I will have you killed.
Raba said to him: Let him kill you, but you must not kill.
What do you think, your blood is redder than another man's?
Perhaps his blood is redder than yours.

Commendation

When Akabia ben Mahalalel was dying, his son said to him:
Father, commend me to some of your comrades.
Akabia said to him:
I will not commend you.
His son said to him: Is it because of some fault you have
found in me?
He said to him:
No. But your deeds will endear you, and your deeds will es-
trange you.

They that love Him

Our masters have taught:
They that are shamed, and do not shame others,
that hear their disgrace, and do not retort,
that act out of love, and rejoice in chastisements—
it is of them that Scripture says:
"But they that love Him be as the sun when he goeth forth in
his might" (Judg. 5:31).

Today

Rabbi Eliezer said:

Turn to God one day before your death.
His disciples asked him: Does a man know on which day he
     will die?
He answered them:
Just because of this, let him turn to God on this very day, for
     perhaps he must die on the morrow, and thus it will
     come about that all his days will be days of turning to
     God.

Judgment

When a man is led in to be judged,[29] he is asked:
Have you done your business faithfully?
Have you set yourself regular periods to study the Torah?
Have you begotten children after you?
Have you looked forward to redemption?
Have you used all your wits in the study of the Law?
Have you understood how one thing will follow from another?
Yet even so—if "the fear of the Lord is his treasure" (Isa.
     33:6), it will go well with him,
if not, it will not.

Revelation and the Study of the Law

FROM THE TALMUD AND MIDRASH

The awesome event of the revelation on Mount Sinai lay in the past,
and the voice of the prophets, spokesmen of divine will, became silent in the
time of Ezra the Scribe, so taught the talmudic masters. However, the Scriptures are a living record of divine revelation. It is incumbent upon man to
penetrate the surface of what is written and to discover the divine thought and
will. That is the meaning of study: through immersion into the text of Torah,
the learner will perceive anew the word spoken on Sinai.

As a statue

"I am the Lord thy God" (Exod. 20:2):[30]

The Holy One, blessed be he, appeared as a statue which can
be seen from everywhere.
A thousand men gaze at it, and it gazes back at all.
So looked the Holy One, blessed be he, when he was speaking
to Israel.
Each and every one of Israel said to himself:
It is to me the Word is speaking.

All at one time

"And God spoke all these words" (Exod. 20:1).
—All at one and the same time:
taking life and giving life at one and the same time,
afflicting and healing at one and the same time.
Answering the woman in her travail,
those who go down to the sea and the desert farers,
those locked in the prison house,
one in the east and one in the west, one in the north, and one
in the south;
"Forming the light, and creating darkness; making peace and
creating evil'" (Isa. 45:7),
—all at one and the same time.

As the desert

Why was the Torah given in the desert [of Sinai]?
To teach you
that if a man does not hold himself as unpossessed as the
desert,
he does not become worthy of the words of the Torah.

The Torah was given in public, for all to see, in the open.
For if it had been given in the land of Israel, Israel would have
said to the nations of the world, You have no share
in it;
therefore the Torah was given in the wilderness, in public, for
all to see, in the open,
and everyone who wishes to receive it, let him come and receive it.

Israel and the nations

When the Omnipresent revealed himself to give the Torah to
    Israel,
he revealed himself not to Israel alone, but to all the nations.
At first he went to the children of Esau, and said to them:
Will you accept the Torah?
They said to him: What is written in it?
He said to them: "Thou shalt not kill."
They said to him: Master of the Universe, our father was a
    killer by nature;
as it is said [. . .]: "And by the sword shalt thou live"
    (Gen. 27:40).
Then He went to the children of Ammon and Moab and said
    to them:
Will you accept the Torah?
They said to him: What is written in it?
He said to them: "Thou shalt not commit adultery."
They said to him: Master of the Universe, immorality is our
    nature [. . .].
He went and found the children of Ishmael, and said to them:
Will you accept the Torah?
They said to him: What is written in it?
He said to them: "Thou shalt not steal."
They said to him: Master of the Universe, our father was a
    thief by nature [. . .].
There was not a nation of all the nations to whom He did not
    go, and to whom he did not speak, and on whose
    threshold he did not knock, to ask whether they wished
    to receive the Torah. . . .
But even the seven commandments which the children of
    Noah did accept[31] they could not persevere in,
until he lifted their yoke off them, and gave the laws to Israel.

The children

When Israel stood to receive the Torah,
the Holy One, blessed be he, said to them:

I am giving you my Torah. Bring me good guarantors that you
will guard it, and I shall give it to you.
They said: Our patriarchs are our guarantors.
The Holy One, blessed be he, said to them:
Your patriarchs are unacceptable to me,[32]
yet bring me good guarantors, and I shall give it to you.
They said to him:
Master of the Universe, our prophets are our guarantors.
He said to them:
The prophets are unacceptable to me:
"The rulers transgressed against Me; the prophets also proph-
esied by Baal" (Jer. 2:8).
Yet bring me good guarantors, and I shall give it to you.
They said:
Behold, our children are our guarantors.
The Holy One, blessed be he, said:
They are certainly good guarantors.
For their sake I give the Torah to you.

The keepers of the city

Rabbi Judah the Prince asked Rabbi Dosa and Rabbi Ammi
to go forth and inspect the cities in the Land of Israel.
They came to a city and said to the people: Have the keepers
of the city brought before us.
They brought the overseer and the senator.
Then they said to them: Are these the keepers of the city?
Why, these are the destroyers of the city!
Then the people asked them: Who are the keepers of the city?
Thereupon they answered: The teachers of the Scriptures and
of the Tradition, who keep watch by day and by night,
in accordance with the words:
"This book of the law shall not depart out of thy mouth, but
thou shalt meditate therein day and night" (Josh. 1:8).

Witnesses

"And ye are My witnesses, saith the Lord, and I am God"
(Isa. 43:12).

If ye are "my witnesses," I am the Lord,
and if ye are not my witnesses,
I am not, as it were, the Lord.

In thy heart

"For this commandment which I command thee this day, it is
        not too hard for thee, neither is it far off. It is not in
        heaven. . . . Neither is it beyond the sea . . ." (Deut.
        30:11-13).
They said to Moses:
Our master, lo, you say to us it is not in heaven and it is not
        beyond the sea;
then where is it?
He said to them:
In a place that "is very night unto thee, in thy mouth, and in
        thy heart, that thou mayest do it" (v. 14)—
It is not far from you, it is near to you.

What animals teach

Had the Torah not been given us, we could have learned
        modesty from the cat, the command not to rob from
        the ant, chastity from the dove, and propriety from
        the cock.

The core of the commandments

Six hundred and thirteen commandments were given to
        Moses, three hundred and sixty-five prohibitory laws,
        equaling the number of the days of the solar year,
and two hundred and forty-eight mandatory laws,
corresponding to the parts of the body.
David came and brought them down to eleven;
as it is written:
"Lord, who shall sojourn in Thy tabernacle? . . .
He that walketh uprightly, and worketh righteousness, and
        speaketh truth in his heart; that hath no slander upon
        his tongue, nor doeth evil to his fellow, nor taketh up

a reproach against his neighbor; in whose eyes a vile person is despised, but he honoreth them that fear the Lord; he that sweareth to his own hurt, and changeth not; he that putteth not out his money on interest, nor taketh a bribe against the innocent" (Ps. 15:1-5).

Isaiah came and brought them down to six;
as it is written:

"He that walketh righteously and speaketh uprightly; he that despiseth the gain of oppressions, that shaketh his hands from holding of bribes, that stoppeth his ears from hearing of blood, and shutteth his eyes from looking upon evil" (Isa. 33:15).

Micah came and brought them down to three;
as it is written:

"It hath been told thee, O man, what is good . . .: Only to do justly, and to love mercy, and to walk humbly with thy God" (Mic. 6:8).

Isaiah came again and brought them down to two;
as it is said:

"Thus saith the Lord,
Keep ye justice, and do righteousness" (Isa. 56:1).

Amos came and brought them down to one;
as it is said:

"For thus saith the Lord unto the house of Israel:
Seek ye Me, and live" (Amos 5:4).

Or:

Habakkuk came and brought them down to one;
as it is said:

"But the righteous shall live by his faith" (Hab. 2:4).

A greater principle

"Thou shalt love thy neighbor as thyself" (Lev. 19:18).
Rabbi Akiba says: This is the great principle of the Torah.
Ben Azzai says: "This is the book of the generations of Adam: In the day that God created man, in the likeness of God made He him" (Gen. 5:1)—
this is a principle greater than that.

The yoke of freedom

Had Israel gazed deep into the words of the Torah when it
    was given them,
no nation or kingdom could ever rule over them.
And what did it say to them?
Accept upon yourselves the yoke of the kingdom of heaven,
and subdue one another in the fear of heaven,
and deal with one another in charity.

Fire and light

"Now mount Sinai was altogether on smoke, because the Lord
    descended upon it in fire" (Exod. 19:18):
this tells us that the Torah is fire, and was given in the midst
    of fire, and is compared to fire.
As the way of fire is, that when a man is near it, he is burned,
    when far from it, chilled—
so the only way for a man to do is to warm himself in the
    light.

The Torah is called a "fiery law" (Deut. 33:2):
Let all who come to engage in the Torah
see themselves as standing in the midst of fire.

Not in heaven

. . . On that day Rabbi Eliezer [in dispute with other sages]
    brought all the proofs in the world [in support of his
    opinion], but the sages would not accept them.[33]
He said to them: If the law is according to me, let this locust
    tree prove it.
The locust tree moved a hundred cubits. (And some say: four
    hundred cubits.)
The sages said to him: The locust tree cannot prove anything.
Then he said to them: If the law is according to me, let this
    stream of water prove it.
The stream of water turned and flowed backward.
They said to him: The stream cannot prove anything.

Then he said to them: If the law is according to me, let the
walls of the House of Study prove it.

The walls of the House of Study began to topple.

Rabbi Joshua reprimanded the walls:

If scholars are disputing with one another about the law, what
business is it of yours?

They did not fall down out of respect for Rabbi Joshua, and
did not straighten up out of respect for Rabbi Eliezer,
and they are still inclined.

Then Rabbi Eliezer said to them: If the law is according to
me, let the heaven prove it.

A voice came forth from heaven and said:

Why do you dispute with Rabbi Eliezer? The law is according
to him in every case.

Thereupon Rabbi Joshua rose to his feet and said:

"It is not in heaven" (Deut. 30:12):

the Torah has already been given once and for all from Mount
Sinai;

we do not listen to voices from heaven.

For Thou hast already written in the Torah on Mount Sinai:

"After the majority must one incline" (Exod. 23:2).

[Later on] Rabbi Nathan came upon Elijah [the prophet].[34]

He said to him: What was the Holy One, blessed be he, doing
at that moment?

Elijah said to him:

He was smiling and saying: My children have defeated me,
my children have defeated me!

The trapper

[The Prophet] Elijah,[35] of blessed memory, said:

Once I was on a journey and came upon a certain man who
began to mock and scoff at me.

I said to him: What will you answer on the Day of Judgment,
since you have not learned Torah?

He said: I will be able to answer: I was given no understanding and knowledge and intelligence by heaven.

I said to him: What is your trade?

He said to me: I am a trapper of birds and fish.

I said to him:

Who gave you the knowledge and intelligence to take flax
and to spin and to weave it, and to make nets, and to
take fish and birds in them, and to sell them?

He said to me: The understanding and knowledge for that
were given me by heaven.

I said to him: You were given understanding and knowledge
to take the flax, to spin and to weave it, and to take fish
and birds in the nets,

but you were given no understanding to gain Torah?

Yet it is written:

"But the word is very nigh unto thee, in thy mouth, and in
thy heart that thou mayest do it" (Deut. 30:14).

At once he considered the matter in his heart, and lifted up
his voice and wept.

The vessels

A parable:

A man came to the shopkeeper to buy a measure of wine.

The shopkeeper said to him: Bring me your vessel.

But the man opened his bag.

Then he said to the shopkeeper: Give me some oil.

The shopkeeper said to him: Bring me your vessel.

But the man opened the corner of his garment.

Said the shopkeeper to him: How can you buy wine and oil if
you have no vessel at hand?

Similarly:

God says to the wicked:

You have no good deeds with you—how then do you wish to
learn Torah!

They questioned Rabban Johanan ben Zakkai:

A sage who fears sin—what is he like?

He answered them: He is an artisan with the tools of his craft
in his hands.

A sage who does not fear sin—what is he like?

He answered them: He is an artisan without the tools of his
    craft in his hands.
A man who fears sin, but is not a sage—what is he like?
He answered them: He is a man who is no artisan, but one
    who has the tools of the craft in his hands.

For love of Torah

Rabbi Johanan[36] was walking from Tiberias to Sepphoris, and
    Rabbi Hiyya bar Abba was supporting him.
They came to a certain field, and Rabbi Johanan said:
This field was mine, and I sold it in order to gain the Torah.
They came to a certain vineyard, and he said:
This vineyard was mine, and I sold it in order to gain the
    Torah.
They came to a certain olive grove, and he said:
This olive grove was mine, and I sold it in order to gain the
    Torah.
Rabbi Hiyya began to cry.
Rabbi Johanan said: Why are you crying?
He said to him: Because you left nothing for your old age.
He said to him: Is what I have done a small thing in your eyes?
For I have sold things which [belong to the world] created in
    the course of six days,
and I have gained a thing which was given in the course of
    forty days;
as it is said [of Moses]: "And he was there with the Lord forty
    days and forty nights" (Exod. 34:28).

Should you say:
Lo, I am learning Torah that I may become rich,
and that I may be called "Master,"
and that I may receive a reward
—therefore it is said: "to love the Lord your God" (Deut.
    11:13), all that you do you must do only out of love.

The free gift

. . . [God] showed Moses all the treasures that are the reward
    of the righteous for their deeds.

Moses asked: Whose treasure is this?

God answered: The masters of the Torah.

—And whose treasure is this?

—Those who honor them.

Then He showed Moses a treasure greater than all the rest.

Moses said: Master of the Universe, whose is this great treasure?

He said to him:

He who has good deeds, I give him his reward from his own treasure;

and he who has none of his own, freely give from this;

as it is said: "And I will be gracious to whom I will be gracious, and I will show mercy on whom I will show mercy" (Exod. 33:19).

The mark of a man's foot

"And the Lord said unto Moses . . . Behold I will stand before thee there upon the rock in Horeb" (Exod. 17:5-6).

The Holy One, blessed be he, said to him:

Wherever you find the mark of a man's foot,

there I am before you.

Equality

Should you say:

There are children of the elders,

and there are children of the great,

and there are children of the prophets,

—it is said:

"If ye shall diligently keep *all* this commandment" (Deut. 11:22):

Scripture tells us that *all* are equal in the Torah.

And so it is said:

"Moses commanded us a law, an inheritance of the congregation of Jacob" (Deut. 33:4).

—"Priests, Levites, and Israelites" is not written here, but: "the congregation of Jacob."

Why is it that sages do not have sons who are also sages?
So that no one shall think the Torah can be inherited.
Also:
So that they shall not consider themselves superior to the rest
of the community.
Rabbi Hanina said:

Much have I learned from my teachers,
and more from my comrades than from my teachers,
and from my disciples the most.

A man

Whence do we know that even a Gentile who engages in the
Torah is like a high priest?
We learn it from: "Ye shall therefore keep My statutes, and
Mine ordinances, which if a man do, he shall live by
them" (Lev. 18:5).
"Priests, Levites, and Israelites" was not said,
but "a man";
thus you may learn that even a Gentile who engages in the
Torah
—lo, he is like a high priest.

Humility

If a man lowers himself for the sake of Torah,
eats dried-out dates and wears mean clothing,
and sits diligently at the doors of the sages,
every passerby says: This might be a fool!
But in the end you will find that the whole Torah is within
him.

"The small and great are there [in afterlife] alike;
and the servant is free from his master" (Job 3:19):
Don't we know that "the small and great are there"?
The meaning is:
He who makes himself small for the sake of Torah in this
world,
will be great in the world to come;

he who makes himself a servant for the sake of Torah in this
world,
will be a free man in the world to come.

Scholars and kings

A sage takes precedence over a king of Israel;
if a sage dies, we have none like him—
if a king dies, all Israel are eligible for kingship.

The gates

There is no creature the Holy One, blessed be he, rejects,
but he accepts them all.
The gates are open at every hour,
and all who wish to enter, may enter.
Therefore it is said:
"My doors I opened to the wanderer" (Job 31:32)
—meaning the Holy One, blessed be he, who suffers his creatures.

Israel: A Holy Community

FROM THE TALMUD AND MIDRASH

Is Israel a people, a nation or a religion? The argument persisted for
centuries and various definitions were put forward and rejected. The talmudic
Haggadah, in describing Israel, offers an indication of what the Jewish people
considered themselves to be after the loss of the last vestiges of national independence, and (in the passage, "Jacob's Ladder") how they interpreted
their precarious position in the framework of the nations of the world, which,
following the law of historic life, rise and fall.

Three signs

This people is known by three signs:
Being compassionate, shamefaced, and charitable.
Everyone who has these three signs is worthy of cleaving to
this people.

Poverty

What is the meaning of the Scriptural verse:
"Behold, I have refined thee, but not as silver; I have tried
     thee in the furnace of poverty" (Isa. 48:10)?
It teaches that the Holy One, blessed be he, went over all the
     good qualities that he might give Israel, and found
     poverty the best.
That is what people say:
Poverty is becoming to Jews, like a red halter on a white horse.

Like oil

"Thy name is as oil poured forth" (Cant. 1:3).[37]
As oil is bitter to begin with, but sweet in the end,
so: "And though thy beginning was small, yet thy end should
     greatly increase" (Job 8:7).
As oil improves only through being pressed,
so Israel cannot turn from sin,
except through chastisement.
As oil which when a drop of water falls into a full cup of oil,
     a drop of the oil spills out,
so, when a word of Torah enters the heart, a word of scoffing
     leaves it;
when a word of scoffing enters the heart, a word of Torah
     leaves it.
As oil brings light to the world,
so Israel brings light to the world;
as it is said: "And nations shall walk at thy light, and kings at
     the brightness of thy rising" (Isa. 60:3).
As oil is soundless,
so Israel is soundless in this world.

Jacob and Esau

"The voice is the voice of Jacob, but the hands are the hands
     of Esau" (Gen. 27:22).
The nations of the world entered before Abnimos the weaver.[38]
They said to him:

Can we attack this nation?
He said to them:
Go and pass before their Houses of Study and Houses of
      Prayer.
If you there hear children chanting, you cannot attack them.
But if you do not hear children chanting, you can attack them.
For thus their father assured them:
"The voice is the voice of Jacob";
So long as the voice of Jacob is chanting in Houses of Study
      and Houses of Prayer,
the hands are not "the hands of Esau."[39]

Sharing

Every distress that Israel and the nations of the world share
is a distress indeed.
Every distress that is Israel's alone
is no distress.

In that night when Israel crossed the Red Sea,
the angels desired to sing a song before God.
But the Holy One, blessed be he, forbade it, and said to them:
My legions are in distress, and you would sing a song in my
      presence?

Jacob's ladder [40]

"And he dreamed, and behold a ladder set up on the earth,
      and the top of it reaching to heaven; and behold the
      angels of God ascending and descending on it" (Gen.
      28:12).
—Teaching us that Holy One, blessed be he, showed to our
      father Jacob
the lord of Babylonia[41] ascending and descending,
and the lord of Media ascending and descending,
and the lord of Greece ascending and descending,
and the lord of Rome ascending and descending.
The Holy One, blessed be he, said to him: Jacob, you must
      ascend too!
Then our father Jacob grew very fearful and said:

But perhaps, as they shall have to descend, I, too, shall have
to descend.
The Holy One, blessed be he, said to him:
"Be not dismayed, O Israel" (Jer. 30:10). If you ascend, you
shall never have to descend.

But Jacob did not have faith, and did not ascend.
The Holy One, blessed be he, said to him:
If you had had faith and ascended, you would never have
descended again.
But now that you have not had faith, and have not ascended,
your children will be enslaved to four kingdoms in this world,
through duties, taxes in kind, fines and poll taxes.
Then Jacob grew very fearful and said to the Holy One,
blessed be he: Will that last forever?
He said to him (ibid.): "Be not dismayed, O Israel,
for behold I will save thee from afar"—from Babylonia.
"And thy seed from the land of their captivity will return"—
from Gaul and Spain and the neighboring lands.
"And Israel shall return"—from Babylonia.
"And be quiet"—from Media.
"And at ease"—from Greece.
"And none shall make him afraid"—from Rome.

Peace

FROM THE TALMUD AND MIDRASH

The very numerous sayings on the importance of peace in personal,
communal, political, or religious life, scattered over the talmudic and midrashic
literature, represent a tradition of some four centuries. They are documents of
nonpolitical Judaism in the form it took after the destruction of Judaea. Here
Israel apprehends its activities as culminating in peace, utilizing the Torah as
an instrument of peace and as a blueprint of the worship of God, conceived
as a God of peace. In addition to scattered sayings, certain portions within
the talmudic-midrashic works can be recognized as anthologies, or remnants of
anthologies on peace. As a rule the individual maxims are introduced by the
phrase, "Great is peace."

Great is peace, because peace is for the earth what yeast is for
    the dough.
If the Holy One, blessed be he, had not given peace to the
    earth,
it would be depopulated by the sword and by hosts of animals.

The world rests upon three things: On justice, on truth, on
    peace.
Yet, those three are one and the same thing.
For if there is justice, there is truth, and there is peace.
And these three are expressed in one and the same verse:
"Execute the judgment of truth and peace in your gates"
    (Zech. 8:16).
Wherever there is justice, there is peace, and wherever there is
    peace, there is justice.

See how great is his reward who makes peace between men.
It is written: "Thou shalt build the altar of the Lord thy God
    of unhewn stones" (Deut. 27:6).
If these stones which cannot hear and cannot see and cannot
    smell and cannot speak,
because they make peace between men through the sacrifices
    that are offered upon them
Scripture saves them from the sword and declares:
"Thou shalt lift no iron tool upon them" (*ibid.* v.5)
—man, who can hear and see and smell and speak,
how much more is this true of him, when he makes peace be-
    tween his fellow-men.

Great is peace,
for Aaron the priest was praised only because he was a peace-
    able man.
For it was he who loved peace, who pursued peace, who was
    first to offer peace, and who responded to peace;
as it is written:
"He walked with Me in peace and uprightness" (Mal. 2:6).
And what is written thereafter?
"And did turn many away from iniquity."
This teaches: If ever he saw two men who hated each other,

he went to one of them and said to him: "Why do you
hate that man? For he came to my house, and prostrated himself before me and said: 'I have sinned
against him!' Go and pacify him!"
And Aaron left him and went to the second man and spoke to
him as to the first.
Thus it was his wont to set peace and love and friendship between man and man, and he 'did turn many away from
iniquity.'

Great is peace,
for we seal all benedictions and all prayers with "peace."
The recitation of "Hear, O Israel" we seal with "peace":
"Spread the tabernacle of peace."
The benediction of the priests is sealed with "peace":
"And give thee peace" (Num. 6:26).

Thus spoke the Holy One, blessed be he, to Israel:
"You have caused my house to be destroyed and my children
to be banished—
but ask for Jerusalem's peace and I shall forgive you."
He, however, who loves peace, who pursues peace, who offers
peace first, and responds to peace,
the Holy One, blessed be he, will let him inherit the life of
this world and the world to come,
as it is written:
"But the humble shall inherit the land, and delight themselves in the abundance of peace" (Ps. 37:11).

Exile and Redemption

FROM THE TALMUD AND MIDRASH

That the fall of the Temple in the year 70 was proof that God had
forsaken Israel was an argument used by the early Christian community that
called itself the new Israel. The talmudic sages rejected this argument. It was
their contention that the divine presence (*Shekhinah*) never left Israel. It

accompanies Israel into exile, partakes in its sufferings, and will partake in its ultimate redemption. The date and the manner of redemption mattered less (especially in the first generations after the year 70) than people's internal preparedness. If they would "but hearken to His voice," Messiah would come today.

The keys of the Temple

When the Temple was about to be destroyed, the young
          priests assembled in bands with the keys of the Temple
          in their hands, and went up to the roof of the Temple,
          and said before Him:
Master of the Universe, seeing that we have not been worthy
          to be faithful treasurers, let the keys be given back to
          you,
and they threw them heavenwards.
Then something like a hand came forth and received the keys
          from them.
Whereupon they leaped and fell into the fire.

Love

"For I am love-sick" (Cant. 2:5).
The congregation of Israel said to the Holy One, blessed be
          he:
Master of the Universe, all the ills you bring upon me—are to
          bring me to love you the more.
Another interpretation:
The congregation of Israel said to the Holy One, blessed be he:
Master of the Universe, all the ills the nations of the world
          bring upon me—
are because I love you.

Divine Presence in exile

You find:
Every place where Israel was exiled, the Divine Presence was
          with them.
They were exiled to Egypt, the Presence was with them.
They were exiled to Babylon, the Presence was with them.
They were exiled to Elam, the Presence was with them.

They were exiled to Rome, the Presence was with them.
And when they shall return, the Presence, as it were, will be
    with them.

Waiting

"For with thee is the fountain of life; in Thy light do we see
    light" (Ps. 36:10).
As one who was journeying at the time of the sinking of the
    sun,
and someone came and lit a candle for him, and it went out;
and another came and lit a candle for him, and it went out.
He said: From now on, I shall wait for the morning light
    alone.
So, Israel said to the Holy One, blessed be he:
Master of the Universe, we made a lamp for you in the days of
    Moses, and it went out;
ten lamps in the days of Solomon,[42] and they went out.
From now on we will wait for your light alone:
"In Thy light do we see light."

Today

Rabbi Joshua, son of Levi, came upon the prophet Elijah[43]
    and asked him: "When will the Messiah come?"
The other replied: "Go and ask him yourself."
"Where is he to be found?"
"Before the gates of Rome."
"By what sign shall I know him?"
"He is sitting among poor lepers: the others unbind all their
    sores at once, and then bind them up again, but he
    unbinds one wound at a time, and binds it up again
    straightway, thinking, should I perhaps be needed [to
    appear as the Messiah] I shall not be delayed."
So he went and found him and said: "Peace be with you, my
    master and teacher!"
He answered him: "Peace be with you, son of Levi!"
Then he asked him: "When are you coming, master?"
He answered him: "Today!"

Thereupon he returned to Elijah and said to him: "He has deceived me, he said he would come today, and he has not come."

Elijah answered: "This is what he meant: 'Today—if ye would but hearken to His voice' (Ps. 95:7)."[44]

The real redemption

Israel said to the Holy One, blessed be he:

Have you not redeemed us already through Moses and Joshua and all the judges and kings?

Yet now are we to return to be enslaved and be ashamed, as though we had never been redeemed?

The Holy One, blessed be he, said to them:

Seeing that your redemption was at the hands of flesh and blood,

and your leaders were men, here today, tomorrow in the grave;

therefore your redemption has been redemption for a space.

But in time to come I myself will redeem you;

I, who am living and enduring,

will redeem you with a redemption enduring forever;

as it is said:

"O Israel, that art saved by the Lord with an everlasting salvation" (Isa. 45:17).

The Messiah

The garment in which [God] will clothe the Messiah will shine forth from one end of the world to the other.

Those of Israel will make use of his light, and will say:

Blessed the hour in which the Messiah was created;

blessed the womb from which he came;

blessed the generation which sees him;

blessed the age that waited for him.

The opening of his lips is blessing and peace;

his speech is pleasure of spirit;

his garment is glory and majesty;

his words bring confidence and rest,

his tongue pardon and forgiveness;
his prayer is a sweet savor,
his supplication holiness and purity.
Blessed are you, Israel, for what is in store for you.

Messiah and the world to come

Samuel[45] said:
There is no difference between this world and the days of the
    Messiah except [that they will be free of the] servitude
    to the [foreign] kingdoms.
Rabbi Johanan[46] said:
All the prophets prophesied only for the days of Messiah, but
    what concerns the world to come—
"no eye hath seen, oh God, beside Thee, what He will do for
    him that waiteth for Him" (Isa. 64:3).[47]

Rav used to say:
Not like this world is the world to come.
In the world to come there is no eating nor drinking;
no procreation of children or business; no envy, or hatred, or
    competition;
but the righteous sit, their crowns on their heads,
and enjoy the splendor of the Divine Presence.

Planting

Rabban Johanan ben Zakkai used to say:
If there be a plant in your hand when they say to you:
Behold the Messiah!
—Go and plant the plant, and afterward go out to greet him.[48]

Reflections on the Book of Job

FROM THE TALMUD AND MIDRASH

In contradistinction to the author of the Testament of Job, the talmudic
sages acknowledge Job as a rebel and an accuser of God who multiplies his

wounds "without cause." They contrast Job, whom they consider one of the
heathen prophets, with Abraham, the lover of God. But, although Job is
known as one "who feared the Lord" the talmudic masters try to understand
this "fear" as implying the motive of "love." It is the Lord's work to inform
Job that in spite of the apparent injustice and anarchy, He is still concerned
with His creation and with man. The personal element, missing in God's
answer to Job in the Bible, is restored by the sages.

Heathen prophets

Seven prophets prophesied to the nations of the world.
Balaam and his father, Job [and his friends] Eliphaz the Te-
    manite, Bildad the Shuhite, Zophar the Naamathite,
    and Elihu the son of Barachel the Buzite.

Unaided knowledge

There are four persons who came to know the Holy One,
    blessed be he, out of their own thinking:
Abraham: There was no man who would have taught him how
    to know God; he reached this knowledge by himself;
Likewise Job, of whom it is said: "I have treasured in my
    bosom the words of His mouth" (Job 23:12).
Likewise Hezekiah, King of Judah, about whom it is said: ". . .
    when he knoweth to refuse the evil, and choose the
    good" (Isa. 7:15).
The King Messiah, too, by himself did he reach the knowledge
    of the Holy One, blessed be he.

Who can hinder Thee

". . . Although Thou knowest that I shall not be condemned;
    and there is none that can deliver out of Thy hand"
    (Job 10:7).
Raba said:
Job sought to free the whole world from judgment.
He said: Lord of the Universe, Thou hast created the ox with
    his cloven hoofs and Thou hast created the ass with his
    whole hoofs;
Thou hast created Paradise and Thou hast created Gehin-
    nom;[49]

Thou hast created the righteous ones and Thou hast created
    the wicked ones—
who is it that can hinder Thee?[50]
What did Job's friends answer him?
"Yea, thou doest away with fear, and impairest devotion be-
    fore God" (15:4);
The Holy One, blessed be he, did create the evil impulse,
but he also created the Torah with which to season it.

Fear of God and love of God[51]

It is written of Job, "one that feared God" (1:1)
and it is written of Abraham, "Thou fearest God" (Gen.
    22:12):
now, just as "fearing God" with Abraham implies [that he
    acted] from love,
so "fearing God" with Job implies [that he acted] from love.

Rabbi Joshua ben Hyrcanus expounded:
Job served the Holy One, blessed be he, only from love,
as it is written: "Though He slay me, yet will I trust in Him"
    (13:15),
or, clearer still: "Till I die I will not put away mine integrity
    from me" (27:5)—
teaching that he acted from love.
Rabbi Joshua [ben Hananiah] said:
Who will remove the dust from your eyes, Rabban Johanan
    ben Zakkai,
for all your life you have used to expound that Job served God
    only from fear,
as it is said: "That man was whole-hearted and upright, and
    one that feared God and shunned evil" (1:1)
and now, Joshua, the disciple of your disciple, taught us that
    Job acted from love.

Abraham and Job

Rabbi Levi said:
The statement made by Abraham is like the statement made
    by Job;

but Job expressed it rashly and Abraham deliberately.

Job said: "It is all one—therefore I say: He destroyeth the
    innocent and the wicked" (9:22);

but Abraham said: "Wilt Thou indeed sweep away the right-
    eous and the wicked?" (Gen. 18:23).

Rabbi Johanan said:

Greater is what is said of Job than what is said of Abraham.

Of Abraham Scripture says: "For now I know that thou fear-
    est God" (Gen. 22:12),

whereas of Job it is said: "That man was whole-hearted and
    upright, and one that feared God and shunned evil"
    (1:1).

Rabbi Levi said:

Satan [in speaking to God]⁵² acted out of a sacred intention:

When he saw that the Holy One, blessed be he, favored Job,
    he thought:

Far be it that He should forget the love of Abraham.

[Later,] when Rav Aha bar Jacob reported this interpretation
    in Papunia,

Satan came and kissed his feet.

Satan

Rabbi Yitzhak said:

The pain of the Satan⁵³ was stronger than that of Job;

the Satan can be compared to a servant to whom his master
    said: Break the barrel but preserve the wine therein.

No resurrection

"As the cloud is consumed and vanisheth away, so he that
    goeth down to the grave shall come up no more" (7:9);

this shows that Job denied the resurrection of the dead.

Job the rebel

"Oh that my vexation were but weighed, and my calamity
    laid in the balances altogether!" (6:2).

Rav said:

Dust should be put into the mouth of Job
[because he spoke as if there were] an equality with heaven
    [on the part of man].
"There is no arbiter betwixt us, that might lay his hand upon
    us both" (9:33).
Rav said:
Is there a servant who may argue against his master?

Enemy of God?

"He would break me with a tempest and multiply my wounds
    without cause" (9:17).
Job said to Him:
Master of the Universe, perhaps a tempest has passed before
    Thee and thus Thou confusest Iyob [Job] and Oyeb
    [enemy]? [54]
He answered him out of the tempest:
"Gird up now thy loins like a man; for I will demand of thee,
    and declare thou unto Me" (38:3):
Many hairs have I created in man, and for every hair I have
    created a groove of its own, so that two hairs should
    not suck from one groove . . .
I do not confuse grooves, how could I confuse Iyob and Oyeb?
"Who hath cleft a channel for the waterflood?" (38:25):
Many drops have I created in the clouds, and for every drop
    a mould of its own, so that two drops should not come
    forth from one mould; for should two drops come forth
    from one mould they would wash away the soil and it
    would not bring forth fruit.
I do not confuse drops, how could I confuse Iyob and Oyeb?
"Or a way for the lightning of the thunder" (ibid.):
Many thunderclaps have I created in the clouds, and for each
    clap a path of its own, so that two claps should not
    issue in the same path . . .
I do not confuse thunderclaps, how could I confuse Iyob and
    Oyeb?
"Knowest thou the time when the wild goats of the rock bring
    forth?" (39:1):

The wild goat is cruel to her young. When she crouches to
   give birth, she goes up to the top of the mountain so
   that the young should fall off and die; so I prepare an
   eagle to catch it in his wings and put it before her;
   should the eagle be one second too early or one second
   too late the young would be killed.
I do not confuse the seconds, how could I confuse Iyob and
   Oyeb?
"Or canst thou mark when the hinds do calve?" (*ibid.*)
The calf has a narrow womb. When she crouches to give birth,
   I prepare a serpent that bites her at the opening of the
   womb and she is delivered from her young; were the
   serpent one second too early or too late, she would die.
I do not confuse the seconds, how could I confuse Iyob and
   Oyeb?
"Job speaks without knowledge and his words are without
   wisdom" (34:35).

The turning point

As long as Job stood against his friends and his friends against
   him,
the attribute of divine justice[55] prevailed;
only after they made peace with each other and Job prayed
   for his friends,
the Holy One, blessed be he, returned to him,
as it is said:
"And the Lord turned the fortune of Job, when he prayed for
   his friends" (42:10).

Blessing

When Rabbi Johanan finished the Book of Job, he used to
   say:
The end of man is death
the end of cattle is to slaughter—
all are doomed to die.
Blessed is he who has grown in the Torah
and whose toil is in the Torah,

and who is giving pleasure to his Maker;
who has grown up with a good name
and with a good name departs from this world.

Prayers of the Masters

FROM THE TALMUD TRACTATE BERAKHOT

In addition to the regular order of daily devotion it was the custom of
the talmudic masters to utter a self-composed private prayer. The following is
a brief collection quoted in the talmudic tractate Berakhot ("Benedictions").
As public worship developed, many such meditations were incorporated into
the regular prayer book.

May it be Thy will, O Lord our God,
to cause to dwell in our lot, love, brotherliness, peace and
      friendship;
to enrich our boundaries through disciples,
to prosper our goal with hope and with future,
to set us a share in Paradise,
to cause us to obtain good companions and good impulse in
      Thy world;
that we may rise in the morning and find
our heart longing to hear Thy name.

May it be Thy will, O Lord our God,
to look upon our shame,
to behold our misery;
clothe Thyself in Thy mercy,
and cover Thyself in Thy power,
and wrap Thyself in Thy love,
and gird Thyself in Thy grace;
may the attribute of Thy kindness and mildness
come before Thee.

May it be Thy will, O Lord our God,
that we do not sin,
so that we fall not into shame or disgrace before our fathers.

May it be Thy will, O Lord our God,
that Thy Torah be our occupation,
that our hearts be not grieved
nor our eyes darkened.

May it be Thy will, O Lord our God,
to grant us long life, a life of peace, of good,
a life of blessing, of sustenance, of bodily vigor;
a life in which there is fear of sin
a life free from shame and disgrace, a life of prosperity and
          honor,
a life in which we may have the love of Torah and the fear
          of heaven,
a life in which Thou shalt fulfil all the wishes of our heart for
          good.

Master of the Universe,
it is known and apparent before Thee
that it is our will to do Thy will.
But what hinders us?
The ferment in the dough,[56] and servitude to the [foreign]
          kingdoms.
May it be Thy will to save us out of their hands,
so that we may again do the commandments of Thy will
with a whole heart.

My God, before I was formed
I had no worth
and now that I am formed,
it is as though I had not been formed.
Dust I am in my life,
and how much more in my death!
Here am I, in Thy presence,
like a vessel filled with shame and disgrace.
May it be Thy will, O Lord my God,
that I sin no more,
and the sins I have committed before Thee
purge them away in Thy great mercy,
but not through suffering and grave disease,

My God,
Keep my tongue from evil,
and my lips from speaking guile.
To those who slander me, let my soul be silent,
my soul shall be to all as dust.
Open my heart to Thy Torah,
let my soul pursue Thy commandments.
And deliver me from evil schemes, from the evil impulse,
and from an evil woman,
from all evil that rushes to come into the world.
But as for those who think evil against me,
speedily break their plots and destroy their thoughts.
Let the words of my mouth
and the meditation of my heart
be acceptable in Thy presence,
O Lord, my rock, my redeemer.

O my God, the soul that Thou hast given me is pure!
Thou didst create it, Thou didst form it, Thou didst breathe
it into me, Thou preservest it within me,
In time Thou wilt take it from me, and return it to me in the
life to come.
As long as the soul is within me, I will give thanks unto Thee,
O Lord my God, and the God of my fathers,
master of all deeds, lord of all souls!

Reflections on Life

FROM SEDER ELIYAHU RABBA

Using older material, a tenth-century author, whose country of residence is in doubt (Palestine? Babylonia? Italy?), composed a collection of
teachings, maxims and parables on the wide scope of nonlegal talmudic-midrashic themes: Creation and world order; law and commandments; study and
teaching; repentance and charity; joy of life and humility; and divine love that

encompasses all His creatures. The title of the book, *Tanna debe Eliyahu*, or *Seder Eliyahu*, refers to the teachings of the prophet Elijah, whom the talmudic legend pictures as frequenting the academies of Palestine, imparting moral and religious advice. The book, written in Hebrew and divided into two parts (*Seder Eliyahu Rabba*, The Large Order of Elijah, and *Seder Eliyahu Zutta*, The Small Order of Elijah), is characterized by stylistic beauty and warm human appeal. Little known in the Middle Ages, it became popular when it appeared in print (Venice, 1598). A critical edition appeared in 1902, based on a manuscript in the Vatican Library dating from the year 1073.

Every day

Every day man is sold, and every day redeemed.

Every day man's spirit is taken from him and [. . .] returned to him in the morning.

Every day miracles are worked for him as for those who went out of Egypt.

Every day redemption is worked for him, as for those who went out of Egypt.

Every day he is fed on the breasts of his mother.

Every day he is chastised for his deeds, like a child by his teacher.

Surpassing both

King David said:

I, what am I in this world?

I have been fearful in the midst of my joy, and have rejoiced in the midst of my fear,

and my love has surpassed them both.

Preparation

Let a man do good deeds, and then ask Torah from the Omnipresent.

Let a man do righteous and fitting deeds, and then ask wisdom from the Omnipresent.

Let a man seize the way of humility, and then ask understanding from the Omnipresent.

Man's deeds

I call heaven and earth to witness:
whether it be heathen or Israelite,
whether it be man or woman, manservant or maidservant,
all according to his deeds
does the holy spirit rest upon a man.

Heaven and man

. . . The Holy One, blessed be he, continued to appease
   Moses.
He said to him:
Am I not your Father, and you my children,
you my brothers, and I your brother;
you my friends, and I your friend;
you my lovers, and I your lover;
Have I allowed you to lack?
All that I ask you in this, as I have examined myself and found
   eleven qualities,
so all I ask of you is eleven qualities;
and they are:
"He that walketh upright, and worketh righteousness,
And speaketh truth . . . " (Ps. 15:2-5).

The Holy One, blessed be he, continued to appease Moses.
He said to him:
Do I at all favor an Israelite or a Gentile,
a man or a woman, a manservant or a maidservant?
But whoever he is who keeps a commandment, the reward is
   at its heels.
Hence it was said:
He who honors heaven more, heaven's honor is more, and his
   own honor is more, as well.
He who honors heaven less, and honors himself more,
heaven's honor continues the same, but his own honor is less.

Provision

I call heaven and earth to be my witness,
that the Holy One, blessed be he, is sitting and dividing pro-

visions with his own hand
among all who come into the world,
and among all the handiwork that he created in the world;
from man to beast, to creeping thing, and to the bird in the
    sky.

Prayer

David, King of Israel, said:
My Father who art in heaven
blessed be Thy great Name for all eternity
and mayest Thou find contentment from Israel, Thy servants,
    wherever they may dwell.
Thou hast reared us, made us great, sanctified us, praised us;
Thou hast bound on us the crown of the words of Torah
they that reach from end to end of the world.
Whatever of Torah I have fulfilled, this came only through
    Thee;
whatever loving-kindness I have shown, this came only through
    Thee;
in return for the little of Torah that I have done before Thee
Thou hast given me a share in this world, in the days of the
    Messiah, and in the world to come.

In the midst of sorrow

When Moses descended from Mount Sinai, and saw the
    abominations of Israel,
he gazed at the tablets and saw that the words had flown away,
and broke them at the foot of the hill.
At once he fell dumb. He could not say a word.
At that moment a decree was passed concerning Israel,
that they were to study these same words
in the midst of sorrow and in the midst of slavery,
in migration, and in confusion,
in pressing poverty, and in lack of food.
For the sorrow they have suffered,

the Holy One, blessed be he, shall reward them during the
        days of the Messiah,
many times over.

Meeting

How does a man find his Father who is in heaven?
He finds him by good deeds, and study of the Torah.
And the Holy One, blessed be he, finds man
through love, through brotherhood, through respect,
through companionship, through truth, through peace,
through bending the knee, through humility,
through studious session, through commerce lessened,
through service of the masters, through the discussion of
        students,
through a good heart, through decency,
through No that is really No,
through Yes that is really Yes.

The Oral Law

Once I was on a journey, and I came upon a man who went
        at me after the way of heretics.
Now, he accepted the Written Law, but not the Oral Law.[57]
He said to me:
The Written Law was given us from Mount Sinai;
the Oral Law was not given us from Mount Sinai.
I said to him:
But were not both the Written and the Oral Law spoken by
        the Omnipresent?
Then what difference is there between the Written and the
        Oral Law? To what can this be compared?
To a king of flesh and blood who had two servants, and loved
        them both with a perfect love;
and he gave them each a measure of wheat, and each a bundle
        of flax.
The wise servant, what did he do?
He took the flax and spun a cloth.

Then he took the wheat and made flour.
The flour he cleansed, and ground, and kneaded, and baked,
    and set on top of the table.
Then he spread the cloth over it, and left it so until the king
    should come.
But the foolish servant did nothing at all.
After some days, the king returned from a journey and came
    into his house and said to them:
My sons, bring me what I gave you.
One servant showed the wheaten bread on the table with a
    cloth spread over it,
and the other servant showed the wheat still in the box, with
    a bundle of flax upon it.
Alas for his shame, alas for his disgrace!
Now, when the Holy One, blessed be he, gave the Torah to
    Israel,
he gave it only in the form of wheat, for us to extract flour
    from it,
and flax, to extract a garment.

To walk humbly

Thus said the Holy One, blessed be he, to Israel:
My children, have I allowed you to lack?
What do I seek of you?
All I ask is that you love one another,
and honor one another, and respect one another,
and let there be found in you neither transgression nor theft
    nor any ugly thing;
so that you never become tainted;
as it is said: "It hath been told thee, O man, what is good
    . . . and to walk humbly with thy God" (Mic. 6:8)
—do not read: "Walk humbly with thy God,"
but rather: "Walk humbly, and thy God will be with thee"
—as long as you are with Him in humility,
He will be with you in humility.

Notes

1. I. F. Baer, "The Historical Foundations of the Halacha," *Zion*, XVII (1952); "The Ancient Hasidim in Philo's Writings and in Hebrew Tradition," *Zion*, XVIII (1953).

2. H. A. Wolfson, *Philo: Foundations of Religious Philosophy in Judaism, Christianity and Islam* (Cambridge: Harvard University Press, 1947).

3. E. Bickerman, *The Maccabees* (New York: Schocken Books, 1947).

4. W. F. Albright, *From the Stone Age to Christianity* (2d ed.; Baltimore: Johns Hopkins University Press, 1940), ch. VI.

5. E. Schürer, *A History of the Jewish People*, (New York: Schocken Books, 1961), p. 21.

6. *See* A. Kaminka, "Hillel's Life and Work," *The Jewish Quarterly Review*, N.S., XXX, 107-122.

7. W. Jaeger, *Paideia: the Ideals of Greek Culture*, trans. G. Highet (3 vols.; New York: Oxford University Press, 1939 seq.).

8. Flavius Josephus, *War*., II, 8:14.

9. Flavius Josephus, *ibid*., II, 8:7.

I

1. Creation of man by God implies to the author that evil was not intended; evil resulted from man following freely his "inclination" (Hebrew, *Yetzer*). The theological difficulty still remains.

2. God knows what a man has chosen.

3. Comp. Prov. 13:24: "He that spareth his rod hateth his son."

4. The father lives on in his son.

5. The author tries to justify the physician's job before the adherents of the "old ways" who saw in the physician too modern a figure.

6. *See* Exod. 15:23 f.

7. Sickness is here considered a punishment for wrongdoing.

8. Note the emphasis on travel as aiding in the scribe's education.

9. Simon, surnamed "the Righteous" lived at the beginning of the second century B.C.

10. The Temple.

11. The Holy of Holies; the passage refers to the high priest's service on the Day of Atonement; *see* Lev. 16.

12. This refers to the ceremony of the Feast of Weeks; *see* Num. 28:26.

13. "A covenant of peace to maintain the sanctuary" and the promise of the high priesthood "for ever" (Ben Sira 45:24). Phinehas was the grandson of Aaron.

14. Note the Stoic idea of the world soul.

15. Man's actions are the cause of evil that befalls him.

16. God's mercy is to lead man to repentance.

17. According to a Stoic saying, quoted by Philodemus (*ca.* 50 B.C.)

"the wise are the friends of God and God of the wise."

18. Wisdom as a prerequisite of prophecy is also Stoic teaching.

19. Xenophon's *Memorabilia* (memoirs of Socrates), II, 1, offers a statement parallel to this section.

20. The four cardinal virtues according to Plato and the Stoics.

21. This refers to the temptation of Eve.

22. The righteous are immortal. "The wise man who appears to have departed from this mortal life lives in a life immortal" (Philo).

II

1. He was kept in Rome for twelve years after the defeat of Syria at Magnesia, 190 B.C.

2. The so-called "Seleucid Era" is counted from October 1, 312, on the accession of Seleucus I of Syria.

3. The reference is to the Jewish Hellenists.

4. An operation with the purpose of undoing circumcision by which the heathens recognized a Jew; the athletic exercises in the gymnasium were practiced in the nude.

5. However, Egypt rose again; Antiochus returned to besiege Alexandria and failed.

6. Apollonius (II Macc. 5:24).

7. This citadel was called Acra and was held by a Syrian detachment.

8. The policy of paganization was supported by Jewish Hellenists.

9. The term is taken from Dan. 12:11.

10. "The sons of Joarib" is one of the twenty-four classes of priests.

11. Modin lies east of Lydda (Lud).

12. Num. 25:7 f.

13. "The Pious," members of communities of peasants who adhered strictly to ideals of Torah and the prophets; seeing the threat to the practice of religion they abandoned their peace-loving tenets.

14. The "sacrifice" of Isaac, Gen. 22.

15. Gen. 39.

16. Num. 25:7 f.

17. Josh. 1:2 ff.

18. Num. 13:30 ff.

19. I Sam. 24:4 ff.

20. II Kings 2:1.

21. Dan. 3 and 6.

22. *Ibid.*

23. Judah and his men have won victories over superior Syrian armies; they defeated Apollonius, the governor of Samaria, and Seron, commander of Coele-Syria; they checked three Syrian generals with 40,000 foot soldiers and 7,000 horsemen near Emmaus. An attack by Lysias of Syria who came up from the south, at Beth Zur, was repelled.

24. Exod. 20:25; Deut. 27:5 f.; no iron could be used in cutting the stones.

25. First reference to the Hanukkah (Feast of Lights) celebration.

26. Idumaea, land of Edom, southern neighbor of Judaea.

27. That is, after Simon, Judah the Maccabee's brother, had achieved

the goal of the twenty-years' rebellion: independence from Syria. He captured the Citadel (Acra). The Jewish Hellenists submitted to the newly established government of Simon, or left the country.

28. The modern Jaffa. Simon's capture of the fortress Gazara (the Biblical Gezer) in the plain of Judaea, to assure an easy connection between Jerusalem and Jaffa.

29. After the death of Judah, his brother Jonathan carried on the cause of the rebellion.

30. Jonathan had concluded a treaty of "confederacy and friendship" with Sparta, and renewed the treaty Judah had made with Rome.

31. Approximate value of $35,000.

32. The high priestly office as a part of the Maccabean rule had started with Jonathan; the high priests preceding Jonathan were Hellenists.

33. Simon's descendants (John Hyrcanus, Aristobulus I, Alexander Jannaeus, Salome Alexandra, Aristobulus II, Hyrcanus) ruled the country up to 63 B.C. when Pompey made Judaea tributary to Rome.

III

1. Comp. "the day of the Lord," a term applied by the Biblical prophets to the final day of judgment.

2. The text of this line is possibly corrupt.

3. The netherworld.

4. Note in the following the arguments of "the sinners" (Sadducees?) and the writer's affirmation of the future bliss of the righteous.

5. This refers to the resurrection of the dead which doctrine was variously defined.

6. Title of the Messiah.

7. After "their punishment shall have come from the Lord." The new priesthood, which is to follow the immoral Hellenization of this sacred office, is pictured in Messianic terms.

8. A rare image in Jewish literature.

9. Beliar (Belial): angel of lawlessness, chief of evil spirits.

10. This most probably refers to the Hasmonaean ruling house.

11. The high priesthood.

12. Pompey, who in 63 B.C. entered Jerusalem and established Roman rule in Judaea.

13. *Ibid.*

14. Pompey carried the Hasmonaean Aristobulus II and his children captive to Rome.

15. The society of the Hasidim.

16. Political calamity gave rise to the renewed expectation of the Messianic kingdom.

IV

1. Considered the legitimate family of priests.

2. Or, multitude.

3. A surrogate for the name of God.

4. The perverse men, i.e., the non-sectarians, may not even after puri-

fication touch "the Purity" (food, vessels, rites) of the holy men, i.e., the sectarians.

5. The true Israel is identified with the sectarian brotherhood.

6. The term "Many" appears to be used as a technical term for the membership.

7. Or, as Brownlee suggests, religion.

8. In the original: HUHA, a surrogate of God.

9. In the original the word for "the Lord" is substituted by four dots.

10. The original has the Hebrew letter Aleph, possible esoteric reference to the name of God.

11. The members were to keep secret the teachings of the brotherhood.

12. Belial (Beliar): angel of lawlessness, chief of evil spirits.

13. By observing the laws governing ritual purity.

14. Philo introduces his presentation by contrasting the order of the Therapeutae with the Egyptian animal worship which caused the Egyptians to lose "the most vital of the senses, sight."

15. This notion is Platonic (*Phaedrus*) and goes back to Hesiod.

16. The corresponding Greek word suggests duties performed in rotation (F. H. Colson).

17. Without the aid of a midwife.

18. A Platonic phrase (*Timaeus*).

19. The reference is to the ancient Israelites crossing the Red Sea after the exodus from Egypt.

VI

1. The double meanings of *polis* ("city" and "state"), and of *pheugein* ("to flee," "to be exiled," hence "to be outlawed") clarify this passage. According to the Cynics and the Stoics, the wise man does not regard himself as a citizen of any single state, but as a member of the world state. Citizenship in this world state is based on the possession of reason; Philo interpreted this ethically.

2. This is an allusion to the third meaning of *polis*—the urban in contrast to the rural. The Greeks considered the peasant (*agroikos*) uneducated, just as the Jews so regarded the Am ha-Aretz, and the Romans the *rusticus*.

3. This is the reading of the Septuagint. The Hebrew text reads: "He [God] made them houses."

4. This and the following refers to Exod. 16, Num. 11, Exod. 15:22-25.

5. This refers to Herod and to the Hasmonaean kings who preceded Herod.

6. In A.D. 37, Caligula appointed Agrippa king over the northeastern districts of Herod's kingdom, previously ruled by Herod's son, Philip. His realm was expanded later.

7. Minister in the service of Emperor Augustus and friend of Herod. *See* Flavius Josephus, *War* I, 20:4; *Antiquities* XVI, 2:1; the visit took place in 15 B.C.

8. Comp. "In Praise of the High Priest Simon, Son of Johanan," from the Wisdom of Ben Sira.

9. Succeeding Augustus, Tiberius ruled from 14 to 37.

10. Pontius Pilate, procurator of Judaea (26 to 36) and judge in the trial of Jesus.

11. The residence of the Roman procurators.

12. Another instance of Pilate's outrages is reported by Josephus in *Antiquities* XVIII, 3:1 and *War* II, 9, 2-3.

13. The Day of Atonement. *See* Lev. 16.

14. Edicts of Augustus concerning the Jews' rights "to follow their own customs according to the law of their forefathers" are recorded by Josephus in *Antiquities* XVI, 6:1-3.

15. On other donations of Augustus to the Temple, *see* Josephus, *War* V, 13:6.

16. Julia Major, a daughter of Augustus, married emperor Tiberius, Caligula's grandfather.

17. Emperor Tiberius kept Agrippa in prison.

18. Teacher of rhetoric in Rhodes and in Rome; Cicero and Julius Caesar were his disciples.

19. Alexandrian writer.

20. *Nomos*, law, appears first in Hesiod.

21. In contradistinction to the Greek deities who are born.

22. An adaptation of the four cardinal virtues of the Platonic School.

23. The reference is to Skeptics.

24. The Epicureans.

25. Plato (*Timaeus*), in part followed by Philo, thought of God as creating the world with the aid of collaborators.

26. The Pentateuchal laws (Exod. 23:8, Deut. 16:19 and 27:25) do not impose the death penalty in this case; with some exceptions Josephus follows Scriptural laws.

27. Republic III, 398 A.

28. Fifth century B.C.

29. Fifth century B.C.; known as "the atheist."

30. Fifth century B.C.; he wrote: "Regarding the gods, I am unable to know whether they exist or do not exist."

31. Visited Athens in the time of Solon.

VII

1. The first destruction of Jerusalem (by Babylon) took place in 586 B.C. The author, however, uses the image of the first Temple period to suggest the second Temple, destroyed by Rome in A.D. 70. The date thus refers to A.D. 100.

2. Salathiel (Shealtiel) is the father of Zerubbabel, leader of the Jews, who returned to Zion after the Babylonian Exile, in 538 B.C. (Ezra 3:2; 5:2). The identification of Salathiel with Ezra is fictitious; Ezra appeared in Jerusalem a century later.

3. Babylon stands here for Rome.

4. The apocalyptic starts his argument with Adam, not with Abraham or the Exodus from Egypt.

5. The apocalyptic maintains the idea of the hereditary weakness of human nature. Comp. Romans 5:12 f. Classical Judaism has a more optimistic view of man.

6. The concept of angels (as distinct from "divine messengers") belongs to the late-Biblical and post-Biblical tradition.

7. The human body is the "vessel" of the mind.

8. Comp. the view of the pessimistic School of Shammai against the optimistic view of the School of Hillel, in "Man" (chapter "Hillel the Elder").

9. The habitations of the righteous dead.

10. Hebrew, Yerahmiel.

11. The end will come when the divinely pre-ordained number of the righteous has been completed.

12. The course of history is predetermined; man's action is not a factor.

13. The Antichrist, the eschatological arch-enemy.

14. "We who have received the Law and sinned must perish, together with our heart, which has taken it in: the Law, however, perishes not, but abides in its glory" (IV Ezra 9:36-37).

15. The three years count from Solomon's ascension to the throne to the building of the Temple. Mystically interpreted, the three years refer to three millennia from Creation to the foundation of the Temple.

16. This refers to the "heavenly Jerusalem" which is the model of Jerusalem on earth.

17. The interpretation is based on the inclusiveness implied in the word "all" in the verse quoted.

VIII

1. Over food, the promised land, and over Jerusalem.

2. The Mediterranean.

3. Probably refers to the Sadducees who rejected the belief in a future world.

4. At certain times it may be advisable to void or amend a law in order to preserve the Law as a whole.

5. About 3 P.M.

6. A communal institution for the support of the poorest.

7. This refers to every participant, not only to the poor.

8. A dish of nuts and fruit pounded together and mixed with vinegar. The bitter herbs were dipped into this to mitigate their bitterness.

9. Some texts add: "On other nights we eat all other manner of vegetables, but this night bitter herb."

10. Some texts add: "On other nights we dip but once, but this night twice."

11. Egyptian slavery and idolatry.

12. Son (or grandson) of Hillel the Elder.

13. Exod. 12:27 and 39; 1:14.

14. This refers to the "Hallel" Psalms, 113 to 118.

15. End of Ps. 113.

16. End of Ps. 114.

17. Hebrew *afikoman*, Greek *epi komon*, or *epikomios*, meaning festival procession. The solemn Passover meal with its symbolism must not be followed by an after-dinner revelry which was a customary sequel to the banquet in the Hellenist world, especially for the young.

IX

1. Leader, with Nehemiah, of the Judaean community after the establishment of the Second Temple (*see* Introduction).

2. Quoted from the "Sayings of the Fathers," Mishnaic collection of ethical maxims.

3. The phrase indicates conversion to Judaism.

4. This saying is an affirmation of divine justice; the victim of drowning must himself have drowned somebody. However, the first drowning and its cause remains unexplained and outside of human reasoning.

5. The negative version of the Golden Rule.

6. Seat of the central academy, established after the fall of Jerusalem.

7. Menahot 110a.

8. Prov. 15:1.

9. *Supra* note 7.

10. Learning and wealth.

11. Rabbi Johanan lost ten sons; he carried a bone (or a tooth) of the tenth son with him.

12. God. *See* Dan. 7:9.

13. In the talmudic tradition the term God (*Elohim*) is interpreted as referring to the divine attribute of stern justice, while "Lord" (JHVH) indicates the attribute of love and mercy.

14. Hebrew, *Shekhinah*: the divine element indwelling in the world; the presence of the divine among men.

15. This passage is part of the address by which the Court impressed the witnesses with the seriousness of their testimony.

16. Pico della Mirandola, a representative Renaissance thinker, borrowed this passage for his description of "modern man" (*De hominis dignitate,* Rome 1486).

17. "Evil desire" (Hebrew, *Yetzer ha-Ra,* an urge which is opposed to the desire to do good (*Yetzer ha-Tov*). It is not considered as evil per se, but as a power abused by men. It is rather the "passion" in which all human action originates. Man is called upon to serve God "with both desires."

18. This refers to the miraculous feeding of the Israelites in the wilderness.

19. On this verse later Jewish thought based the doctrine of the "thirteen attributes" of God.

20. Honi, or Onias, a Hasid and miracle worker in the Hasmonean period (*see also* Josephus, *Antiquities* XIV, 2:1).

21. Talmudic tradition considers him to be the youngest disciple of Hillel the Elder. He lived in the period of the destruction of the Second Temple.

22. Gifts to the poor.

23. Festival, liturgic, and ritual requirements.

24. According to the law, the negligent worker is responsible for the loss.

25. Rav (Babylonia, third century) applied the moral rather than the civil law.

26. Editor of the Mishnah, end of second century, and descendant of Hillel the Elder.

27. Be Hozae: Khuzistan, a province in southwest Persia.
Be Lapat: capital of Khuzistan in the Sasanian period.

28. After his ascent to heaven, Elijah, according to legend, continued to appear as a divine messenger, teaching, helping, befriending the pious.

29. The reference is to judgment after death.

30. The starting words of the first commandment.

31. Seven basic laws (prohibition against idolatry, incest, murder, profanation of the name of God, robbery, the duty to form instruments of justice, prohibition against eating parts cut from living animals) to be accepted by the descendants of Noah, i.e., by all men. Hugo Grotius (17th century) took the Noahide commandments as the foundation for his "natural law."

32. Biblical sentences are quoted to justify the rejection.

33. The discussion concerned the question whether an oven of a particular construction was liable of ritual uncleanness. Rabbi Eliezer declared it as clean, the sages as unclean. Both Rabbi Eliezer and Rabbi Joshua (mentioned later) were disciples of Johanan ben Zakkai.

34. *Supra* note 28.

35. *Ibid.*

36. Johanan bar Nappaha of Tiberias, a leading third century scholar.

37. The Song of Songs is interpreted by the Talmud as an allegory on the love between God and Israel.

38. Oinomaos of Gadara (second century B.C.), a member of the school of the younger Cynics. The Midrash (Lam. Rabba, Introd. 2) calls Biblical Balaam and Oinomaos *the* philosophers of the pagans.

39. That is, in this case the hands are without power.

40. This passage, attributed to Rabbi Meir (second century A.D.), should be read as an example of talmudic reflection on Israel's precarious position in world history, here represented by the "four kingdoms," and an expression of her hope in redemption.

41. Each nation is said to have its angelic representation in heaven.

42. The reference is to the desert sanctuary in the time of Moses and Solomon's temple in Jerusalem.

43. *Supra* note 28.

44. A strong affirmation of the belief that redemption depends on the action of man.

45. Leading scholar in Babylonia (third century A.D.).

46. Johanan bar Nappaha of Tiberias, a leading third century scholar.

47. Both sayings militate against a supernatural conception of the Messianic age. The "world to come," on the other hand, is a purely spiritual concept from which historical and national notions are removed. The following saying by Rav (Babylonia, third century A.D.) is especially significant for this understanding of the world to come.

48. For the understanding of this saying it should be remembered that its author lived around the period of the destruction of Jerusalem when many Jews engaged in Messianic and apocalyptic visions.

49. Gehenna; hell.

50. That is, there is no freedom of will and action.

51. Fear and love are considered to be the two possible human atti-

tudes to the divine, the two motives of man's moral action. Naturally, love ranks higher than fear.

52. The Tempter in the prose introduction to the Book of Job.

53. The Satan was given permission to put Job through various trials but was bidden to preserve his life.

54. That is, consider me as your enemy.

55. Strict justice and forgiving mercy are considered to be the two possible divine attitudes to man and world.

56. The evil impulse.

57. Written Law refers to Torah; Oral Law to Tradition; the Sadducees accepted the first, the Pharisees both.

Sources

I

IN PRAISE OF WISDOM: The origin of wisdom, Wisdom of Ben Sira, 1:1-10; The fear of the Lord is true wisdom, *ibid.*, 1:11-20 and 26-30; On free will, *ibid.*, 15:11-20; A man's duties, *ibid.*, 7:11-28 and 32-36; Of women, *ibid.*, 9:1-9 and 25:16-26:4; The training of children, *ibid.*, 30:1-13; The physician, *ibid.*, 38:1-15.

THE IDEAL SCRIBE: *Ibid.*, 39:1-11.

MANIFESTATION OF GOD IN NATURE: *Ibid.*, 43.

THE HIGH PRIEST, SIMON, SON OF JOHANAN: *Ibid.*, 50:1-24.

WISDOM AND THE ORDER OF THIS WORLD: Wisdom is a spirit that loveth man: Wisdom of Solomon, 1:1-15; God—lover of souls, *ibid.*, 11:21-12:2; Wisdom is a breath of the power of God, *ibid.*, 7:22-8:1; Solomon desired wisdom as a bride, *ibid.*, 8:2-18; Immortality, *ibid.*, 2:23-3:9.

II

THE ORIGIN OF THE MACCABEAN REBELLION: First Book of Maccabees, 1-2.

THE REDEDICATION OF THE TEMPLE: *Ibid.*, 4:36-61.

SIMON'S BENEFICENT RULE: *Ibid.*, 14:4-49.

MARTYRDOM OF THE SEVEN BROTHERS AND THEIR MOTHERS: Second Book of Maccabees, 7.

III

THE DAY OF JUDGMENT: Book of Enoch, 102:1-103:4.

THE VICTORY OF THE RIGHTEOUS: *Ibid.*, 50-51.

THE ELECT ONE: *Ibid.*, 49.

A NEW PRIESTHOOD: Testament of Levi, 18:2-14.

THOU ART OUR KING: Psalms of Solomon, 17.

IV

THE RULES OF THE DEAD SEA, OR QUMRAN, BROTHERHOOD: Manual of Discipline, column 5, line 1 to column 6, line 8, and col. 8, lines 1 to 19.

FROM THE SOURCE OF HIS KNOWLEDGE: A Psalm: *Ibid.*, col. 10, line 23 to col. 11, line 15.

HYMNS OF THE DEAD SEA BROTHERHOOD: Streams in dry ground, Thanksgiving Hymns, VIII, 4-12; They seek Thee with a double heart, IV, 5-37.

THE ORDER OF THE ESSENES: Philo, "Every Good Man Is Free" (Probus), XII-XIII.

THE SECT OF THE THERAPEUTAE: Philo, "On the Contemplative Life," II-IV and VIII-XI.

V

JOB THE SAINT: Testament of Job, edited and translated by K. Kohler, *Semitic Studies in Memory of Alexander Kohut*, Berlin, 1897.

VI

HELENISTIC EXPOSITION OF SCRIPTURE: On Hiding From the Presence of God: Philo, *Allegorical Commentary*, III, 1-6 and 28-31; Revelation in the Sinai desert, Philo: *The Decalogue*, I-IV and X; The Sabbath, *The Special Laws* II, ch. XV.

THE EMPEROR'S STATUE: Philo, *Legacy to Gaius*, XXXVI-XLII. (Translation based on C. D. Yonge, *The Works of Philo Judaeus*, vol. IV, London 1855.)

I TAKE REFUGE: Prayer of Asenath. P. Batiffol, Studia Patristica, Paris 1889–1890.

INSPIRED REASON: Fourth Book of Maccabees, 18.

IN DEFENSE OF JUDAISM: Flavius Josephus, *Against Apion*, II, 15-42. (Translation based on *The Works of Flavius Josephus*, by Whiston, revised by A. R. Shilleto, vol. V, London 1890.)

VII

THE HEROES OF MASADA: Flavius Josephus, *The Jewish War*, VII, 8:7.

THE VISION OF A NEW ERA: Fourth Book of Ezra, 3:1-5:15.

THE VISION OF THE DISCONSOLATE WOMAN: *Ibid.*, 9:38-10:57.

THE CONSOLATION OF ZION: Apocalypse of Baruch, 44-46.

THE TEN MARTYRS, Asarah Haruge Malkhut, in *Bet ha-Midrash*, ed. A. Jellinek, vol. VI; Midrash Ele Ezkera, Jellinek, *ibid.*, vol. II. Sanhedrin 14a, Abodah Zarah 17b-18b, Semahot VIII.

VIII

THE ORDER OF BENEDICTIONS: Mishnah Berakhot, VI and IX.

THE SEDER CEREMONY: Mishnah Pesahim, X, 1-8.

HILLEL THE ELDER: The re-established Torah, Sukkah 20a; Education, Soferim XVI, 9; Disciples, Abot de R. Nathan, First Version, III; On disseminating knowledge, Berakhot 63a; Peace, Abot I, 12; The ignorant cannot be a hasid, *ibid.* II, 6; Torah, *ibid.*, II, 8 and 5; With people, Tosefta Berakhot II, 21; cf. Derekh Eretz Zutta V; Teachings, Abot I, 14; II, 8; I, 13; II, 7; Lev. Rabba I, 5; The human body, Lev. Rabba XXXIV, 3; Beautiful bride, Ketubot 16b f; Disaster, Berakhot 60a; The poor man, Ketubot 67b; The wager, Shabbat 30b; The entire Torah on one foot, Shabbat 31a; Every day, Betzah 16a; Man, Erubin 13b; The rival schools, *ibid.*; The heavenly voice, Sotah 48b. (Translations from N. N. Glatzer, *Hillel the Elder*, Washington 1959.)

THE WAYS OF GOOD LIFE: Every day, Berakhot 63b; The gist of it, *ibid.*, 17a; The gates of Torah, *ibid.*; My neighbor, *ibid.*; Brothers, *ibid.*; The final goal, *ibid.*; Chastisements of love, *ibid.*, 5a; Old men, *ibid.*, 8b; Animals first, *ibid.*, 40a; Sinners, ibid., 10a; Far and near, *ibid.*, 34b and 60b f; Beauty, *ibid.*, 5b; The blessing, *ibid.*, 28b; In farewell, *ibid.*, 17a.

CREATION AND MAN: In its time, Gen. Rabba IX, 2; In the beginning, *ibid.*, XII, 15; Between heaven and earth, Tanhuma Gen. 2:4 (Buber, p. 11); Origins, Sanhedrin 38a f, Gen. Rabba XXII, 4; The crown of creation, Sanhedrin 38a; Singularity, Mishnah Sanhedrin IV, 5; For you, Eccles. Rabba VII, 28, Gen. Rabba V, 10; Grow!, Gen. Rabba X, 7; Evil desire, *ibid.*, IX, 9, Yoma 69b; Coming and going, Eccles. Rabba V, 21; Order, Yoma 38a f, Abot de R. Nathan, First Version, XXXIX.

GOD—MAN—WORLD: Justice, Gen. Rabba XXXIX, 6; Sustenance, Mekhilta 16:14 (47b); Ascent, Abodah Zarah 20b; The imitation of God, Sifre Deut. 11:22 (85a), Sotah 14a; Four answers, Pesikta de R. Kahana 158b; Of their own free will, Numbers Rabba VIII, 2; The heart, Midrash Hagadah Gen. 38:1, Sota 5a; Destiny, Erubin 13b; Rain, Taanit 23b; Mercy not sacrifice, Abot de R. Nathan, First Version, IV; Honor due to parents and to God, Yer. Peah I, 1, Kiddushin 30b. Captivity, Horayot 13a; The law and more, Baba Metzia 83a; Let everyone enter, Baba Batra 8a; The sufferings, Baba Metzia 85a; Jesters, Taanit 22a; The guardian of chastity, Yer. Taanit 64b; Demands, Erubin 100b; Blood, Pesahim 25b; Commendation, Mishnah Eduyot V, 7; They that love Him, Shabbat 88b; Today, *ibid.*, 153a; Judgment, *ibid.*, 31a.

REVELATION AND THE STUDY OF THE LAW: As a statue, Pesikta de R. Kahana 110a; All at one time, Tanhuma Exod. 20:1; As the desert, Pesikta de R. Kahana 107a; Mekhilta 19:2 (62a); Israel and the nations, Sifre Deut. 33:2 (142b); The children, Cant. Rabba I, 24; The keepers of the city, Pesikta de R. Kahana 120b; Witnesses, *ibid.*, 102b; In the heart, Deut. Rabba VIII, 7; What animals teach, Erubin 100b; The core of the commandments, Makkot 23b f.; A greater principle, Sifra 19:8 (89b); The yoke of freedom, Sifre Deut. 32:39 (138b); Fire and Light, Mekhilta 19:18 (65a); Pesikta de R. Kahana 200a; Not in heaven, Baba Metzia 59b; The trapper, Tanhuma Deut. 31:1; The vessels, Abot de R. Nathan, Second Version, XXXII, and First Version, XXII; For love of Torah, Lev. Rabba XXX, 1; Sifre Deut. 11:13 (79b); The free gift, Tanhuma Exod. 33:19; The mark of man's foot, Mekhilta 17:6 (52b); Equality, Sifre Deut. 11:22 (84b); Nedarim 81a; Taanit 7a; A man, Abodah Zarah 3a; Humility, Abot de R. Nathan, First Version, XI, and Baba Metzia 85b; Scholars and kings, Horayot 13a; The gates, Exod. Rabba XIX, 4.

ISRAEL: A HOLY COMMUNITY: Three signs, Yebamot 79a; Poverty, Hagigah 9b; Like oil, Cant. Rabba I, 21; Jacob and Esau, Pesikta de R. Kahana 121a; Sharing, Deut. Rabba II, 14; Jacob's ladder, Pesikta de R. Kahana 151; Lev. Rabba XXIX, 2.

PEACE: Perek ha-Shalom and Num. Rabba XI, 16-20.

EXILE AND REDEMPTION: The keys of the Temple, Taanit 29a; Love, Cant. Rabba II, 14; Divine presence in exile, Mekhilta 12:51; Waiting, Pesikta de R. Kahana 144a; Today, Sanhedrin 98a; The real redemption, Midrash Tehillim 31:2; The Messiah, Pesikta de R. Kahana 149a f; Messiah and the world to come, Berakhot 34b and 17a; Planting, Abot de R. Nathan, Second Version, XXXI.

REFLECTIONS ON THE BOOK OF JOB: Heathen prophets, Baba Bathra 15b; Unaided knowledge, Num. Rabba XIV, 7; Who can hinder Thee, Baba

Bathra 16a; Fear of God and love of God, Sotah 31a; Abraham and Job,
Tanhuma Vayera 5; Baba Bathra 15b f; Satan, Baba Bathra 16a; No resurrec-
tion, *ibid.*; Job the rebel, *ibid.*; Enemy of God?, *ibid.*; The turning point,
Pesikta Rabbati 165a; Blessing, Berakhot 17a.

PRAYERS OF THE MASTERS: Berakhot 16b to 17a.

REFLECTIONS ON LIFE: Every day, Seder Eliyahu Rabba II; Surpassing
both, *ibid.*, III; Preparation, *ibid.*, VI; Man's deeds, *ibid.*, IX; Heaven and
Man, *ibid.*, XIV; Provision, *ibid.*, XV; Prayer, *ibid.*, XVIII; In the midst of
sorrow, *ibid.*, XIX; Meeting, *ibid.*, XXIII; The Oral Law, Seder Eliyahu Zutta
II; To walk humbly, Seder Eliyahu Rabba XXVI.

Abbreviations employed in quotations from Scripture

Gen.	Genesis	Hos.	Hosea
Exod.	Exodus	Zeph.	Zephaniah
Lev.	Leviticus	Hag.	Haggai
Num.	Numbers	Zech.	Zechariah
Deut.	Deuteronomy	Mal.	Malachi
Josh.	Joshua	Prov.	Proverbs
Judg.	Judges	Lam.	Lamentations
Sam.	Samuels	Eccles.	Ecclesiastes
Isa.	Isaiah	Dan.	Daniel
Jer.	Jeremiah	Neh.	Nehemiah
Ezek.	Ezekiel	Chron.	Chronicles

Acknowledgments

Thanks are due to the following authors and publishers for permission to use their translations: American Schools of Oriental Research and Professor William Hugh Brownlee for passages from the latter's translation of the Dead Sea Manual of Discipline (Bulletin of the American School of Oriental Research, Supplementary Studies Nos. 10-12 [1951] and No. 135 [1954]); Harvard University Press for *Philo*, translated by F. H. Colson (Loeb Classical Library edition, vols. VII [*The Decalogue, The Special Laws*] and IX ["Every Good Man Is Free," "The Contemplative Life"]); Oxford University Press for selections from *Apocrypha and Pseudepigrapha of the Old Testament*, edited by R. H. Charles (Oxford, 1913) and the Mishnah, translated by Herbert Danby; Schocken Books, Inc. for selections by N. N. Glatzer, translated by Jacob Sloan, from *Hammer on the Rock* (New York, 1948), and from *In Time and Eternity* (New York, 1946); the Viking Press for excerpts from *The Dead Sea Scrolls*, by Millar Burrows (copyright 1955 by Millar Burrows).

Suggestions for Further Reading

Good historical introductions to the period as a whole or to major parts of it are Salo W. Baron, *A Social and Religious History of the Jews* ("Ancient Times," Vol. I-II [2d ed.] New York: Columbia University Press, 1952); Robert H. Pfeiffer, *History of New Testament Times*, New York 1949; and Emil Schürer, *The Jewish People in the Time of Jesus Christ*, New York 1961.

For information on post-Biblical Apocrypha, see the notes to the English translation of *The Apocrypha and Pseudepigrapha of the Old Testament*, edited by R. H. Charles, 2 vols., Oxford 1913; Charles Cutler Torrey, *The Apocryphal Literature*, New Haven 1945; Bruce M. Metzger, *An Introduction to the Apocrypha*, New York 1957, and the second part of Pfeiffer's *History of New Testament Times*.

Hellenism and Hellenistic Judaism is discussed in Victor Tcherikover, *Hellenistic Civilization and the Jews*, Philadelphia 1959; Moses Hadas, *Hellenistic Culture*, New York 1959; Erwin R. Goodenough, *By Light, Light: the Mystic Gospel of Hellenistic Judaism*, New Haven 1935; Hans Jonas, *The Gnostic Religion* (Boston: Beacon Press, 1958); Elias Bickerman, *The Maccabees* (New York: Schocken Books, 1947); Harry A. Wolfson, *Philo: Foundations of Religious Philosophy in Judaism, Christianity and Islam* (2 vols.; Cambridge: Harvard University Press, 1947), a classical study of Philo's position in the history of thought; H. St. J. Thackeray, *Josephus the Man and the Historian*, New York 1929; N. N. Glatzer, *Jerusalem and Rome: From the Writings of Josephus*, New York 1960.

The Dead Sea (Qumran) brotherhood is surveyed by Millar Burrows, *The Dead Sea Scrolls*, New York 1955, and *More Light on the Dead Sea Scrolls*, New York 1958; Frank Moore Cross, Jr., *The Ancient Library of Qumran*, New York 1958; *The Scrolls and the New Testament* (a collection of scholarly essays), edited by Krister Stendahl, New York 1957; *The Dead Sea Scriptures*, trans. by Theodore H. Gaster, New York 1956.

On Pharisaism, Talmud and Midrash: George Foot Moore, *Judaism in the First Centuries of the Christian Era*, 3 vols., Cambridge, Mass. 1927-1930; Solomon Zeitlin, *The Sadducees and the Pharisees*, Philadelphia 1937; Gerson D. Cohen, "The Talmudic Age," *Great Ages and Ideas of the Jewish People*, New York 1956; N. N. Glatzer, *Hillel the Elder: the Emergence of Classical Judaism*, Washington 1959; *The Living Talmud*, ed. by Judah Goldin, New York 1957.

Index